PAPERS ON WELFARE AND GROWTH

PAPERS ON
WELFARE AND GROWTH

TIBOR SCITOVSKY
Professor of Economics
University of California, Berkeley

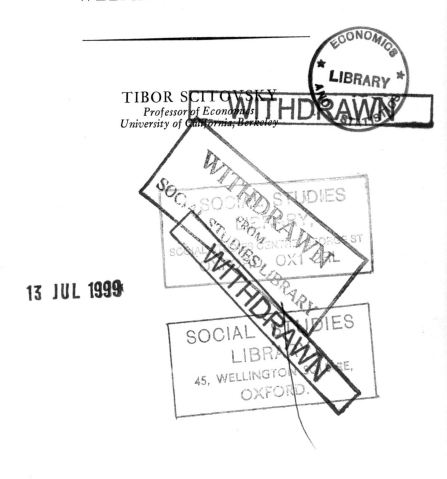
London
GEORGE ALLEN & UNWIN LTD
RUSKIN HOUSE MUSEUM STREET

PRINTED IN GREAT BRITAIN
in 11 point Janson type
BY SIMSON SHAND LTD
LONDON, HERTFORD AND HARLOW

PREFACE

Of the papers assembled in this volume, fifteen have been published before, two have been given as lectures but not previously printed. They range in time over a period of more than twenty years; but all of them exemplify the approach of exploring the logical implications of a few simple and plausible postulates. Rereading them with a view to their inclusion in this volume, I was pleased with my progress towards shorter and simpler ways of saying what I had to say and struck by the recurrence of a relatively few ideas. The latter is a sobering thought for an author but also the main justification for publishing this volume.

After all, an economist is not a man of letters, with devotees who want to read all he has written, because they like his style, or his psychological insight, or the world he creates. People who read economics do so for the subject's not the author's sake. If there is a reason, nevertheless, for assembling in one volume the writings of a single economist, it is that they complement each other, carry further the same thought, explore different implications of the same postulate, or round out the treatment of the same subject. The essays in this volume deal with two subjects; but these are broad and broadly interpreted. There are much closer ties between the essays of the kind just mentioned. The first and second are of a piece, both try to reconcile Keynes's employment and interest theory with the classical theory of interest and capital accumulation. Essays three to six also form a group; three and four deal with different subjects but these are pulled together in five and developed a little further in six. Eleven and twelve again belong together, since both deal with the economic implications of imperfect knowledge; but this to some extent is the subject also of the third and fourteenth essays. Again, fourteen and fifteen continue the argument first stated in thirteen; but it is thirteen, sixteen and to some extent five that explore different implications of the same event: uneven economic progress. Seven, eight and nine form a group only as exercises in economic geometry; a more important common feature, which also ties them together with most of the other essays in this volume, is that they all deal with exceptions, flaws and difficulties in that best of all possible worlds, the competitive system.

Apart from the correction of minor printer's and author's errors, the essays previously published have been reprinted unchanged, with two exceptions. The thirteenth essay was originally published in the *Yale Review* whose editorial policy precludes footnotes and limits length. In the present volume the footnotes and omitted passages have been restored. In the original version of the eighth essay, the main argument was qualified and weakened in a way that has since been shown to have been unnecessary. The argument has been simplified and the qualifications omitted in the present version. Also, in this and the preceeding paper, footnotes have been added to draw the reader's attention to subsequent modifications or corrections of my original argument.

Thanks for letting me reprint these essays are due to my wife, with whom I wrote and published the thirteenth paper, and to Macmillan & Co., the Stanford University Press, and the editors of the *American Economic Review, Economica*, the *Journal of Political Economy*, the *Quarterly Journal of Economics*, the *Review of Economic Studies*, and the *Yale Review*. I am indebted to Miss Ruth Westheimer for preparing the index.

TIBOR SCITOVSKY
Berkeley, California

CONTENTS

ACKNOWLEDGMENTS

Chapter 1 Originally published in *Economica*, August 1940; 2 in *Review of Economic Studies*, February 1941; 3 in *Journal of Political Economy*, April 1954; 4 in *Quarterly Journal of Economics*, November 1955; 5 in M. Abramovitz *et. al.*, *The Allocation of Economic Resources* (Stanford University Press, Stanford, 1959), a slightly different version appeared in *Economie Appliquée*; 6 in E. A. G. Robinson (ed.) *Economic Consequences of the Size of Nations* (Macmillan & Co. Ltd, London, 1960); 7 in *Review of Economic Studies*, November 1941; 8 in *Review of Economic Studies*, Summer 1942; 9 in *Review of Economic Studies*, Winter 1943; 10 in *American Economic Review*, June 1951; 11 in *Review of Economic Studies*, 1944-45; 12 in *American Economic Review*, May 1950; 13 jointly with Anne A. Scitovsky in *Yale Review*, Autumn 1959; 14 in *American Economic Review*, May 1960; 15 in *American Economic Review*, May 1962; 16 Lecture delivered in 1963; 17 Lecture delivered in 1963.

A

ECONOMIC GROWTH AND
RELATED PROBLEMS

Chapter 1

A STUDY OF INTEREST AND CAPITAL[1]

1940

The aim of this paper is to study the determination and interdependence of the rates of interest yielded by different kinds of securities. The complexity of the subject makes it necessary to divide it into three parts. In Part I we make an attempt to determine the price and rate of output of securities in a general way; and as securities are a commodity of which large stocks are always extant, we shall begin with a short discussion on the general theory of supply and demand of commodities of which large stocks are usually held, and so derive the price of securities in analogy with ordinary supply and demand analysis. It will be seen that in this way we arrive at a theory of interest rates which is fundamentally a generalization of Mr Keynes's liquidity preference theory for any number of securities. In Part II we shall analyse the several criteria according to which securities differ from each other. This will lead us to a more complete understanding of the interdependence of different rates of interest and to a new explanation of the relative movements of long- and short-term rates. In Part III we shall restate the theory in a slightly different form and compare it with the 'real' theory of interest and capital.

It is possible to conceive of the rate of interest as being determined by the supply and demand either of capital goods, or of securities, or of money. In this paper we shall always think of it as being determined in the market for securities, and to make the analogy with the supply and demand analysis of

[1] The writing of this paper was made possible by a special grant from the Leon Bequest Fund. I am very much indebted to Professor O. Lange and Mr G. Jászi for reading the manuscript and making valuable suggestions.

consumers' commodities easier, we shall have to think in terms of security prices as well as in terms of yields. This may be a little inconvenient at first because of the inverse relationship between the price and yield of a security, but I hope that the advantage of this approach will outweigh the additional trouble. The 'physical' quantity of securities will be measured by their nominal value.

In Parts I and II we shall deal generally with any number of different kinds of securities. Money is just one of these. Securities differ from each other not because the capital goods they represent are physically heterogeneous, but according to their promised yield, life-time and risk of default. For goods must always be differentiated from the buyers' point of view, and yield, life-time and riskiness are the only characteristics of a security that matter to the investor. For example, beet and cane sugar, or natural and artificial rubber, are identical commodities if consumers do not or cannot distinguish between them; similarly, two securities are homogeneous whatever the nature of the capital goods they stand for *if* they are equally safe and offer the same income for the same period.[1] The meaning of these characteristics will be discussed in detail in Part II. Until then we shall simply have to accept the fact that securities differ from each other in several ways, just as consumers' goods differ in taste, colour, consistency and a hundred other respects.

We shall have to make two simplifying assumptions, to be retained throughout this article. The first is the exclusion of ordinary shares and all other non-fixed-interest-bearing securities. This is admittedly a limitation. I believe that the co-existence of stocks and shares has some very important and interesting consequences, but I also think that this problem is additional to ours, in the sense that its solution would supplement rather than distort our results, so that its discussion may be reserved for some future date. For the time being our analysis will be considerably simplified by the absence of all non-fixed-interest-bearing securities.

Our second assumption is rigid money wages within the short period, in the sense that money wages in any short period are independent of changes *in the same* short period. Dropping

[1] We abstract from the problem of shifts in consumers' demand from the *services* of one capital good to that of another.

this assumption would lead to interesting and rather un-expected results,[1] but the discussion of such problems is beyond the scope of this paper. Besides, I believe the assumption to be a realistic one.

I

In the supply and demand analysis of an ordinary consumers' good, supply is represented by the flow of production, demand by the flow of consumers' demand—both functions of price—and the quality of these two is said to determine the equilibrium price and flow of output. This is a legitimate approach to reality in the case of many commodities which cannot be stored or the stocks of which are small and independent of price—depending only on storage costs and the rate of turn-over. When, however, the volume of stocks is a function of price and is large relatively to current production,[2] then supply will no longer be equivalent to production, but will—at certain prices—be temporarily augmented by a reduction, or temporarily reduced by an accumulation, of stocks; and this factor may become so important relatively to current production as to render the above picture of the determination of short-period equilibrium incorrect and misleading.

The reason for a general theory of stocks being as yet non-existent seems to lie in the fact that the desire to hold stocks is usually a very complicated function of price, involving derivatives with respect to time and relative prices at different dates.[3] For the following argument, however, we shall make the simple assumption that the form of this function is exactly similar to an ordinary demand function, i.e. that the desire to hold stocks is a diminishing function of price. This will be

[1] These will be discussed in the next essay.

[2] The *volume* of stocks and the *flow* of production have different dimensions and are therefore incomparable quantities. We can, however, compare the volume of stocks with the volume of production per unit of time. The choice of this unit is not entirely arbitrary. To be useful it must correspond to the Marshallian short period to which most economic analysis refers. While few economists have assigned a definite length to the short period, the order of magnitude we think of when talking about short-period adjustment and short-period equilibrium seems to be about half a year. This assumption will be made use of at a later stage.

[3] Since the writing of this paper, however, there has appeared a very important article on the subject by Mr N. Kaldor, 'Speculation and Economic Stability', in the October 1939 number of *The Review of Economic Studies*.

shown to be true of the demand for holding securities, and in the short run it also represents—at any rate approximately—speculative demand for commodity stocks whenever speculation is based on the notion of normality.

Let us consider an equilibrium situation where price is such that current production equals current consumption and the volume of stocks corresponds to the volume demanded by 'stockholders' at that price. Then assume a shift in consumers' demand. In the absence of stocks there would be an immediate change in price, followed by the adjustment of production, and a new equilibrium would be established at the new point of intersection of the two curves. In the presence of stocks, however, the situation will be different, because the establishment of the new equilibrium will be retarded by the adjustment of the volume of stocks to the new price. So a diminished consumption demand (leftward or downward shift of the consumption curve) will be temporarily supplemented by the demand of stockholders who want to increase their stocks as price falls[1]—thereby checking the fall in price and the consequent adjustment of production.[2] Similarly, an increased consumption demand will be temporarily satisfied—and the rise in price and production checked—by the dishoarding of stocks. The nature of this retardation can best be described by saying that the existence of stocks sets a limit to the time-rate at which price can change, the limit depending on the size of stocks and the price-elasticity of stockholding. For to each price change there corresponds a certain quantity of stocks which must be released (if price rises) or accumulated (if it falls) before the new equilibrium price can be established; and given the price change, this will be the greater the more elastic the demand for stockholding and the greater the total quantity of stocks. The time needed for the adjustment—and for the new equilibrium to be established—will be the longer the greater is this quantity in relation to the gap between current production and consumption opened up by the initial change in data (and not immediately closed by the requisite

[1] We have assumed above (see end of previous paragraph) that speculation in commodity stocks is based on the notion of a normal and 'just' price which is expected to return and deviations from which are believed to be temporary. In other words, we have assumed the elasticity of expectations to be zero.

[2] Throughout this paper we shall assume production to be price-determined.

change in price), since—to put it crudely—stocks can only be released or accumulated through this gap. If this ratio is very large, because, for example, stocks are very large, then the adjustment of price will proceed so slowly that we can say the influence on price of primary changes in production or consumption is negligible in the short run, and it will be more correct to say that price depends on the quantity of stocks than that it is determined by the intersection of the production and consumption curves.

If the existence of stocks keeps the price of a commodity temporarily at a level where current production and consumption are not equal, this disparity will cause a change in the level of income which may—if the commodity is important and its stocks large—equate its production and consumption before price has had time to equate them. The way in which this happens has often been described and is known as the theory of the multiplier. A disparity in any particular industry between receipts and income paid out causes a similar but opposite disparity in the rest of the economy. This will disappoint (favourably or unfavourably) the expectations of entrepreneurs in those industries and induce them to change their rate of production and with it the rate at which they pay out income to the owners of the factors of production. This process is cumulative and will continue while the disequilibrium in the first industry subsists, i.e. until current demand is equated to current production, partly by the change in incomes causing a change in demand, partly—to the extent that stocks have adjusted themselves in the meantime—by the change in price.

For a further elucidation of the above argument let us take a specific example. Imagine a community which always spends all its income and has a margin of unemployed resources.[1] We further assume that there is speculation in one of the staple commodities consumed by this society—let us call it wheat— and that the average value of speculative wheat stocks is large relatively to the value of all other speculative stocks taken together. Now imagine a shift in consumers' demand away from wheat. The prices of all the goods which now are demanded more urgently will rise, causing an increased production and a higher level of employment in the industries

[1] The compatibility of these two assumptions will appear presently.

B

affected. The price of wheat would fall and cause an offsetting diminution of production and employment in the wheat industry *if* it were not for the existence of speculation. But when the price of wheat begins to fall, people, who believe that the former price of wheat was 'normal' and therefore expect it to return after a while, will find it profitable to hoard wheat, thereby checking the fall in its price and production. So we get a net increase in employment in the community, and corresponding to it a rise in the level of incomes. This will increase consumers' demand for most commodities. The increased demand for goods other than wheat will cause employment and incomes to rise yet further; the increased demand for wheat will check and ultimately stop the accumulation of wheat stocks. Short-period equilibrium will be re-established when incomes have risen sufficiently to make the consumption of wheat again equal to its production *in spite of the change in tastes*. This will probably happen at a wheat price somewhat below the original, corresponding to the now greater wheat stocks. It should be obvious that the argument for a shift in demand towards wheat is perfectly symmetrical.

All this, of course, will happen only if prices in those other industries are flexible. If they were as rigid as the price of wheat (e.g. because of the existence of equally large stocks), then the disequilibrium between receipts and outgoings in the wheat industry caused by the adjustment of its stocks would merely cause an exactly offsetting adjustment of stocks in all the other industries, without inducing entrepreneurs to any action. Thus the degree to which the equality between the current demand and current production of any particular commodity is brought about by a change in the level of income rather than by a change in its price, depends on the value of its stocks relatively to the value of all other stocks taken together. The greater the relative value of its stocks, the more sticky will be its price, and the more quickly will the level of income adjust itself through changes in the activity of other industries.

The reader may object here that speculators will not keep stocks at their unnaturally high (or low) level indefinitely; in fact, that speculators' demand for stocks cannot be represented by a simple diminishing function of price. He will be perfectly right. The change in the level of income described above is only a temporary effect of the shift in consumers' tastes, and the whole argument may be taken as an illustration of the harmful destabilizing nature of speculation. But it is also an illustration by analogy of the *permanent* effect on the level of income of changes in the propensity to consume. For it will be shown on p. 20 that unlike commodity stocks, the stocks of securities *are* simple decreasing functions of price, so that as regards the latter it will be true to say that they determine security prices while the level of income equates the flow of saving ('current consumption') to the flow of investment. This is the more true because securities are the commodity with large stocks *par excellence*. Another respect in which securities differ from other goods is that the current demand for them represents not consumption, but what may be called *normal* additions to stock. It will become apparent that this fact cannot affect the argument, but it will make the exposition easier if we assume for the moment that new securities are bought out of new savings for an entirely different purpose from that which induces people to hold the stock of 'secondhand' securities. (In Part III the same argument will be repeated without this analytical dodge.) In this way we can split up the individual's economic problem into two parts: firstly he has to decide in what forms to hold his already accumulated stock of wealth, secondly he has to allocate his flow of income between the flows of different kinds of consumers' goods and securities.

The second of these, to be dealt with later, is the familiar problem of the subjective theory of demand and is generally considered to be solved. The first is exactly analogous to the second. Each security promises a certain yield, distributed over time in a certain way, and each promise inspires a certain degree of confidence.[1] The individual aims at the highest possible average yield, subject to the limitations of his wealth and preference for safety and liquidity. At each constellation of market prices, which to him are given, there exists an optimum selection of securities which, in his opinion, involves the exact amount of risk and illiquidity he is willing to bear and at the same time maximizes his average yield.

From the community's point of view the quantity and not

---

[1] While the yield is an objective quantity, the degree of confidence depends on subjective valuation.

the price of each security is given in the short period, and these, together with the individuals' preference scales and the level of income determine security prices.[1] Just as in the general theory of demand for consumers' goods, it can be shown that, neglecting capital-gain and capital-loss effects (these correspond to the income effects of the theory of consumers' demand), the price of each security is a diminishing function of its quantity, while an increase in the quantity of another security will lower or raise its price according as the securities are substitutes or complements.

The effects of variations in the quantity of money need special consideration. They can be analysed most easily if we think of the price of a security as the ratio of its marginal utility to the marginal utility of money, the *numéraire*. Then an increase in the quantity of money will lower the marginal utility of money, i.e. lower the value of the denominator in the expression for price, and raise or lower the value of the numerator according as the security in question is a complement or substitute of money. So an increase in the quantity of money will cause *all* security prices to rise, those of complements most and those of substitutes least. In the limiting case the price of a perfect substitute for money would remain unchanged, because both the denominator and numerator of the expression for its price would fall in the same proportion.

This is little more than a generalization of Mr Keynes's liquidity preference theory of the rate of interest. In the special case when there are only securities of one kind besides money, *the* rate of interest is an index of their relative prices which is a function of their relative quantities. The rate of interest, therefore, will rise equally whether the quantity of securities is increased relatively to that of money, or the quantity of money is diminished relatively to that of securities. For short-period analysis it is better to think of the rate of interest as a function of the quantity of money, simply because a change in the quantity of money is easily conceivable within

---

[1] The level of income must be given because money not only satisfies preference for safety and liquidity, it is also demanded for transaction purposes, and this demand is an increasing function of income and the level of employment. Hence an increase in employment is equivalent to a diminution of the quantity of money—available to the investor.

the short period while a significant change in the quantity of other securities is impossible by definition.[1]

When we distinguish between different kinds of securities, the crude picture of *the* rate of interest as the demand price of money breaks down because of the multiplicity of interest rates. But it still remains true that the quantity of each kind of capital and hence each kind of security is practically fixed within the short period—securities not representing physical capital (war loans), however, form an important exception—and only the quantity of money is variable. We can say, therefore, that while the prices of different kinds of securities are determined by their quantities and individuals' preference scales, in the short run the quantity of securities representing 'real' capital is fixed by the technical limitations of the rate at which they can be consumed, added to or converted into other kinds of capital; so that changes in their prices and yields can only be accounted for by changes in preference scales and in the quantity of money and incomes.[2]

The above argument contains an explanation of the exact relationship between Mr Keynes's theory of interest and the so-called classical theory. The classical theory never distinguished between the stock of capital and the flow of saving

[1] The concept of the short period originally arose in connection with partial equilibrium analysis. As the equipment of an individual firm can only be changed discontinuously, partial adjustment with constant equipment can be analysed in the intervals between two discontinuous changes in equipment. This was called short-period analysis, and the minimum length of this interval: that period of time which is too short for the entrepreneur to adjust his equipment in response to changes in price, was defined by Marshall as the short period. Its length, therefore, was determined by the gestation period of equipment, which we have assumed above (footnote 2, p. 15) to be of the order of magnitude of half a year in industry. When we use the concept of the short period in total analysis we tacitly redefine it to mean a period sufficiently short to make changes in total equipment (which are continuous!) negligible. Statistics of the stock of capital and of current investment suggest that we may legitimately retain the order of length of the short period of partial analysis also when dealing with total quantities. The national capital in England and the USA has been estimated at about six times the annual national income, i.e. twelve times the national income of our short period; while net investment and depreciation of equipment are both about (a maximum of) 12 per cent of the national income. So the maximum increase and the maximum possible decrease of the stock of capital is not more than approximately 1 per cent during a short period of six months.

[2] For the problem arising from the fact that securities are not issued *pari passu* with the progress of the investment they represent, see J. M. Keynes: 'The "ex ante" theory of investment', *Economic Journal*, vol. 47, pp. 663-4.

in this context. If, therefore, we interpret it as meaning that the rate of interest is a function of the stock of securities, it is identical with Mr Keynes's theory, though for precision's sake one should say 'stock of securities relatively to the quantity of money'.[1] If, on the other hand, it meant that the rate of interest is determined—analogously with the price of a non-storable commodity—by the equality of current production (investment) and consumption (saving), then it is not identical with the liquidity preference theory; moreover it is also wrong, being based on a false analogy.[2] We have seen so far how security prices are determined in the market where capitalists choose the form in which to hold their wealth—the quantity of securities and the level of income being given. With the exception of money and other securities representing non-tangible capital, the quantity of securities is technically fixed in the short period, but there remains the determination of the level of income by (current) supply conditions and the allocation of the flow of income between different uses. We are not here concerned with the determination of the relative prices of consumers' goods, nor with the effect on income of a shift in demand from one consumers' good to another. As to the relative rates at which different securities and different kinds of capital goods are produced, they, as we know, do not affect security prices directly in the short run,[3] while for the determination of income and employment only total investment (i.e. the horizontal sum of all security production curves) and total saving are of importance. So we can concentrate on the relation between investment and saving.

We shall assume that the rate of supply of securities, or, shortly, investment activity, is an increasing function of the level of security prices (diminishing function of the structure

[1] At the same time Mr Keynes cannot be charged with a lack of precision when he does not mention the stock of securities. For he is primarily concerned with the short period within which that stock is constant.

[2] We do not propose to criticize here all those writers who have asserted that the Keynesian theory of interest is identical with the classical theory. But the reader's attention may be drawn to an article by Mr Peter Bauer, 'Die allgemeine Theorie von Keynes und ihre Kritiker', *Zeitschr. für Nationalökonomie*, vol. 9, p. 99, who criticizes Professor Hicks for not noticing that in the liquidity preference theory the rate of interest equates the supply and demand of a *stock*, while in the classical theory it equates the supply and demand of a *flow*.

[3] In the long run they do affect relative prices by determining the relative quantity of the stocks of different securities.

of interest rates). This seems plausible enough, but is by no means obvious, nor always true, and will be justified in part three. Until then it must be regarded as an arbitrary assumption. Saving is an increasing function of employment and income. Whether it also depends on the rate of interest is an open question, but makes little difference to our argument. For simplicity's sake we shall assume that it does not.

We have seen that the secondhand market links the structure of security prices to the level of income.[1] Hence the level of income determines, *via* the secondhand market, the level of investment activity; and it also determines directly (and indirectly if saving is also a function of interest rates) the flow of saving. When the level of income is such that these two are equal we have short-period equilibrium. What happens if they are unequal, if, for example, investment exceeds saving?[2] This, as we know from page 17, causes receipts in consumption-good industries to exceed expected receipts (costs), which will induce entrepreneurs to increase current production and with it the level of employment and income. The rise in incomes increases the flow of savings, but—by increasing the transaction demand for money—it also lowers the level of security prices. This latter will have the effect of checking investment activity, and with investment falling and saving rising equilibrium will be established.

So we see that an excess of investment over saving will not only raise the level of income until savings have caught up with investment; it will also lower security prices. This latter effect, however, is brought about not directly by the supply of securities exceeding the demand for them, but indirectly, through increasing employment, raising the transaction demand for money and thereby diminishing the quantity of money available for purposes of investment. Whether changes in the rate of saving or in the level of security prices are more important in bringing about short-period equilibrium is a

[1] Because the level of income determines the quantity of money available for purposes of investment.
[2] It must be borne in mind that while saving may be unequal to investment the supply and demand of securities will always be equal—even in an 'ex ante' sense—because the gap between saving and investment is filled in either by holders or secondhand securities who at that price find it profitable to go into money, or by holders of money who find it profitable to swap money for securities, as the case may be.

question of fact. But the great fluctuations in employment and the surprising stability of the gilt-edged rate suggest an answer to it.

II

It has been shown on pp. 19-20 how, given the quantity of different kinds of securities, the price of each of them is determined by the individuals' preference scales. We now proceed to investigate more closely the factors that account for the differences between different securities and cause their prices and yields to be different, and to move differently. It has already been mentioned that from the investor's point of view —which alone is relevant for the determination of price and yield—securities differ according to nominal yield, life-time and risk of default. Nominal yield and life-time are both characteristics of the time-shape of a security and will, therefore, be treated together. In fact, it is often said that a lower nominal yield (coupon rate) is equivalent to a longer life-time.[1] While this is only true approximately, it is a convenient simplification which we propose to adopt, thereby reducing the number of our criteria to two: currency and risk of default. Differences in currency cause differences in yield and price again for two reasons: first, because expected future interest rates vary over time, and secondly, because these expectations are not certain. We shall consider variations in expected future rates first, and assume for the moment that all securities are equally risky both as regards the danger of default and that of changing market valuations.

Having thus excluded the problems of riskiness and of the uncertainty of expectations, it is clear that the demand for different kinds of securities will always be such as to equalize their true yields over any given period of time. In other words, security prices must so adjust themselves as to make investment in all types of securities equally profitable (yield the same interest) whatever length of time one invests for. It should also be obvious that this does not necessarily imply that the market rate of interest on every security must always be equal. For the market rate of a security expresses the rate of interest it

[1] Cf. F. R. Macaulay: *Some Theoretical Problems suggested by the Movements of Interest Rates, Bond Yields and Stock Prices in the United States since 1856*, 1938, p. 45.

will yield on its present value *if held to maturity*.[1] Its yield for a shorter period of time depends on the relation between its market value at the beginning and at the end of that period, and may be greater or smaller than its market rate. If then, given the quantities of different securities, demand conditions are such as to make the yield of a given security (say) 4 per cent, and the yield of another security with a longer currency 5 per cent, this implies that the market expects the yield of the more durable security to rise by the date of maturity of the first security to such a level as to make its true yield over the life-time of the first security also 4 per cent. It follows from this argument that the present market rates of securities of different currency express the expected future course of the market rate of any given security, and that differences in the amplitude of the fluctuations of different market rates can be accounted for by the expected future course of security yields.[2] In the following we shall try to explain the divergence of present market rates from the gilt-edged rate in terms of the future course of gilt-edged rates. Theoretically we could have chosen the future yields of any type of security, but in practice the horizon of expectations is likely to stretch farthest in relation to gilt-edged securities.

The way in which future expectations are based on past experience can be conveniently expressed in terms of Professor Hicks's elasticity of expectations. The simplest and most important case is that of unit elasticity, when people expect present rates to continue unchanged in the future. It is easy to see without further explanation that if the quantity of securities and demand conditions are such as to make the present gilt-edged rate 4 per cent, and people expect it to remain 4 per cent also in the future, then the true yield of gilt-edged securities will be 4 per cent over any period of time. Consequently the market rate of *all* securities (i.e. securities of all life-times) must also be 4 per cent. So we can establish our first rule: if the elasticity of yield expectations is unity, security prices must be such and must move in such a way as to make

[1] We define the market rate as that rate of discount which will make the discounted sum of all future payments promised by a security equal to its present market value.
[2] A somewhat similar argument can be found in Chapter 11 of Professor J. R. Hicks' *Value and Capital*, 1939, where it is also proved that this kind of argument is not circular.

the *market rate* of all securities always equal. We next consider the case of an elasticity of expectations smaller than one. Assume as an example that a change in data causes the gilt-edged rate to rise from 4 per cent to 5 per cent, but people expect it to return in the near future to either 4 per cent or to some intermediate level between 4 per cent and 5 per cent. In other words, people expect an appreciation in the value of gilt-edged securities, and if anybody buys them now and sells after their yield has again fallen, he will make a capital gain, and will have earned interest over that period at a rate higher than the gilt-edged rate of the date of purchase by the capital appreciation. So if the yield on shorter-term securities is to be the same as the true yield on gilt-edged over the life-time of the short-term securities, their market rates must rise more than the gilt-edged rate has risen, and when the latter falls their rate will fall by more. In the limiting case of zero elasticity of expectations the market rates of securities with a shorter duration will fluctuate so much more violently as to make their *prices* move proportionately with the prices of gilt-edged securities.[1] We shall not discuss elasticities greater than unity, but the reader ought to be able to work it out for himself that in such a case it is the market rates of the longer-term securities that would fluctuate more violently in consequence of a change in data.

So far we have not considered speculation. But whenever the elasticity of expectations is greater than zero, the prices of securities with a shorter currency will be more stable than the prices of those with a longer duration, and this will induce people to go into long when they expect a general price rise, and into short (and money) when they anticipate a fall. This will further accentuate the disparity between price movements, while it will stabilize relative market rate movements when the elasticity of expectations is less than one and destabilize them when it is unity or above it.

The outcome of this rather involved argument is that it depends entirely on the elasticity of yield expectations whether —and to what extent—it is the differences in life-time that account for the different amplitudes in the fluctuations of different market yields. We shall see presently that our other

---

[1] This is strictly correct only if the gilt-edged securities are non-redeemable. Otherwise it is only approximately true.

criterion, risk of default, can account equally well for the observed fact that short-term rates are more volatile than long-term rates; and personally I also believe that this factor is the more important. For it seems unlikely that the elasticity of yield expectations should so consistently be always below unity. But a true assessment of the relative importance of the two factors could only be made on the basis of statistical investigation.

Hitherto we have excluded the problem of riskiness by assuming all securities to be equally risky. Henceforth we shall exclude the problem of different durations, not by adopting a uniform life-time for all securities, but by assuming the elasticity of yield expectations to be unity. In this way we can let differences in the amplitude of price variations to be taken care of by differences in currency, while we leave differences in yields to be explained by varying degrees of riskiness. We do not regard this as a correct representation of reality (although we suspect it to be fairly near), only as a convenient method of separating the discussion of the two criteria.[1]

Before we can go on to the discussion of risk of default, we shall have to consider another kind of risk: the risk of future changes in capital values. Liquidity preference proper is an insurance against this risk only. We have seen above how the expectation of falling security prices will lead speculators to buy money and short-term bills for long-term securities. In addition to this speculative demand there will also be a more permanent demand for money and bills arising from the uncertainty of expectations, and coming from people who cannot be compensated for a danger of capital loss by the chance of capital gain. Much has been written recently on this motive for the preference of money and low-income-yielding bills over high-income-yielding securities, and we have nothing to add to it. Two things, however, may be pointed out. Firstly that arguments showing an equally strong preference for long-term securities (e.g. by investors who want to stabilize the yield of their investment rather than its capital value) do not affect the liquidity preference theory.[2] Secondly that *in*

---

[1] To be quite correct, if we admit speculation, the elasticity of expectations must be slightly below unity to equalize yields.

[2] For even if there are people who prefer the cinema to the theatre and do not regard it merely as an imperfect substitute for it, their relative prices will still depend on their relative quantities.

a purely formal sense the propositions of this paper do not depend on the validity of the liquidity preference theory. This will appear below.

Risk of default is the next criterion of differentiation between securities. It is obvious that securities do differ according to the confidence attached to the fulfilment of their promises and that such differences can and do account for differences in their yields. The problem is, in what order does this risk range the different types of securities? Since all securities promise the future payment of money sums, money itself must occupy the first place as the completely riskless security. Gilt-edged securities come next. Their 'nearness' to money seems to be the most satisfactory explanation of the great stability of the gilt-edged rate: we have seen on page 20 that it is the yield of the closest substitutes to money which is least affected by changes in the quantity of money and in the level of employment. We have not yet explained, however, the relatively high level of the gilt-edged rate. One reason must be liquidity preference, another, perhaps equally important one, seems to be the high transaction costs (brokerage charges, stamp duties, commissions, etc.) on long-term securities. Assuming a certain stability in the frequency of transactions, this would be an element in long-term rates which is independent of tastes and relative quantities.

In what exact order the stocks, bills and overdraft facilities of all the different private companies and foreign governments and municipalities range on our list would be difficult to decide. Nor is this necessary for our purposes, as we are only interested here in the relation between long- and short-term rates, and that is explained by the special position of short-term securities. It is an important feature of short-term capital that it is mainly held by the banking system. In particular, all bank advances are 'held' by the banks and the greater part of bills is also held by them. Now it is well known that banks usually tend to keep a fixed proportion between their cash reserves, advances to industry, commercial bill holdings and security holdings; and we also know that such 'joint demand' establishes a relation of complementarity between the goods jointly demanded. This will not affect long-term securities, of which banks only hold a very small proportion, but it will make all forms of short-term capital complementary with money. On

p. 20 we have discussed the relative *price* movements of substitutes and complements. But having assumed the elasticity of yield expectations to be unity, the argument must now hold about relative changes in *yields*. So we can say that an increase in the quantity of money will affect the yield on gilt-edged securities least, while it will cause the short-term rate to fall most. The degree to which changes in the quantity of money (and in the level of employment) affect the yield on gilt-edged securities depends on their riskiness and on liquidity preference. If we could exclude liquidity preference and assumed for a moment that gilt-edged securities are completely riskless, then a change in the quantity of money would leave the gilt-edged rate unchanged, but it would still cause a large change in the short-term rate and smaller changes in the yields of long-term securities other than gilt-edged.

III

We have attempted, in Part I of this paper, to apply ordinary supply and demand analysis to the special case of securities, and hope to have shown both the analogy and the difference between the determination of security prices on the one hand and of the prices of consumers' goods on the other. We have seen that security prices and interest rates are mainly dependent on the demand for the stock of securities, while current investment and current saving have only an indirect influence *via* the level of income and the demand for money. The demand for the stock of securities has been analysed in greater detail in Part II, and we should now proceed to a detailed discussion of current investment. This is of especial interest, because it is here that 'real' elements enter into the present theory which so far must have seemed to be merely a theory of risk and money. To show the relationship between real capital theory and the present theory more clearly, we shall summarize what we understand under real capital theory in the form of two diagrams, and then restate the argument of Part I in the same form. It will be seen that this alternative statement also makes the discussion of the factors determining current investment very simple.

From our point of view the two important concepts of real capital theory are the marginal productivity of capital and the rate of human impatience or time preference. The definition of the former is that rate of interest at which the stream of the marginal value products of a capital good must be discounted in order to make its present value equal to the (replacement) cost of the capital good. Time preference is defined as that rate of interest which must be offered to induce the community to save a certain part of its income. The marginal productivity of capital as well as time preference are functions both of the quantity of capital and of the rate at which capital is being accumulated. For the marginal productivity of a capital good is a diminishing function of the number of capital goods in existence, while its replacement cost is an increasing function of the rate at which capital goods are produced. Similarly, the larger the community's capital equipment, the higher is its real income (assuming full employment), and the less inducement is necessary for people to save; while given the level of income the rate of saving is an increasing function (according to classical theory) of the rate of interest. To spare ourselves the trouble of drawing three-dimensional diagrams we shall have to introduce two new concepts: *stationary* time preference and *stationary* marginal productivity of capital. The former is defined as that rate of interest at which the community wishes neither to save nor to dissave, the latter as that marginal productivity of capital which would rule if net investment were zero.

We can now show the dependence of these two rates on the quantity of capital in a diagram (fig. 1) where we measure the rate of interest on the vertical and the quantity of capital on the horizontal axis. The s.m.p. curve will be downward sloping, representing the law of non-proportional returns,[1] and the s.t.p. curve will fall too, though not so steeply. The intersection of these two curves determines long-period equilibrium. In a progressive economy we are to the left of this point, in a regressive economy to the right. The two curves determine the rate of interest in long-period equilibrium; in a progressive or regressive economy they only set the approximate limits within which the rate of interest must be determined by the equality of the rate of saving and the rate of investment. Let us consider the special case of short-period

---

[1] When the quantity of capital is increased—that of other factors being kept constant—its marginal productivity must fall.

r, with a total quantity of capital: $O\,r$, and a short-period of six months as our unit of time. We can then draw a new diagram (fig. 2) measuring the rate of interest on the y axis as before, but on the x axis we measure net investment (net saving) per unit of time: ΔK, instead of the quantity of capital: K. Having estimated the ratio $\dfrac{\Delta K}{K}$ to have the approximate value $\dfrac{1}{100}$,[1] if we want to get a picture comparable to fig. 1, the unit of ΔK must be a hundred times smaller than the unit of K. In this plane we can redraw the s.t.p. and s.m.p. curves: they will be minute portions of the two curves of fig. 1 at point r, magnified in the horizontal direction. (Because of the difference in the horizontal scales in figs. 1 and 2.) As this reduces the slope of the curves a hundred-fold, both will be virtually horizontal.

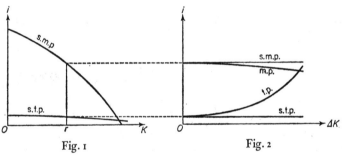

Fig. 1   Fig. 2

At this stage a further elucidation of the exact relationship of the two diagrams becomes necessary. So far it seemed that fig. 2 is just a distorted (horizontally magnified) reproduction of a thin slice of fig. 1 along the vertical line erected in point r. While this interpretation is correct, a glance at the horizontal s.t.p. and s.m.p. lines suggests that this alone would not justify the drawing of another diagram. The two curves of fig. 1 belong to the realm of comparative statics: different points on them represent alternative situations (different quantities of capital equipment), without paying attention to the problems of transition. Fig. 2 aims at remedying this defect, and different

[1] See p. 21, footnote 1. To be exact, we estimated, not the ratio of the quantity of net investment per unit of time to the total quantity of existing capital equipment, but the ratio of their values. The two, however, must be approximately the same.

points in its plane represent not only different quantities of capital, but also different rates of investment and saving. (More correctly: volumes of investment and saving per unit of time.) The fact, however, that the s.t.p. and s.m.p. curves are virtually horizontal in fig. 2 suggests that the first interpretations of ΔK can be neglected in the short run: in other words *we can treat the quantity of capital equipment as fixed when analysing the rate of investment and the rate of saving in the short period.*

It will now be obvious that the s.t.p. and s.m.p. curves, belonging to the realm of comparative statics, have no place in fig. 2. They have been drawn to illustrate the above argument, but they have a real existence only at their point of intersection with the ordinate axis, for it is only there that time preference and marginal productivity are stationary. The 'dynamic' t.p. and m.p. curves will have to start from these points, and the time preference curve will now be drawn with an upward slope, representing the rate of saving as an increasing function of the rate of interest. The marginal productivity of capital is an increasing function of the marginal productivity of the physical capital good and a diminishing function of the replacement cost of that capital good. When investment activity increases, the opportunity cost of capital goods will rise,[1] but the marginal productivity of the capital goods themselves may either rise or fall, according as capital-good industries are less or more labour-saving than consumption-good industries. The combined effect of these two factors may make the marginal productivity curve slope upwards as well as downwards. There is no indication of Böhm Bawerk or any other real capital theorists having been aware of this complication; so if we wanted to represent their theory truthfully we would have to draw the m.p. curve as a horizontal line. But to emphasize the fact that marginal productivity depends on investment activity as well as on the quantity of capital, we shall make the curve slope downward. There are two reasons which make this more probable than a rising

---

[1] Only if the factors of production are combined in different proportions in the capital-good and consumption-good industries respectively. We are, of course, assuming full employment here, but for future reference the reader's attention may be drawn to the fact that the result of this analysis: namely that the marginal productivity curve may equally rise or fall with investment activity, is true also when we do not assume full employment.

m.p. curve. Firstly, many forms of investment activity—like residential and industrial building, rail-road and other construction—are notoriously labour-intensive; secondly, real wages usually rise with increasing employment.[1] So in fig. 2 we get a t.p. curve which is rising and a m.p. curve which may be either rising (though not so steeply) or falling; and their intersection, according to real capital theory, determines the rate of interest and the volume of saving and investment per short period.

It is best to think of these two curves as being the sum of two components: one (illustrated by the s.t.p. and s.m.p. lines of fig. 2) depending on the quantity of capital in existence and practically fixed within the short period, and the other (given by the vertical difference between the t.p. and s.t.p., and the m.p. and s.m.p. curves, respectively) depending on the rate of capital accumulation. Mr Lerner seems to have been the first to realize that the marginal productivity of capital is a function not only of the quantity of capital, but also of its rate of accumulation.[2] He separated the two components in a fashion somewhat similar to ours and called our marginal productivity of capital the marginal efficiency of investment, reserving the first name for our stationary marginal productivity. What he has not realized, however, is that while the s.m.p. curve is always downward-sloping—because of the law of non-proportional returns—this is not necessarily true of the marginal productivity curve (his marginal efficiency investment). It is indeed curious how long this fact has gone unnoticed. Economists have assumed the marginal productivity of capital to be a function of its quantity and of its construction cost, and considered relative demand for goods embodying capital in varying proportions as among the 'other things

---

[1] As a rule, increasing employment means an increase in the relative importance of investment industries. If investment-good industries are more labour-intensive than consumption-good industries this will cause a *rise* in the marginal productivity of labour in exactly the same way as a shift in consumers' demand from motor-cars and wireless sets to butlers and maids would increase the marginal productivity and hence the earnings of labour. The argument is not affected by the fact that the shift from consumption to investment is not absolute but only relative, and it remains true—though the effect may be less strong—when marginal labour cost curves are rising in each industry.

[2] A. P. Lerner: 'Capital, Investment and Interest'. Manchester Statistical Society, Group Meetings, 1936-37.

C

being equal'; not noticing that a faster capital accumulation itself may constitute such a change in relative demand. The importance of this singular omission is not to be minimized, for it contains the simplest and most orthodox explanation of why real wages so often rise in prosperity and why sometimes the marginal productivity of capital rises with investment activity.

The theory of this paper differs from the above formulation of real capital theory in that it takes account of risk and introduces money. In order to restate the argument of Part I in terms of the above two diagrams we shall have to relinquish our general system of any number of different kinds of securities and retain one distinction only: that between long- and short-term capital. The individual investor can choose between holding his wealth in long-term securities or in money, while we shall assume that short-term capital is provided exclusively by the banking system. Furthermore we shall also assume that the quantity of securities and of capital goods is closely correlated, so that we can interpret K as an index both of the stock of securities and of the community's capital equipment.[1] We can then (fig. 1a) draw the two curves of fig. 1 in exactly the same way as we have drawn them above. But in addition we now have a third curve which may be called the security preference curve, showing the quantity of securities (capital) the community is willing to hold at each rate of interest. This is not identical with the s.t.p. curve which shows that interest rate at which the community's expenditure exactly equals its income, for now there are two alternatives to holding capital: spending it and *holding money*.[2] As money is only held when there is uncertainty and risk, the yield of securities must include a premium on bearing risk. Therefore the security preference curve will be higher than the s.t.p. curve. More-

[1] This is a rather drastic simplification and excludes many important problems, which, however, I believe to be at an altogether lower level of abstraction and therefore outside the scope of this article. The most important of these is the effect on the rate of interest of investments that are financed, not through the capital market but, e.g. out of undistributed profits. It has been pointed out to me by Mr Melvin Reder that on the basis of the above theory such investments would *lower* (instead of raising) the rate of interest by increasing the demand for securities, without at the same time increasing their supply.

[2] Security preference is identical with the demand for holding (the stock of) securities. It has been renamed, so as not to confuse the reader with the paradoxical shape and position of the demand curve when drawn in a plane where the ordinate represents yields instead of security prices.

over, given the quantity of money, it will be slightly upward-sloping, because an increase in the quantity of securities means an increase relatively to the quantity of money.

Let us now draw a short-period diagram appertaining to the quantity of capital: $O\,r$ (fig. 2a). The m.p. curve will have the same shape as before, though we must remember that it could, and sometimes does, rise instead of falling. In a risky economy investment will not be pushed to the point where the marginal productivity of capital is equal to the market rate of interest, but only to the point where the marginal productivity *minus* marginal risk is equal to it. This principle, first stated by Mr Kalecki, has been described in detail on several occasions—which makes it unnecessary that we should expand

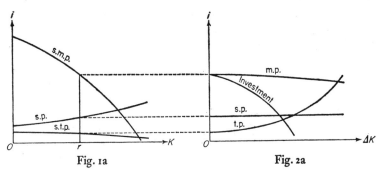

Fig. 1a   Fig. 2a

upon it.[1] To summarize it shortly we can say that there is a risk of new investment turning out unsuccessfully, and this risk increases with the number and size of investments started per unit of time. It ties up the liquid funds either of the investing entrepreneur himself, or of the bank that gave him advances, or of the promoter who is going to float his securities, *until the securities are floated.*[2] The cost of bearing this risk—either in the form of interest on the bank-advances, or

[1] M. Kalecki: 'The Principle of Increasing Risk', *Economica* (NS), vol. 4; J. M. Keynes: 'The "ex ante" Theory of the Rate of Interest', *Economic Journal*, vol. 47; and N. Kaldor: 'Capital Intensity and the Trade Cycle', *Economica* (NS), vol. 6, February 1939.

[2] Securities are usually floated when the new concern is already going. If they were floated before 'construction' began, the initial risk would have to be borne by the purchasers of the securities and the entrepreneur would have to pay for initial risk-bearing throughout the life of the securities. He usually finds it cheaper to pay initial cost for initial risk-bearing and to get his long-term capital at a lower rate of interest.

in the form of promoter's premium, or as a bonus to the entrepreneur for risking his own liquid funds—is an initial cost of investment; as such it enters into the cost of securities, and hence causes the investment curve to fall more steeply. The 'additional steepness' of this marginal-productivity-cum-marginal-risk curve (hereafter called investment curve) depends on the policy and liquidity of the banks.

The time preference curve presents no new problems and can be drawn as it was drawn in fig. 2.

The security preference rate depends only upon the quantity of securities and the quantity of money and is therefore independent of the rate of accumulation—as long as we assume full employment. So we can draw it as a virtually horizontal straight line.

The problem now arises: what happens if the investment curve cuts the s.p. curve as shown in fig. 2a? Clearly, their intersection must determine the market rate of interest, but at that rate, saving—shown by the t.p. curve—exceeds investment. As this cannot lower the rate of interest directly, it must lower the level of income until savings become equal to investment. We could draw a family of t.p. curves corresponding to each level of income, but we prefer to retain the one only which corresponds to full employment, so that we can use the (horizontal) distance between this curve and the point of intersection of the s.p. and investment curves as an index of unemployment. We must be careful now, because the two other curves were also drawn on the assumption of full employment. But redrawing them will not be difficult, because the family of t.p. curves assigns a definite level of employment to each point of the plane. We have first to draw the family of t.p. curves and the family of investment curves, and join together the points where two curves corresponding to the same level of employment cut each other. This will be our new investment curve. We then repeat the same procedure with the family of t.p. and s.p. curves and get our new s.p. curve. The investment curve will retain its main features, so we shall not bother to describe its transformation. The new s.p. curve on the other hand will now be slightly rising, because the higher the level of income, the smaller is the quantity of money available as an alternative to holding securities. Fig. 2b represents the redrawn diagram. The intersection of the in-

vestment and s.p. curves determines investment activity, the
rate of interest and the level of employment. The first two can
be read off the two axes, the level of employment can be
judged by the horizontal distance between the point of intersection and the t.p. curve which is purely hypothetical and
only shows what saving would be if there were full employment.

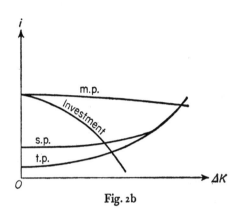

Fig. 2b

A comparison of figs 2 and 2b will show that the introduction of risk and money has made the investment curve steeper
and the demand-for-securities curve less steep. The former is
due to the fact that in a risky economy marginal risk must be
deducted from marginal productivity, the latter to the substitution of security preference for time preference as demand
for securities. In Part I it has been described in some detail
why security preference—which is identical with stockholders' demand—must be represented by a flat curve. This
can now be elucidated yet further.

Our demand for an ordinary commodity is a diminishing
function of price not only because its marginal utility to us
falls as we get more of it, but also because to be able to buy
more of it we must restrict our purchases elsewhere. In other
words, as we buy increasing quantities of a particular good its
marginal utility falls and the marginal utility of our expenditure on everything else (loosely called the marginal utility of
money) increases; and price is refined as the ratio of the

marginal utility of the good in question to the marginal utility of the rest of our income.

Investment adds to the community's stock of securities and thereby reduces its marginal utility, but it will increase the marginal utility of expenditure *only* when it involves real abstinence, i.e. when there is full employment. When there are unemployed resources in the economy, increased investment will not necessitate a 'restriction of purchases elsewhere', indeed consumption usually increases *pari passu* with investment, so the demand price for securities will not fall because the marginal utility of expenditure increases, but only because the marginal utility of securities falls—and we know that new securities produced during the short period are such a small fraction of the total stock that this effect is practically nil. From the individual's point of view, of course, buying a security does imply restricting consumption. But the communal demand curve for securities is not a simple sum of the individuals' demand curves, as these are not independent of each other.

The above argument also implies that when there is full employment the t.p. curve comes into its own again; that is the reason why in fig. 2b we have not continued the s.p. curve beyond its intersection with the t.p. curve. This can also be expressed by saying that the t.p. and s.p. curves coincide beyond their meeting point. For once full employment is reached, any attempt at increasing investment beyond saving will result in sharply rising prices and costs which, by increasing the transaction demand for money, will send up interest rates in the secondhand market. Of course, as there is no definite point where full employment begins and underemployment ends, so the kink in the s.p. curve will not be a mathematical kink either.

We have now completed the restatement of our main argument. This formulation of it is less general than the first, admitting one kind of long-term security only, but it simplifies the consideration of specific problems. For example, a rise in the marginal efficiency of capital can be represented in fig. 2b by a rise in the investment curve, and we can read off immediately that this will increase investment activity and the level of employment, and raise the market rate of interest. An increase in the quantity of money causes the s.p. curve to fall and the investment curve to become less steep.[1] The greater the community's confidence in the liquidity and risklessness of the securities, the smaller will be the shift in the s.p. curve. In the limiting case an increase in the quantity of money would only affect the investment curve. This shows how changes in the quantity of money can cause changes in the level of investment and employment *via* the short-term rate and without affecting the long-term rate of interest at all.

---

[1] The latter because the increased liquidity of the banks induces them to charge less for initial risk-bearing. This effect need not manifest itself in a fall of the short-term rate; the banks have also other means at their disposal for restricting credit than raising its price, and their increased liquidity may just induce them to be more generous in their credit policy.

Chapter 2

CAPITAL ACCUMULATION, EMPLOYMENT AND PRICE RIGIDITY[1]

1941

The primary aim of this article is to analyse the significance, implications, and legitimacy of such notions as 'flexible prices' and 'rigid wages'. While this problem is of vital importance for business cycle theory, it can be treated most conveniently in the framework of a long-period theory of capital accumulation. The following analysis, therefore, is presented as such, but we wish to emphasize our belief that most of the conclusions we shall arrive at in this way are equally applicable, and perhaps more important, as tools in business cycle analysis.

The theory of capital accumulation is often identified with the theory of the business cycle. Yet there is no conceptual difficulty in imagining capital accumulation to proceed smoothly if we assume extra economic data (like technical invention) to change continuously, and if we also abstract from discontinuities and time-lags in the mechanism of the economic system. In the following we shall study this imaginary cycle-free capital accumulation, which may also be regarded as the long-run trend round which the economic system fluctuates owing to the time-lags, delayed actions and discontinuities inherent in its working. Whether cyclical fluctuations are maintained by outside shocks (in which case cycle and trend would be additive), or whether they are maintained by the accumulation of capital itself is irrelevant for our argument. For we believe in the usefulness of analysing the

---

[1] This is the second of a series of articles summarizing a piece of research I carried out on a special grant from the Leon Bequest Fund. The first, 'A Study of Interest and Capital', appeared in *Economica*, August 1940; but the present article forms a complete and independent whole.

problem of capital accumulation separately from that of the business cycle even if the latter is due to and unthinkable without the former. It may be thought that long-run trend is best described by static equilibrium theory. Such a 'dynamic interpretation' of static theory is well-known to be legitimate if in addition to the absence of discontinuities we also assume perfectly flexible prices. But our exclusion of discontinuities implies nothing about price-flexibility, about which we are going to make, in turn, various definite assumptions.

THE NON-CAPITALISTIC ECONOMY

We shall begin our analysis with a simple non-capitalistic economy where all factors of production are original (in the sense that their birth-rate is independent of economic considerations) and inalienable. Only their services can be hired. For the time being we shall also assume the quantities of all factors of production to be constant and technical conditions of production to be unchanged. Only at the end of this article shall we consider the effects of technical advance and population growth. Owners of the factors of production are paid a flow of income for their productive services which they use for buying flows of different consumption services. They can also keep a hoard of purchasing power in the form of money but in no other form. This restriction will be removed when we come to the discussion of our capitalistic model. Money can be neither consumed nor produced (unlike gold which is mined and has its industrial uses), and its stock will be considered as fixed.[1] We shall also admit the existence of small stocks of other commodities, used for averaging out seasonal variations and smoothing over discontinuous changes in consumption and production. But we assume that there is no speculation in such stocks, that they are not generally held as a store of value, and that entrepreneurs aim at keeping them at their (seasonally) normal level. We can now proceed to analyse the behaviour of this simple model, first in the limiting cases of perfectly flexible and perfectly rigid prices, and then in the more important intermediate cases.

[1] It will become evident as we go along that the alternative assumption of a fixed banking policy—keeping the quantity of money as a given function of the level of employment—would lead to identical results.

Flexible Prices

When all prices, including, of course, those of the factors of production, are perfectly flexible, we can regard static equilibrium theory as a dynamic theory. In this case, therefore, there will always be full employment in the sense that all resources will be employed to the extent their owners wish them to be. The effect of changes in consumers' tastes will not interest us here, and we shall be concerned exclusively with the consequences of changes in the desire to hold wealth. A once-and-for-all increase in the desire to hold wealth will cause a once-and-for-all drop in the general price-level, down to the point where the unchanged stock of money represents the new greater hoard of purchasing power now demanded. A diminished desire to hold wealth will have the converse effect. More important is the case when the community regularly wants to save a given proportion of its income. This will result in a continuous fall of the general price-level at such a time-rate as to make the percentage fall of prices over the average reaction-period of consumers equal to the percentage that savings form of income;[1] where by consumers' reaction-period we mean the time that elapses before a change in money-incomes induces a full adjustment of money-expenditure. That this must be so will become obvious to the reader when he recalls that we have contracted out the possibility of investment and assumed entrepreneurs to aim at keeping commodity stocks constant. For when there is no investment, all incomes originate from current production, and when entrepreneurs keep stocks constant—that it, when they sell all their produce at whatever prices they will fetch—the value of current output, and hence that of total income, must be equal to total expenditure at any moment, or during any period of time.[2]

---

[1] Because it is at this time-rate of price-fall that forced dissaving exactly counterbalances voluntary saving. We have avoided this terminology because the term 'forced saving' has in the past been used in too many different senses not to lead to misunderstanding and muddle.

[2] It may be well to remark here that continuously falling prices need not imply losses for entrepreneurs. As soon as they get accustomed to such a state of affairs, they will calculate the marginal value productivities of the factors of production on the expectation of falling prices and pay them correspondingly. On the other side the ever-increasing value of consumers' money hoards does not correspond to any 'material' gain either. Holders of money may indeed derive a psychological satisfaction out of their bigger stores of purchasing power, and this should properly be considered as a real

Thus, the rate of fall (or rise) of the general price-level depends on the rate of saving (or dissaving) and on the average length of consumers' reaction time. The latter may be thought at first to be identical with the average time that elapses between the receipt and expenditure of incomes—Wicksell's 'average interval of rest of money'—which is determined by the ratio of the total stock of money to national income per unit of time.[1] (It can easily be seen that this ratio has the dimension of time.) This, however, would only be true if the sole function of money were to bridge over discontinuities in receipts and disbursements. If, as in our case, it is also held as a store of value, this mechanical relationship ceases to hold good, and the reaction-time of consumers has to be regarded as an independent datum.

As to the determinants of the rate of saving, we shall assume that the proportion people save out of their income is an increasing function of the level of real income, an increasing function of the *real* rate of interest, and a diminishing function of the stock of purchasing power already accumulated. The first of these, originally propounded by Mr Keynes, has recently been assailed as not being 'a general psychological law which may be relied upon to describe the actions of all men at all times'.[2] No doubt this criticism is formally correct; but the fact alone that all Mr Keynes's work in economic theory was always closely related to actual economic problems of the day, should in itself be sufficient to convince one that he never meant his law in the above sense. We believe that the law that an increase in income leads to a more than proportionate increase in saving and less than proportionate increase in expenditure should be interpreted not as a psychological law relating to all individuals at all times, but as a statistical law relating to modern industrial communities, given their usual distribution of income, the psychology of their members and the spending habits of their governments (e.g. the payment of

gain. But as soon as the community as a whole tried collectively to make more tangible use of its stores by dishoarding them, it could derive no real benefit but would continue to consume the same real income as before at ever-increasing prices.

[1] If this were correct, the rate of fall of prices would have to be equal to the rate of accumulation of savings, i.e. to the proportion current savings bear to the total stock of money in existence.

[2] Elisabeth W. Gilboy: 'The Propensity to Consume', *Quarterly Journal of Economics*, vol. 53, p. 140.

relief to the unemployed). In this sense the law is borne out by statistical evidence and in the present article at any rate it will be so interpreted. The second assumption—that saving increases with rising interest rates—used to be generally accepted by the classical economists, although they were conscious of the existence of exceptions to the rule.[1] These can best be dealt with if we think of saving as the purchase of a stream—perpetual or finite—of future income. Saving represents expenditure on the 'commodity' future income, and a rise in the rate of interest represents a fall in its price; for the higher the rate of interest the smaller will be the capital sum which is necessary to secure a given stream of income. The demand curve for future income may be taken to be downward-sloping (since it is not an inferior good), and a fall in its price to lead to increased purchases. But increased purchases at a lower price may mean either increased or diminished expenditure (saving), according as demand is elastic or inelastic. It would be beyond the scope of this article to analyse the nature and weigh the relative importance of the several psychological motives for saving; instead we shall postulate as an arbitrary assumption that the communal demand curve for future income is elastic in the relevant range, and that, therefore, the rate of saving of the community as a whole is an increasing function of the *real* rate of interest, both in the long and in the short run. It will appear later that this assumption implies nothing about the relationship (or the lack of such) between the rate of saving and the *market* rate of interest. The third of our assumptions—that the accumulation of wealth diminishes the desire to save—I have never as yet seen mentioned and it is only stated here tentatively for completeness' sake. It is unlikely to hold good about individuals but is probably true when we consider several successive generations. Statistics in England point to the existence of such a tendency;[2] on the other hand, they also show that the public's secularly diminishing propensity to save is largely offset by the increasing importance of corporate saving. It will be seen as we go along how our results would be affected if the rate of saving were independent of the last two factors.

[1] Cf. A. Marshall: *Principles of Economics*, definitive edition, p. 235. These exceptions have since been emphasized more strongly by G. Cassel.
[2] Colin Clark: *National Income and Outlay*, Chapter 12.

In our model, the assumptions of a fixed quantity of factors and no technical change (keeping the productivity of labour constant), and of flexible prices (ensuring full employment) keep the level of real income invariant. The stock of savings is given by the fixed quantity of money. As prices fall the stock of purchasing power which it represents increases, and if our third assumption holds good, this will cause the rate of saving, and with it the time-rate of price-fall, to diminish. Thus, on this assumption, we get an asymptotic approach to long-period equilibrium, where the price-level ceases falling because the stock of money has come to represent such a large store of purchasing power that the community can no longer increase its satisfaction by adding to it and, therefore, spends its entire income. The real rate of interest is represented in our model by the appreciation of money as the price-level is falling. If, as argued above, it is falling at a diminishing rate (because the third assumption holds), this implies a diminishing rate of interest which will (if the second assumption holds too) be yet another reason for the rate of saving to fall as time goes on. If, on the other hand, the third assumption is illegitimate and people go on saving irrespective of what they have saved up already, then, of course, prices will go on falling undiminished.

Our next problem is whether this system with its long-period trend of falling prices, approaching or not a long-period equilibrium, is stable. In static equilibrium theory we call a situation stable if a small change affecting a small section of the economy, or a number of simultaneous but *independent* small changes affecting different sections of the economy in *different* ways, cause equally small reactions. In dynamic analysis we call a system stable if an exogenous change affecting the economy as a whole, or at least a large section of it, in the *same* way leads to an effect which is not out of proportion with its cause. This definition may seem somewhat loose but will become clear in the following. Assume first that we are in long-period equilibrium when, owing to some exogenous disturbance, there occurs a temporary increase in the general flow of production or a temporary diminution in the general flow of consumers' demand, causing a 1 per cent fall in the general price-level. This means that money holdings have yielded a 1 per cent rate of interest in terms of real purchasing power. This initial fall in the price-level will lead to the expectation of a further fall,[1] and will thus enhance the attractiveness of holding money to the public and increase their demand for it—thereby *causing* a further fall in prices and a further increase in the attraction of holding money.[2] Thus, if prices were perfectly flexible, a small but general fall in prices would tend to call forth a further cumulative fall. The argument is exactly analogous for the long-run trend of smoothly falling prices. If an outside shock enhances or diminishes the equilibrium rate of fall of prices, this will set up a tendency away from and not towards the equilibrium rate of fall. The case of an initial *rise* in the general price-level is perfectly symmetrical and has been strikingly illustrated by the German inflation of 1923. As soon as the rise of prices destroyed the traditional belief in the stability of the value of money, i.e. as soon as prices became really flexible, the stage was set for the runaway inflation, brought about largely by people's desire to diminish their stock of purchasing power when they discovered that such holdings 'earned' a negative interest in real terms.

It may be objected at this stage that we are too much concerned about the stability of prices; for—one might say—what does it matter if prices fluctuate, as long as production remains undisturbed and there is no unemployment? Up to a certain point this objection is justified. I do think that economists often take it too much for granted that a stable price-level is the only thing that matters. But the kind of instability described above would rob the pricing system of its function: the allocation of economic resources among different uses. For a short time after instability has set in this would not matter, since production would continue in its accustomed grooves. But after a time tastes may change—owing perhaps to the redistribution of income caused by rapidly changing prices, or to any other cause—and then production will fail properly to adjust itself to changed demand conditions, because relative prices are a very poor index of the relative urgency of wants when the price-level as a whole is galloping up or down.

[1] Under what circumstances it will not lead to that expectation will be discussed below.

[2] This, however, is only true if our assumption that saving increases with the rate of interest holds good.

Rigid Prices

For the discussion of the other limiting case of perfectly rigid prices we must make the meaning of this assumption quite explicit. It may mean the fixing either of all prices at one stage of the productive process only, or of all prices of all commodities, intermediate goods, and factors of production.[1] We shall adopt the second interpretation because it is simpler and not more unrealistic nor less general than the first. The last statement may be objected to, because 'costs' are generally regarded as more rigid than 'prices'. This may be true concerning labour costs; on the other hand raw-material costs are usually the most volatile element in the whole price-structure. It is worth noting, however, that while the following argument is rendered simpler on the second interpretation of rigid prices, it holds good equally well on the first too. For given the production functions and consumers' tastes, and given—in each industry—the degree of monopoly as a function of the level of income, each set of prices fixed at any particular stage of the productive process unequivocally determines all prices at all other stages as well. These may be different for every level of employment but will be fixed for each. As against this, it may be argued that the degree of monopoly cannot be regarded as given since it is price-determined rather than price-determining. This is probably correct as a description of our economic system, but it is incompatible with the assumption that prices are fixed at one stage of the productive process only and are perfectly flexible elsewhere. It seems, therefore, better to begin with the assumption of perfectly invariant prices at all stages of production and to relax this assumption later on in a more realistic manner.

We shall start from an equilibrium situation where the production of each commodity equals the demand for it and the given stock of money represents—at the given price-level —the exact amount of purchasing power the community wishes to hold. As already stated, we also assume the existence of unemployed resources and shall altogether exclude the consideration of problems arising when the full employment of any of the factors of production is reached. Then consider

[1] When we assume prices to be fixed, the quantities of productive resources must be variable. In other words, on this assumption we can only discuss the problems of an underemployed economy.

an increased desire to hold purchasing power. As both prices and the stock of money are fixed, this desire cannot materialize; it will instead lead to an impoverishment of society exactly counteracting its increased desire to hold wealth. The mechanism by which such a change comes about is easily visualized. The desire to hold more money on the part of some (or all) people, not counterbalanced by a desire to dishoard on the part of others, will reduce the flow of demand for some (or all) commodities and induce entrepreneurs in the industries affected to reduce their rate of production. (Entrepreneurs notice the diminished demand for their produce by the accumulation of commodity stocks which they promptly try to remedy by restricting production.) Diminished production means a fall in employment and incomes paid out, and this movement will only come to a stop at the point where the now poorer community is content to hold the exact amount of purchasing power represented by the stock of money (i.e. where expenditures again equal incomes); for we assume that the lower is the level of income and employment the smaller is the community's demand for holding money. The argument is exactly the same if we assume that the community regularly wants to save at a rate which depends on the level of income and employment. (The stock of savings already accumulated, and the rate of interest are invariant in this model.) In such a case the level of employment will always have to be such as to induce the community to perform zero saving, and a change in average thriftiness (propensity to save) will only cause a change in the level of employment and income: upward if people become less thrifty and downward if they turn more economical.

There is an important asymmetry between this case and the behaviour of our first model (flexible prices) in the corresponding case. There, a once-and-for-all increase in the desire to hold wealth caused a simple fall in the price-level, and a given rate of saving caused a continuous fall in prices; while here, both result in a once-and-for-all diminution of employment. The difference is explained by the fact that while a fall in the level of employment is a real change and involves a fall in the community's real income, a fall in the general level of prices implies a change in nominal incomes only and leaves real incomes unaffected. A corollary of this difference is that while under conditions of flexible prices the community's desire to save part of its income resulted in an ever-increasing stock of savings, the possession of which has ultimately obliterated this desire and established long-period equilibrium with a stable price-level; under conditions of rigid prices there is no possibility of a corresponding tendency towards equilibrium, because, with given prices and a given stock of money, the hoard of savings cannot be increased.

After the discussion of the two limiting cases, we can proceed to consider the intermediate cases of different degrees of price-flexibility. There are two ways of relaxing the assumption of perfectly rigid prices. Firstly, by letting all prices change uniformly at a certain maximum time-rate; secondly, by allowing some prices to be more flexible than others.

Prices of Uniformly Limited Flexibility

It is easy to see what difference a uniform flexibility of the price- and cost-structure will make to our models. We have seen that with rigid prices the level of employment and income must always be such as to make society's net saving equal to zero, while with perfectly flexible prices the general price-level will be falling at a time-rate determined by consumers' average reaction-time and the rate of saving at full employment.[1] If the maximum time-rate of price-flexibility is below this time-rate,[2] employment, and with it the rate of saving, must fall to that level at which the time-rate of price-fall exactly equals the maximum time rate of price-flexibility. It follows from this that if the rate of saving is an increasing function of the level of income and employment, the equilibrium rate of employment will be the higher, the more flexible are prices. As prices fall, the fixed quantity of money represents an ever-increasing store of purchasing power, and if this diminishes the community's propensity to save we get a tendency towards long-period equilibrium here too. But while in the case of perfectly flexible prices the diminishing propensity to save resulted in a diminishing rate of price fall, here the

[1] For the moment we abstract from the fact that a system of perfectly flexible prices would be unstable.
[2] We assume here that there is an absolute limit to the time-rate at which prices can rise or fall. This, of course, is a gross over-simplification since that limit depends on the strength of the forces tending to change prices; but it much simplifies the argument without at the same time falsifying it.

time-rate of price-fall (and with it the real rate of interest) will remain the same, because employment always tends to the maximum possible level compatible with the given rate of price-flexibility, so that the diminished propensity to save will be exactly offset by a higher level of employment, and the rate of saving itself will remain the same. Only after full employment has been reached will the time rate of price-fall start diminishing, and from then onwards the system will behave in exactly the same way as that of perfectly flexible prices. Until then the tendency towards equilibrium is the slower (and employment the lower) the less flexible is the price- and cost-structure.

We recall that we have proved our system of perfectly flexible prices to be unstable. The problem, therefore, arises: which is the maximum rate of price-flexibility (yielding the highest level of employment) at which the system will still be stable. It will be remembered that the instability of the system of perfectly flexible prices was due to our assumption that an initial change in the value of money (due to an exogenous disturbance) leads to the expectation of a further change *in the same direction,* i.e. that the elasticity of expectations is greater than unity. To find, therefore, the conditions for the stability of the economic system, we must find out what are the circumstances under which a change in the value of money does *not* lead to such expectations. It seems to me that this will be the case whenever people have a notion of *normal* or *just* prices, because only then will they regard a price-change as something abnormal or temporary, which may not persist and is unlikely to continue. The existence of this notion in people's consciousness does not presuppose completely rigid prices. This has been amply proved by the extraordinary tenacity with which people have clung to their belief in the invariance of the value of money at the beginning of each of the major inflations of history, although most of these were preceded by periods of important price-changes. The limit to the degree of price-flexibility, beyond which it would destroy the belief in a normal price-level seems to be analogous to the 'threshold of consciousness' which must be surpassed by a sensation to become perceptible to our senses. Consumers plan their future expenditure on the basis of their experience over a past period. Prices may have changed during this period, but unless these changes have been substantial, consumers will not interpret them as a change in the purchasing power of money.

Prices of Varying Flexibility

This train of thought becomes more intelligible when we drop our assumption of a uniform flexibility of prices. In reality some prices are flexible, others are rigid. The causes for price-rigidity are many. Some of these have been shortly discussed, and one of them, monopoly power, has been dealt with in detail, in my 'Prices under Monopoly and Competition'.[1] The most important are probably long-term contracts, tradition, and technical and administrative considerations. Tradition fixes prices simply because consumers resent having to change their 'scale of values' too often and too drastically, in exactly the same way as they would resent a continuous flux in their friends' telephone numbers. Their resentment, of course, can only be effective as a factor limiting price-flexibility if it is backed up by sanctions. These are to be sought not so much in consumers' ability to refrain from consumption as in the power of public opinion. No industry, and especially no monopolized one, likes to come into the limelight of public scrutiny, and will avoid unsympathetic publicity even at the cost of somewhat reducing its profits. This will be a check not only on rising prices, but also on price-reductions when-ever producers consider the difficulty of subsequently raising prices again. Technical considerations fix the price not only of slot-machine goods—ranging from chewing gum to under-ground fares—but also of all goods that are advertised at a certain price and must, therefore, be sold at that price for a considerable period afterwards. How deeply the notion of normal price is ingrained in people's minds owing to advertise-ment and tradition is shown by the efficacy of the stunt of selling, say, '£5 suits' at fifty shillings. These and other factors do not, of course, fix prices permanently. They only limit their rate of change and stabilize them for a shorter or longer period of time by setting a lower limit either to the time-inter-val between successive price-changes, or to the magnitude of price-change itself (e.g. it may not be worth the trouble to negotiate a new wage contract for less than a, say, 5 per cent change). When there is a force present—e.g. slack trade and

[1] *Journal of Political Economy*, XLIX, 663-85.

unemployment—making for a change in prices, some prices will respond more quickly than others and some may not move at all. Consumers will regard the movement of a few isolated prices as a normal phenomenon, due to causes inherent in those commodities. Only when price-changes become very general or very drastic will they begin to suspect 'trouble on the side of money' and wake up to the realization of a shift in its value. This threshold of consciousness, we submit, is the boundary line between a stable and an unstable economy. We may be accused here of arguing in a circle and of asserting that the stability of the system depends on the belief in 'normal' prices, while this belief itself is conditional on the stability of prices. This is true to the extent that people's faith in the invariance of the value of money will be the stronger the less often it has been tried, and even the greatest faith will be shaken by a sufficiently strong and persistent force tending to change the price-level. But given this force, the stability of the system will still depend on the community's psychology and on the presence of technical and organizational factors making for price-rigidity.

So far we have only implied but not yet proved that a system in which some prices are rigid and others flexible behaves in the same way as our system of uniformly limited price-flexibility. That this is so can best be shown by an example. Assume that the wages of skilled labour are immutably fixed in terms of money while all other wages, costs and prices are perfectly flexible. Consider then a progressive community that performs (or would perform) positive net saving at full employment so that the receipts of industry will always lie below costs. The ensuing underemployment of productive resources will lower all factor prices except the wages of skilled labour. This will make a substitution of other factors for skilled labour profitable, but such substitution takes time. Not only does it take time to exchange more for less skilled-labour-intensive methods, but those methods must first be invented, and the time-rate of substitution is limited by the rate of technical advance. The faster the rate at which substitution can be effected, the higher will be the employment of productive resources other than skilled labour, and the higher will be the community's real income. The argument is the same if we assume the price of a consumers' good fixed instead of that a factor of production; except that in this case it will be consumers' habits that must be revised and altered instead of productive methods.

The economic effects of the existence of isolated rigidities here and there in the structure of prices and costs are thus seen to be identical in all essentials to those of the lesser but uniform rigidity of all prices. The differences will be due to the distortion of the price-structure when the more rigid prices 'lag behind'; this can be likened to a fisherman's net which is pegged down at a few meshes only and gets out of shape when pulled at its loose ends.

THE CAPITALISTIC ECONOMY

The foregoing analysis of an economy in which people want to save but cannot invest should be regarded merely as a statement of problems and as a preliminary exercise to our analysis of the capitalistic economy. This latter will differ from our previous model by the existence of a factor of production—capital—the birth-rate of which is determined by economic considerations. Moreover, as long as we retain the assumption of fixed quantities of the original factors of production, capital will also be the only factor the quantity of which can change.

If the rate of investment (as a proportion of real income) were given independently of economic considerations, the foregoing analysis would still hold good word for word, except that we would everywhere have to substitute for 'rate of saving' the expression 'difference between the rate of saving and the rate of investment' with its proper algebraic sign. E.g. if the given level of investment were equal to the rate of saving the community wishes to perform at full employment, we would get equilibrium at full employment with a stable price-level, irrespective of whether prices are flexible or rigid. If the rate of investment were below this level but positive, then under conditions of perfectly rigid prices we would get equilibrium at that level of employment at which the community wants to save at a rate equal to the rate of investment (i.e. where the difference between saving and investment is zero); while under perfectly flexible prices we would get full employment and a price-level falling at a time-rate determined as described above by the reaction-time of consumers and the (rate of) excess of savings (i.e. the difference between saving at full employment and investment).

The rate of investment cannot, however, be regarded as given, and we must now see how it is determined. We know from capital theory that whenever the marginal productivity of capital is higher than the rate of interest, capital accumulation will be profitable. How much additional capital is needed to bring its marginal productivity to equality with the rate of interest is shown by the shape of the marginal productivity curve. How fast this additional equipment will be built nobody, until quite recently, has bothered to determine. This singular and important omission of a long line of capital theorists has been remedied by M. Kalecki.[1] His argument is shortly that investment involves risk (that of turning out unsuccessfully), and the cost—in the form of an interest rate —of bearing this risk increases with the rate of investment. The latter will, therefore, always be pushed to the point where the cost of risk-bearing exactly equals the difference between the marginal productivity of capital and the market rate of interest. Whether this cost is borne by the entrepreneur himself and is deducted from the marginal productivity of capital, or whether it is borne by his bank or promoter and is added to the rate of interest, is irrelevant from our point of view. We shall simply assume that the rate of investment is an increasing function of the gap between the marginal productivity of capital and the market rate of interest, and proceed to analyse the determination, first of the rate of interest, secondly of the marginal productivity of capital.

The Rate of Interest

Hitherto we have assumed that the quantity of money, the sole medium in which value can be stored, is fixed. This assumption will be retained throughout this article, but we now introduce other, alternative media of storing and holding wealth: securities. These are imperfect substitutes for money because they involve risk and (potential) illiquidity. To counteract this relative disadvantage and to induce people to hold them in spite of this deficiency, their prices must always be lower than that of money, in other words they must earn

[1] M. Kalecki: 'The Principle of Increasing Risk', *Economica* (NS), vol. 4.

a positive rate of interest in terms of money. We distinguish between securities that promise the future payment of definite sums of money (fixed-interest-bearing securities) and those that promise indefinite payments (shares). With the now fashionable policy of dividend stabilization there is little difference between the two as long as prices are stable or show only temporary fluctuations, but fundamental differences arise when there is a permanent shift in prices. Accordingly we shall treat them together first, and separately when we come to the consideration of the effects of price-changes.

Individuals form (subjective) judgments of the risk and illiquidity embodied in different securities and have a certain preference for safety and liquidity. Given these judgments and preferences, each individual will—when confronted with the system of market rates of interest—choose a definite combination of different securities and money in which to hold his wealth. The parallelism between the individual's behaviour in the securities market and in the market where he buys consumers' goods is complete. There the consumer, facing market prices which to him are given, aims at spending his income on different goods in a way that will maximize his total satisfaction. Here the investor, facing market rates of interest, aims at investing his stock of wealth in different securities and in money so that they should yield him the maximum future income compatible with his limited willingness to bear risk and illiquidity.

From the point of view of the community as a whole it is the quantities of securities and of money that are given, and they, together with the given judgments and preferences of investors, determine the market rates of interest in the short period.[1]

The greater the quantity of any particular kind of security the higher will be its market rate of interest, since, given their tastes and judgments, people need an ever-stronger inducement to increase their holdings of any one type of security. A simultaneous increase in the quantity of all securities relatively to that of money will cause a rise in the general level of market rates, while an increase in the quantity of money relatively to that of securities will lead to a lower level. In

[1] For the moment we also assume the level of employment to be given. The effect of changes in employment on interest rates will be considered below.

the following we shall only be concerned with the average or general level of market rates; the determination and inter-dependence of interest rates on different kinds of securities has been discussed in detail in my 'A Study of Interest and Capi-tal'.[1] It may be interjected here that the quantity of securities cannot be regarded as given while capital accumulation is going on and new securities representing the new equipment are issued. But in a modern industrial community the value of net investment made during the short period is an insignificant and negligible fraction of the total stock of equipment already in existence, and its influence on the average level of interest rates can, therefore, be neglected.[2] In the long run, of course, the quantity of securities will increase absolutely and—what is more important—relatively to the constant quantity of money, causing market rates of interest to rise. But we emphasize once more that owing to the relative smallness of the volume of new investment per short period this is a secular phenomenon and can be neglected in short-run arguments.

So far we have assumed a constant level of employment. This was necessary because given the total quantity of money, the higher is the level of employment, the higher will be the demand for money for transaction purposes and the less money will be left available for investment.[3] Hence, a rise in employ-ment has the same effect as a diminution of the quantity of money: both raise market rates of interest. Another factor which may cause changes in interest rates is a change in the purchasing power of money. A fall in the general price-level means an increase in the store of purchasing power repre-sented by the fixed quantity of money, but it also means a proportionate increase in the store of future income repre-sented by the stock of securities that promise the future pay-ment of predetermined sums of money. There is no special reason why people should continue to hold money and fixed-interest-bearing securities in the same proportions—or rather that they should be induced to hold them in the same

[1] Chapter 1 above.
[2] Taking six months as our short-period, the ratio that the value of new investment bears to the value on already extant equipment is probably of the order of magnitude of 1-2 per cent. Cf. S. Kuznets: *National Income and Capital Formation*, p. 15.
[3] A more elegant though less graphic way of saying the same thing is that relative tastes for securities and money depend on the level of employment.

proportions by the same structure of interest rates—when the real value of their total stock of wealth has increased. Nevertheless, a proportional increase in the quantities of purchasing power represented by money and fixed-interest-bearing securities would be unlikely to affect interest rates significantly. The fall in the price-level, however, diminishes the transaction demand for money and, setting free a greater proportion for purposes of investment, will cause a slight fall in interest rates.

Before proceeding to the discussion of the influence of price-changes on the market rate on shares, it may be worth our while to make a short digression and to inquire into the exact nature of the market rate on fixed-interest-bearing securities. In the first part of this article we have seen that under a system where money is the only form in which purchasing power can be stored the appreciation of money is the 'reward for abstinence'. When money and securities exist side by side as alternative forms of holding purchasing power, the real rate of interest on holding money will still be its rate of appreciation, while the real rate of interest on a fixed-interest-bearing security will be compounded of its market rate (determined by the relation of the security's market value and its promised future money repayments) and the rate of appreciation of money over its life-time. This is due to the fact that the fate of fixed-interest-bearing securities is tied up with that of money: representing definite promises to pay predetermined sums of money, they depreciate or appreciate together. The way in which these two rates are compounded is given by the formula

$$(1 + i_r) = (1 + i_m)(1 + i_a),$$

or approximately by

$$i_r \approx i_m + i_a.$$

Hence, what we customarily call the market or money rate of interest on fixed-interest-bearing securities (i_m) is the difference between the real rate on securities (i_r) and the real rate on money (i_a). It is the additional attraction of securities necessary to induce people to bear the risk and illiquidity of holding them instead of money and can, therefore, be regarded as the reward thereof. This shows the mistake of the classical economists who thought of the market rate of interest as composed of the reward for abstinence and the reward for risk-bearing. That indeed is true of the real rate on securities, but the market rate is always that part of the real rate which is the reward for risk- and illiquidity-bearing only.

This argument does not necessarily imply that the proportion people save out of their income depends only on expected changes in the value of money and not at all on market rates of interest. For it is in the nature of risk- and illiquidity-bearing that they cannot be separated from abstinence, in the same way as butter cannot (with any propriety) be eaten without bread. Thus, when higher market rates make risk-bearing more attractive, not only will people try to keep a greater proportion of their already accumulated wealth in securities, they may also be induced to save more out of their income. But it is important to realize that the relationship between the market rate of interest and the rate of saving is comparable to that between the price of butter and the demand for bread, and not to that between the price, and demand for, the same commodity. The indirect nature of this relationship explains its looseness, and it seems to me that it also provides a satisfactory explanation of the insensitivity of the rate of saving to *short-run* changes in the market rate of interest.

After this digression we can proceed to the analysis of the effects of price-changes on the market rate of interest on shares. We define the market rate on a share as the ratio of its expected dividend payments to its market value. Since dividend payments are likely to move together with the general level of prices, the store (or stream) of future purchasing power represented by the stock of shares will remain approximately unchanged when a general price-fall (price-rise) increases (diminishes) the store of purchasing power represented by money and fixed-interest-bearing securities. As this is equivalent to a diminution (increase) in the quantity of shares relatively to that of money and fixed-interest-bearing securities, it will lead to a fall (rise) in the market rate on shares in exactly the same way as a diminution in the supply of a consumers' good leads to a rise in its price.[1]

Thus far we have computed the market rates on shares on

---

[1] We have seen above that the fall in prices also lowers the market rate on fixed-interest-bearing securities, but—as a comparison of the two arguments will show—always to a lesser extent.

the implicit assumption that the change in prices is regarded as permanent and non-recurring. If, however, the initial price-fall leads to the expectation of a further price-fall, and a corresponding fall in money profits and dividends, then the expected time-rate of fall (p.a.) must be deducted from the market rate and may easily make it negative. This tendency, however, will be partially counteracted by the diminution in the demand for holding shares due to their diminished attraction. One would, indeed, be tempted to argue that it would be totally counteracted were it not for the fact that shares are held not only for the income they yield but also for the control they give over industry. This establishes a significant difference between them and fixed-interest-bearing securities and lowers their elasticity of substitution. (The argument is perfectly symmetrical for the case of an expected price-rise.) It is important to notice that the market rate on fixed-interest-bearing securities is entirely unaffected by price-change expectations.

The Marginal Productivity of Capital

The marginal productivity of capital may be defined as that rate of interest at which the stream of expected future marginal value products (net profits) of a capital-good must be discounted in order to make its (the stream's) present value equal to the cost of building an equivalent capital-good. This rate will fall with capital accumulation, because the greater is the quantity of capital relatively to that of other factors of production, the smaller will be its marginal productivity. Besides the relative quantity of different factors of production, the marginal productivity of capital-goods also depends on the relative demand for different factors. Variations in the level of investment constitute changes in this relative demand if the various factors are not combined in the same proportions in investment-good industries and consumption-good industries respectively. E.g. if investment-good industries are capital-intensive, the marginal productivity of capital-goods will rise as the rate of investment increases, it will fall if investment-good industries are labour-intensive. But the marginal productivity of a capital-good is not the same thing as the marginal productivity of capital. The latter also depends on the replacement cost of capital-goods. This is likely to rise with increasing rate of investment, thereby tending to lower the marginal productivity of capital. On balance, therefore, an increase in the rate of investment is more likely to lower than to raise the marginal productivity of capital, although the latter is not impossible.[1] Another factor affecting the marginal productivity of capital is the degree of utilization of existing equipment. For one of the most significant differences between the productive factors: capital and labour, is that the former must be hired for a much longer period than the latter. Labour can usually be dismissed at a week's notice, but equipment, when once bought or constructed, remains on the hands of the entrepreneur who will have to pay interest on the capital invested irrespective of whether and to what extent he makes use of it. It may be argued that this consideration enters the determination of the marginal productivity of already existing equipment only, and not at all that of new capital, which is always planned for full utilization. (For new investment the latter alone is relevant.) While this is true, I believe that the level of employment of existing equipment is bound to have a strong psychological influence on the mind of new investors, whereas investment in the duplication of already existing equipment (the 'widening' of capital) is altogether unthinkable as long as there is excess capacity. More strictly relevant to our special problems is the question how the marginal productivity of capital is affected by a change in prices. Recalling its definition, we see that the marginal productivity of capital is an increasing function of the expected future prices of finished goods, a diminishing function of expected future costs (because expected net profits are the difference between expected receipts and outlays), and a diminishing function of present replacement costs. It also appears that a proportionate change in all three of these quantities leaves the marginal productivity of capital unchanged, whence it follows that the latter is independent of the absolute level of prices. It is not independent, however, of expected changes in prices since these will affect the relationship between present costs and expected future

---

[1] But even that would not lead to instability, because the risk of investment is likely to rise faster than the marginal productivity of capital, so that even with a fixed rate of interest there would always be a stable equilibrium level of investment at which the difference between the marginal productivity of capital and the money rate of interest is exactly equal to the cost of bearing the risk of that rate of investment.

net profits, and will raise the marginal productivity of capital
when a price-rise is expected and lower it when a price-fall is
foreseen, by the expected time-rate of change of prices.

Rigid Prices

We are now fully equipped for the analysis of the behaviour
of the capitalist economy. We shall consider the case of perfectly rigid prices first, and we shall start from initial conditions that make for full employment. It will appear presently
that this assumption makes no difference to the argument and
that we could equally well have started from any degree of
underemployment. Assume that with given tastes, production
functions, saving and risk-bearing propensities, and with given
quantities of money, securities and equipment, the market rates
of interest and the marginal productivity of capital are such
that the level of investment determined by them exactly equals
the rate of saving performed at full employment. We know
that this leads to full employment. But as time goes on, the
accumulation of capital equipment will depress the marginal
productivity of capital, the corresponding increase in the
quantity of securities will be likely to raise market rates of
interest,[1] and both effects will tend to lower the level of
investment. The propensity to save—that is, the rate of saving
as a function of the level of employment—will rise on account
of rising real incomes (due to the increasing quantity and
roundaboutness of equipment) and rising interest rates, but
this tendency may be partly offset by the increase in the stock
of wealth. As the inducement to invest falls and the propensity
to save rises, the level of employment will have to fall to ensure
the equality of saving and investment, but first there will be
an excess of savings for a short time. This is due to the fact that
since present investment activity is determined to a large
extent by past, and to a small extent only by present investment
decisions (*ex ante* investment), employment and the level of
incomes will not start falling immediately after the rate of
investment decisions has fallen. But the excess of savings so
accumulated will be an insignificant fraction of the total stock

---

[1] It need not raise it since the community's total store of wealth increases
pari passu with the increase in the quantity of securities and, as was pointed
out above, it is not certain that people will want to hold money and securities
in the same proportions when their total wealth has increased.

of wealth, and is, therefore, unlikely to affect the general
level of interest rates, which is determined by the allocation
of the total stock of wealth between the total stock of money
and the total stock of securities. The disparity between
saving and investment will, therefore, lower employment
before the accumulation of excess savings would have had
time to eliminate this disparity by depressing interest rates.
The fall in incomes and employment will lower the rate of
saving directly and also, by causing interest rates to fall, indirectly. It will also depress the marginal productivity of
capital, but this will, to a certain extent, be counteracted by
the fall in interest rates. On balance the level of investment
is likely to fall, but at a slower rate than the rate of saving.[1]
Hence the fall in employment will re-establish short-period
equilibrium, and the trend of short-period equilibria will be
one of diminishing employment, approaching the point of
long-period equilibrium, at which capital accumulation will
have ceased, and the community's desire to save will have been
obliterated by unemployment and the accumulation of wealth.

Flexible Prices

We can now turn to the case where the incipient unemployment leads to a fall in prices. We know that, as long as prices
keep on falling, saving can exceed investment by a quantity
which, expressed as a percentage of total national income, is
equal to the percentage fall of prices over the period of
consumers' reaction-time. But the fall of prices might affect
investment activity and saving, so we must first of all see how
these quantities change.

Saving, as we know, depends among other factors on the
reward for pure abstinence, i.e. on the real rate of interest on
money (the perfectly riskless and liquid security); and on the
reward for risk- and illiquidity-bearing, i.e. on the market rate
of interest on securities. The fall in prices raises the real rate on
money, only if it leads to the expectation of a further general
price-fall, while it always lowers market rates of interest on
securities. We shall see presently that our capitalistic model

---

[1] Cf., however, N. Kaldor: 'A Model of the Trade-Cycle' (*Economic
Journal*, May 1940), where it is contended that the inducement to invest is a
steeper function of the level of employment than the propensity to save, and
this fact is presented as a possible explanation of the trade-cycle.

already becomes unstable at a degree of price-flexibility below that at which an initial price-change begins to undermine the notion of a normal price-level; hence we will not have to consider at all the effect of expected changes in the value of money. As to the fall in market rates of interest, that is likely to leave the rate of saving unaffected in the short run, while it may lower it in the long run. Since we shall mainly be concerned with problems of stability for which short-run considerations alone are relevant, and also because changes in interest rates are unlikely to make a great difference to saving even in the long run, we feel justified in simplifying the argument by assuming the rate of saving to be constant and by concentrating on the inducement to invest.

The marginal productivity of capital will remain unchanged by the fall in prices if that is regarded as permanent and non-recurring (zero elasticity of expectations), it will be raised if the latter leads to the expectation of a future return towards the previous higher level of prices (elasticity negative), and lowered if it makes people expect a further price-fall (elasticity positive).[1] Market rates of interest on fixed-interest-bearing securities are independent of price-expectations and will always be lowered by the price-fall. Since, however, they will be lowered only slightly, we can say approximately that an economy, in which the issuing of fixed-interest-bearing securities is the main form of raising capital (we include bank-advances under fixed-interest-bearing securities), will only be stable if prices are so rigid that a primary price-change does not lead to the expectation of a further change in the same direction. For if it did, the primary excess of savings would, by lowering the inducement to invest, lead to a yet greater excess of saving, and instability in the form of a cumulative price-fall would result.[2]

The market rate on shares will, in the neutral case when no future price-changes are expected, be lowered more than that on fixed-interest-bearing securities; while price-change expec-

---

[1] It will be noticed that our definition of the elasticity of price-expectations is somewhat narrower than Professor Hicks's.

[2] This statement is only approximately true because in order that the inducement to invest be lowered, it is not enough that the marginal productivity of capital should fall; it must fall by more than the market rate of interest has fallen. Hence, the elasticity of expectations which forms the limit between stability and instability is not zero, but slightly greater than zero.

tations will affect it in exactly the same way as they affect the marginal productivity of capital, but always to a much lesser extent. The compound effect of the price-fall and of future price-change expectations will be such as to raise the inducement to invest (i.e. widen the gap between the marginal productivity of capital and the market rate of interest) and to diminish the excess of savings when the elasticity of price-expectations is zero, below zero, or slightly above it, whereas it will lower it (and lead to instability) when the elasticity of expectations exceeds a certain critical value which is somewhat above zero. While this result is fundamentally identical with that which we have reached in the case of fixed-interest-bearing securities (cf. footnote 2 on last page), it also shows that a system in which shares are the dominant form of securities is likely to be more stable than one in which fixed-interest-bearing stocks and bonds are the favourite form of investment. This is due partly to the fact that a price-fall always depresses the market rate on shares more than that on stocks and bonds, and partly to the fact that elastic price-change expectations lower the rate on shares still further while leaving that on stocks and bonds unaffected.

As to the formation of expectations, the reader is referred to our discussion of the subject on pages 49 and the following. There are, however, important differences between the two cases. There, we were concerned with the expectations of consumers in relation to their planned expenditure and saving; here, it is the expectations of entrepreneurs when they plan their investments that are relevant. There, we have argued that past price-changes will affect saving plans and make the system unstable only if they are sufficiently general to be recognized as changes in the value of money. Here, no general price-change is necessary to affect expectations relevant to investment plans, because the inducement to invest depends only on the price of the produce of the equipment to be built and on the cost of co-operating factors. The significance of this difference is that less general and smaller price-changes will be sufficient to lead investing entrepreneurs to unstable expectations than is the case with consumers; whence it follows that a higher degree of price-rigidity will be needed to make the capitalistic economy stable than was necessary for our non-capitalistic system.

Another factor which tends further to accentuate this difference between the two systems is that investment plans are usually based on expectations relating to a much longer future period than consumption plans, because the calculation of the marginal productivity of a capital-good necessitates the approximate assessment of net profits over its entire economic life-time (or over a considerable part of it). Consequently, investing entrepreneurs will, if they are prudent, base their decisions on their experience over a much longer past period than do expenditure-planning consumers; and the longer the period taken into consideration, the sooner are changes in prices noticed. Some may argue here that human beings always base all their decisions on their whole past experience—or on what they remember of it. Yet, I believe, that decisions relating to investment, being more momentous because less easily revocable than consumption and saving plans, will be made more carefully, after a more thorough examination of one's memory and consultation of statistics and other people's opinion and forecasts.

This train of thought could be developed further by the consideration that corresponding to differences in the economic lifetime of various forms of capital equipment, different investment decisions will be made with varying care and caution and based on varying lengths of past experience. Moreover, there are also differences in the rigidity of prices and costs relevant for different industries. For both these reasons it is possible that some sections of the economy should be unstable while others are stable. A detailed analysis of this problem would lie beyond the scope of this article, but because of its importance for business cycle theory (where its significance is somewhat different!) we may give an illustration. Consider an economy in which the past experience of fairly regular cyclical changes in prices and employment is given as a datum. Then assume an initial increase in prosperity and employment, coupled with a rise in prices and a slight rise in interest rates. In industries where equipment is relatively short-lived, entrepreneurs will have a tendency to extrapolate the initial price-rise linearly (i.e. to expect a further rise) and to increase their investments, thereby further increasing prosperity and employment and raising prices. As against the destabilizing behaviour of these entrepreneurs, those whose

E

equipment is of such longevity as to compel them to base their investment policy on past experience over at least one complete trade-cycle will consider the increased prosperity and price-rise as cyclical and temporary and will only be affected by the increase in investment-costs and interest-rates, which tends to reduce their investment plans. Two practical examples of such industries, displaying an anti-cyclical and, therefore, stabilizing behaviour, are the railway industry and residential building.[1]

After this digression we may sum up the foregoing argument by saying that our capitalistic model is less stable than our non-capitalistic model in the sense that it needs more rigid prices for stability; partly because the expectations relevant to its stability relate to a few prices only instead of the general price-level, and partly because they are based on experience over a longer past period. Furthermore, the system will be the less stable the greater is the importance of fixed-interest-bearing securities.

The maximum time-rate of price-fall compatible with the stability of the system is unlikely to be sufficient to counteract completely the secular fall in the marginal productivity of capital and the secular rise in market rates of interest, and thereby to maintain the level of employment in the long run. It is more likely that even in the case of (limited) price-flexibility, the long-run level of employment will fall in a progressive economy, although, of course, at a smaller rate than when prices are perfectly rigid.

It is often said that the contrast between the relatively smooth working of our economic system during the nineteenth century and the chronic unemployment of the 1920s and 1930s is explained by the increasing rigidity of our price- and cost-structure. While personally I do not think that this factor is very important, it has been shown above that it is a possible explanation; yet it does not follow from it that measures aiming at increasing the flexibility of prices and costs would be the proper remedy. For hand in hand with the increasing rigidity of prices went another development: the community's diminishing willingness to bear risk. This tendency manifested

[1] Cf. C. Douglas Campbell: 'Cyclical Fluctuations in the Railway Industry', *Manchester Statistical Society; Transactions*, 1929-30, pp. 3-47. Charles F. Roos: 'Dynamic Economics', Chapter 6.

itself partly in the increased care and caution with which investments were planned, and partly in the shift in investors' tastes from ordinary shares to preferential stock and fixed-interest-bearing securities. Both these changes were shown above to make for lesser stability of the system so that the greater rigidity of present-day prices and costs may well be necessary to maintain the stability of our economy.

Other, and probably more important factors that have contributed to the spectacular progress and relatively high average level of employment of the nineteenth century were population growth, the increase in the quantity of money (in the form of gold rushes and the development of the means of payment other than gold), and, possibly, technical advance. Population growth raises the marginal productivity of capital by diminishing its quantity relatively to that of labour; it diminishes the propensity to save by lowering real income per head (owing to the law of non-proportional returns); and it increases the willingness to bear risk by making misinvestments pay.[1] At the same time, however, it also tends slightly to raise interest rates by increasing the transaction demand for money; but on balance it is likely both to raise the inducement to invest and to lower the propensity to save, and thereby to raise the level of employment. The increase in the quantity of money tends to lower market rates of interest and, if carried further, may also raise prices sufficiently to increase the marginal productivity of capital; both effects tend to increase investment, diminish saving, and therefore to raise employment. Technical advance tends to raise the marginal productivity of capital, and —by creating new needs—it also tends to increase the propensity to consume (diminish the propensity to save). But this is a double-edged weapon, because at the same time it also creates technological unemployment, and it is not impossible that on balance it sometimes increases rather than alleviates unemployment.

To review shortly the main results of this paper, we have shown firstly, how in a non-capitalistic economy people's desire to save leads to unemployment if prices are perfectly

[1] E.g. an important part of the railway construction of the middle of the nineteenth century was misinvestment in the sense that it was far in excess of the needs of the day and did not yield half the profits it was expected to yield; but became profitable (or at least more profitable) in a few years' time through the rapid growth of population.

rigid and to instability when they are perfectly flexible (and when a rise in the interest rate leads to a higher rate of saving!): and we have also determined the optimum degree of price-flexibility which yields the highest level of employment compatible with the stability of the system. We have then proceeded to study the capitalistic economy and have found that it behaves similarly to our non-capitalistic model, except that it is less stable (requires greater price-rigidity for stability) and that its instability does *not* depend on the assumption that saving increases with the real rate of interest. Finally, we have shown that the secular accumulation of capital equipment and of securities is likely to lead to increasing unemployment even if prices and costs are not perfectly rigid (but their flexibility is limited by the requirement of stability), unless employment is maintained by population growth, technical advance, increasing quantity of money, or by at least one of these factors. As regards the more general problem of economic change, the conclusion to be drawn from our results is that on the assumption of fixed prices or limited price-flexibility, there need be no inherent tendency in the economic system towards the full (optimum) employment of productive resources; whereas it is impossible to base a theory of economic change on the assumption of perfectly flexible prices. It is inadmissible even to start out from the assumption of flexible prices as a limiting case, for it is very dangerous to argue or to draw conclusions about our economy on the basis of a model which is essentially unstable. It also follows from this that the criticism of the methods and conclusions of Mr Keynes and his followers on the ground that they assume rigid money wages is totally unwarranted; not only because this assumption is probably less unrealistic than the classical assumption of perfectly flexible wages and prices, but also because the model of rigid wages—fulfilling the condition of stability—is unlikely to differ significantly from the real economy in its essential features, whereas the same certainly cannot be said of the model of perfectly flexible prices and wages, which is unstable.

Chapter 3

TWO CONCEPTS OF EXTERNAL ECONOMIES[1]

1954

The concept of external economies is one of the most elusive in economic literature. Our understanding of it has been greatly enhanced by the active controversy of the '20s over the nature of the 'empty economic boxes'; but full clarity has never been achieved. Definitions of external economies are few and unsatisfactory. It is agreed that they mean services (and disservices) rendered free (without compensation) by one producer to another; but there is no agreement on the nature and form of these services or on the reasons for their being free. It is also agreed that external economies are a cause for divergence between private profit and social benefit and thus for the failure of perfect competition to lead to an optimum situation; but for this there are many reasons, and it is nowhere made clear how many and which of these reasons are subsumed under the heading of 'external economies'. Nor do examples help to clarify the concept. The literature contains many examples of external economies; but they are as varied and dissimilar as are discussions of the subject. Some give the impression that external economies are exceptional and unimportant; others suggest that they are important and ubiquitous. Indeed, one might be tempted to explain this strange dichotomy by ideological differences between the different authors; but such an explanation would be both unwarranted and unnecessary. For, with the increasing rigour of economic thinking and separation of the different branches of economic theory, it is becoming increasingly clear that the

[1] I am indebted to Professor Bernard Haley and Mr Ralph Turvey for many helpful suggestions. The responsibility for errors, however, is entirely mine.

concept of external economies does duty in two entirely
different contexts. One of these is equilibrium theory, the
other is the theory of industrialization in underdeveloped
countries. It is customary to discuss these two subjects at
different levels of abstraction and on the basis of very different
sets of assumptions: no wonder that 'external economies' stand
for very different things in the two contexts. Indeed, I shall
argue that there are two entirely different definitions of
external economies, one much wider than the other; and that
external economies as defined in the theory of industrialization
include, but go far beyond, the external economies of equilibrium theory. The latter have been discussed and rigorously
defined in Professor Meade's 'External Economies and Diseconomies in a Competitive Situation',[1] but, since they form
part of external economies as defined in the theory of industrialization, we shall deal with them briefly here.

I

Equilibrium theory, in both its general and its partial form,
is a static theory, concerned with the characteristics of the
economic system when it is in equilibrium. Most of its conclusions are based on the assumptions of (1) perfect competition on both sides of every market and (2) perfect divisibility
of all resources and products. These assumptions underlie the
main conclusion of general equilibrium theory, viz., that the
market economy leads to a situation of economic optimum
(in Pareto's sense), provided that every economic influence of
one person's (or firm's) behaviour on another person's well-
being (or firm's profit) is transmitted through its impact on
market prices. Expressed differently, equilibrium in a perfectly
competitive economy is a situation of Paretian optimum,
except when there is interdependence among the members of
the economy that is direct, in the sense that it does not operate
through the market mechanism. In general equilibrium theory,
then, direct interdependence is the villain of the piece and the
cause for conflict between private profit and social benefit.

One can distinguish four types of direct (i.e. nonmarket)
interdependence (and one of these—the last one in the following enumeration—is known as 'external economies'): (1)

[1] *Economic Journal*, LXII (1952), 54-67.

The individual person's satisfaction may depend not only on the quantities of products he consumes and services he renders but also on the satisfaction of other persons. In particular, the high income or consumption of others may give a person pain or pleasure; and so may his knowledge that some others are less well off than he is. This is known as the 'interdependence of consumers' satisfaction'. (2) A person's satisfaction may be influenced by the activities of producers not only through their demand for his services and supply of the products he buys but also in ways that do not operate through the market mechanism. These may be called the producer's 'direct' (i.e. nonmarket) influence on personal satisfaction and are best known by the example of the factory that inconveniences the neighbourhood with the fumes or noise that emanate from it. (3) The producer's output may be influenced by the action of persons more directly and in other ways than through their offer of services used and demand for products produced by the firm. This is a counterpart of the previous case, and its main instance is inventions that facilitate production and become available to producers without charge. (4) The output of the individual producer may depend not only on his input of productive resources but also on the activities of other firms. This is a counterpart of case 1 and may be called 'direct interdependence among producers' but is better known under the name of 'external economies and diseconomies'.[1]

Of these four cases of direct interdependence, the first, interdependence among consumers, is undoubtedly important. It is (together with the case mentioned in note 3) among the main reasons for the current controversy in welfare economics and the reluctance of economists to make any welfare statements concerning the consumer. Nowadays, welfare statements are usually confined to the field of production, where the main conclusion of general equilibrium theory seems to stand on firmer ground, primarily because the remaining three cases of direct interdependence (all of which involve the producer) seem exceptional and unimportant. The second case seems exceptional, because most instances of it can be and

---

[1] A fifth and important case, which, however, does not quite fit into the above classification, is that where society provides social services through communal action and makes them available free of charge to all persons and firms.

usually are eliminated by zoning ordinances and industrial regulation concerned with public health and safety. The third case is unimportant, because patent laws have eliminated the main instance of this form of direct interdependence and transformed it into a case of interdependence through the market mechanism.[1] The fourth case seems unimportant, simply because examples of it seem to be few and exceptional.

The last statement appears at first to be contradicted by the many examples of external economies and diseconomies quoted in the literature; but most of these are *not* examples of direct interdependence among producers, which is the only meaning that can be attributed to the term 'external economies' within the context of equilibrium theory. It will be useful in this connection to have a rigorous definition of direct interdependence among producers. Meade gave such a definition when he defined external economies; and I can do no better than to reproduce it. According to him, external economies exist whenever the output (x_1) of a firm depends not only on the factors of production $(l_1, c_1, \ldots)$ utilized by this firm but also on the output (x_2) and factor utilization $(l_2, c_2, \ldots)$ of another firm or group of firms.[2] In symbols,

$$x_1 = F (l_1, c_1, \ldots; \quad x_2, l_2, \ldots),$$

where the existence of external economies is indicated by the presence of the variables to the right of the semicolon. Since $F(\ )$ is a production function, external economies as here defined are a peculiarity of the production function. For this reason it is convenient to call them 'technological external economies'.[3] While this will distinguish them from another category of external economies to be introduced presently, we must bear in mind that technological external economies are the only external economies that can arise because of direct interdependence among producers and within the framework of general equilibrium theory.

The examples of external economies given by Meade are

[1] I.e. patent laws have created a market and a market price for the inventor's services, which in the absence of such laws would often be free goods. The case where the results of government-sponsored research into industrial and agricultural methods are made gratuitously available to industrialists and farmers belongs in the category mentioned in note 1 on the previous page.
[2] *Op. cit.*
[3] The term is used in Jacob Viner's 'Cost Curves and Supply Curves', *Zeitschrift für Nationalökonomie*, III (1931), 23-46.

somewhat bucolic in nature, having to do with bees, orchards, and woods. This, however, is no accident: it is not easy to find examples from industry. Going through the many examples of external economies quoted in literature, I found only two that fit the above definition: the case in which a firm benefits from the labour market created by the establishment of other firms and that in which several firms use a resource which is free but limited in supply.[1] For a more detailed discussion the reader is referred to Meade's article, which will, I think, convince him of the scarcity of technological external economies.

II

The other field in which the concept of external economies occurs frequently is the theory of industrialization of underdeveloped countries, where the concept is used in connection with the special problem of allocating savings among alternative investment opportunities. This last is one of the many practical problems to which economists are wont to apply the conclusions of general equilibrium theory. Most of them realize, of course, that general equilibrium theory is limited in its assumptions and applicability; but the only limitation taken seriously by most economists is that imposed by the assumption of perfect competition; and this—as is well known —is not always a necessary condition for the conclusions of equilibrium theory to hold good. In particular, many economists regard a uniform degree of monopoly as all that is necessary for market forces to bring about an optimum allocation of investment funds; and this weaker condition is held to be more nearly fulfilled in our society. Whether for this reason or for some other, the private profitability of investment is usually considered a good index of its social desirability, at least as a general rule.

To this rule, however, the exceptions are too great and obvious to be ignored, especially in underdeveloped countries; and it is customary to impute most of them to external economies. While the nature of these external economies is

[1] Instances of this are the oil well whose output depends on the number and operation of other wells on the same oilfield; the fisherman whose catch depends on the operations of other fishermen in the same waters; and the firm that uses a public road (or other publicly-owned utility) and is partly crowded out of it by other firms using the same road.

often discussed, I have been unable to find a definition of the concept in the literature dealing with underdeveloped countries. It is possible, however, to infer a definition from the many examples, discussions, and *obiter dicta*. It seems that external economies are invoked whenever the profits of one producer are affected by the actions of other producers. To facilitate comparison with Meade's definition, we can express this in symbols by the function

$$P_1 = G \ (x_1, l_1, c_1, \ldots; \quad x_2, l_2, c_2, \ldots),$$

which shows that the *profits* of the firm depend not only on its own output and factor inputs but also on the output and factor inputs of other firms; and we shall say that in the context of underdeveloped countries external economies are said to exist whenever the variables to the right of the semicolon are present.

This definition of external economies obviously includes direct or nonmarket interdependence among producers, as discussed above and defined by Meade. It is much broader, however, than his definition, because, in addition to direct interdependence among producers, it also includes interdependence among producers through the market mechanism. This latter type of interdependence may be called 'pecuniary external economies' to distinguish it from the technological external economies of direct interdependence.[1]

Interdependence through the market mechanism is all-pervading, and this explains the contrast between the exceptional and often awkward examples of external economies cited in discussions of equilibrium theory and the impression one gains from the literature on underdeveloped countries that the entrepreneur creates external economies and diseconomies with his every move.

What is puzzling, however, is that interdependence through the market mechanism should be held to account for the failure of the market economy to lead to the socially desirable optimum, when equilibrium theory comes to the opposite conclusion and *relies* on market interdependence to bring about an optimum situation. Pecuniary external economies clearly have no place in equilibrium theory. The question is whether the concept is meaningful elsewhere. To answer this

[1] Cf. Viner, *op. cit.*

question we must first investigate the nature of the pecuniary external economies, to which interdependence through the market mechanism gives rise.

Investment in an industry leads to an expansion of its capacity and may thus lower the prices of its products and raise the prices of the factors used by it. The lowering of product prices benefits the users of these products; the raising of factor prices benefits the suppliers of the factors. When these benefits accrue to firms, in the form of profits, they are pecuniary external economies—Marshall called, or would have called, them (together with the benefits accruing to persons) consumers' and producers' surplus, respectively. According to the theory of industrialization, these benefits, being genuine benefits, should be explicitly taken into account when investment decisions are made; and it is usually suggested that this should be done by taking as the maximand not profits alone but the sum of the profits yielded and the pecuniary external economies created by the investment.

This prescription seems to be in direct conflict with the results of equilibrium theory. For, according to the latter and subject to its usual assumptions and limitations, market interdependence in the competitive system insures that the maximization of profit by each firm and of satisfaction by each person brings about an optimum situation, which, as is well known, is sometimes described as a situation in which consumers' and producers' surpluses are maximized. In other words equilibrium theory tells us that in equilibrium the sum of consumers' and producers' surpluses will be maximized, although they do not enter explicitly, as part of the maximand, the economic decisions of any producer.[1] Assuming that these conflicting views are both right, the conflict can be resolved only if we should find that the limitations of general equilibrium theory render it inapplicable to the problems of investment. This, indeed, must often be so; but in the following we shall single out three special cases, which seem especially important and in which the above conflict is resolved.

(*a*) One reason why the conclusions of general equilibrium

[1] Cf. J. R. Hicks, 'The Rehabilitation of Consumers' Surplus', *Review of Economic Studies*, VIII (1941), 108-16. We need not enter here the debate on the usefulness of this terminology. Nor is it necessary to stress that this way of stating the results of perfect competition is characteristic of partial equilibrium analysis.

theory may be inapplicable to the practical problem of investment is that the former's assumption of perfect divisibility is
not always fulfilled. Perfect competition leads to a position of
economic optimum, because under perfect competition the
marginal conditions of economic optimum are contained (in
the absence of direct interdependence) in the marginal conditions of profit maximization by producers and satisfaction
maximization by householders. Indivisibilities, however, may
prevent the producer from fulfilling these marginal conditions.
For example, he may find himself unable to equate marginal
costs to price and, instead, face the choice of producing either
less or more than the output that would equate these two
quantities. In such a case one of the available alternatives will
still yield him a higher profit than all others; but this need no
longer be the one that is also the best from society's point of
view. Hence the need, in such cases, to take society's point of
view explicitly into consideration.

This fact was recognized as early as 1844 by Dupuit.[1] He
was looking for a criterion of the social desirability of investment in such public utilities as canals, roads, bridges, and railways—the typical examples of indivisibilities in economics—
and he found this criterion not in the actual profitability of
such investments but in what their profitability would be in
the hypothetical case in which the operator of the utility
practised price discrimination and thus appropriated to himself the consumers' surplus that would normally (i.e. in the
absence of price discrimination) accrue to the users of the
public utility. In other words, Dupuit's test of social
desirability is whether the sum of profit and consumers' surplus is positive.[2] Dupuit's test and his use of the consumers'
surplus concept underlying it were vindicated by Professor
Hicks;[3] but neither Hicks nor Dupuit makes clear the rôle of
indivisibilities in rendering the above test necessary. For this
last point, as well as for an excellent statement of the entire

[1] Cf. Jules Dupuit, 'De la mesure de l'utilité des travaux publics', *Annales des
ponts et chaussées*, 2d ser., vol. VIII (1844); reprinted in *International
Economic Papers*, No. 2 (1952), pp. 83-110.
[2] This is so whether the consumers' surplus accrues to persons or represents
external economies accruing to firms.
[3] Cf. J. R. Hicks, 'L'Économie de bien-être et la théorie des surplus du
consommateur', and 'Quelques applications de la théorie des surplus du
consommateur', both in *Économie appliquée*, No. 4 (1948), pp. 432-57.

argument, the reader should consult Chapter XVI of Professor Lerner's *Economics of Control*.[1]

(*b*) The second reason for the inapplicability of general equilibrium theory to the problems of investment is that the former is a static or equilibrium theory, whereas the allocation of investment funds is not a static problem at all. According to equilibrium theory, the producer's profit-maximizing behaviour brings about a socially desirable situation *when the system is in equilibrium*; or, to give this result a more dynamic, if not entirely correct, interpretation, profit-maximizing behaviour brings closer the socially desirable optimum if it also brings closer equilibrium. Investment, however, need not bring the system closer to equilibrium; and, when it does not, the results of equilibrium theory may not apply.

Profits are a sign of disequilibrium; and the magnitude of profits under free competition may be regarded as a rough index of the degree of disequilibrium.[2] Profits in a freely competitive industry lead to investment in that industry; and the investment, in turn, tends to eliminate the profits that have called it forth. This far, then, investment tends to bring equilibrium nearer. The same investment, however, may raise or give rise to profits in other industries; and to this extent it leads away from equilibrium. For example, investment in industry A will cheapen its product; and if this is used as a factor in industry B, the latter's profits will rise. This, then, is a case where the price reduction creates, not a consumers' surplus proper, accruing to persons, but pecuniary external economies, benefiting firms. Is this difference sufficient to render the conclusions of general equilibrium theory inapplicable?

To answer this question, we must pursue the argument a little further. The profits of industry B, created by the lower price of factor A, call for investment and expansion in industry B, one result of which will be an increase in industry B's demand for industry A's product. This in turn will give rise to

---

[1] A. P. Lerner, *Economics of Control* (New York: Macmillan Co., 1944). Lerner's solution is slightly different and, I believe, more correct than Dupuit's, in that he takes account also of producers' surplus. It might be added in passing that the type of indivisibility considered by Dupuit establishes a relation among the users of the public utility that is similar in all essentials to direct interdependence among consumers.

[2] However, the absence of profits is not a sufficient condition of equilibrium.

profits and call for further investment and expansion in industry A; and equilibrium is reached only when successive doses of investment and expansion in the two industries have led to the simultaneous elimination of profits in both. It is only at this stage, where equilibrium has been established, that the conclusions of equilibrium theory become applicable and we can say (on the usual assumptions and in the absence of direct interdependence) that the amount of investment profitable in industry A is also the socially desirable amount. This amount is clearly greater than that which is profitable at the first stage, before industry B has made adjustment. We can conclude, therefore, that when an investment gives rise to pecuniary external economies, its private profitability understates its social desirability.

Unfortunately, however, the test of social desirability applicable in the previous case is not applicable here, although it would probably give a better result than a simple calculation of profitability. This can easily be seen by comparing the situation under consideration with that which would obtain if industries A and B were integrated (although in such a way as to preserve the free competition assumed so far). In this case the pecuniary external economies created by investment in industry A would become 'internal' and part of the profits of the investors themselves. Investment in A would be more profitable and pushed further than in the absence of integration; but, *without investment and expansion also in industry* B, it would not be pushed far enough. For what inhibits investment in A is the limitation on the demand for industry A's product imposed by the limited capacity of industry B, the consumer of this product; just as investment in industry B is inhibited by the limited capacity of industry A, the supplier of one of industry B's factors of production. These limitations can be fully removed only by a simultaneous expansion of both industries. We conclude, therefore, that only if expansion in the two industries were integrated and planned together would the profitability of investment in each one of them be a reliable index of its social desirability.

It hardly needs adding that the relation between industries A and B discussed above illustrates only one of the many possible instances of pecuniary external economies that belong in this category. Expansion in industry A may also give rise

Expansion in A leads to an increase in quantity demanded by A for product B → profit of B

to profits (i) in an industry that produces a factor used in industry A, (ii) in an industry whose product is complementary in use to the product of industry A, (iii) in an industry whose product is a substitute for a factor used in industry A, or (iv) in an industry whose product is consumed by persons whose incomes are raised by the expansion of industry A—and this list does not include the cases in which the expansion causes external *dis*economies. It is apparent from this list that vertical integration alone would not be enough and that complete integration of all industries would be necessary to eliminate all divergence between private profit and public benefit. This was fully realized by Dr Rosenstein-Rodan, who, in dealing with the 'Problems of Industrialization of Eastern and South-Eastern Europe',[1] considered most instances of pecuniary external economies listed above and advocated that 'the whole of the industry to be created is to be treated and planned like one huge firm or trust'.[2] To put this conclusion differently, profits in a market economy are a bad guide to economic optimum as far as investment and industrial expansion are concerned; and they are worse, the more decentralized and differentiated the economy.

This entire argument can be restated in somewhat different terms. In an economy in which economic decisions are decentralized, a system of communications is needed to enable each person who makes economic decisions to learn about the economic decisions of others and co-ordinate his decisions with theirs. In the market economy, prices are the signalling device that informs each person of other people's economic decisions; and the merit of perfect competition is that it would cause prices to transmit information reliably and people to respond to this information properly. Market prices, however, reflect the economic situation as it is and not as it will be. For this reason, they are more useful for co-ordinating current production decisions, which are immediately effective and guided by short-run considerations, than they are for co-ordinating investment decisions, which have a delayed effect and—looking ahead to a long future period—should be governed not by what the present economic situation is but by what the future economic situation is expected to be. The

[1] *Economic Journal*, LIII (1943), 202-11.
[2] *Ibid.*, p. 204.

proper co-ordination of investment decisions, therefore, would require a signalling device to transmit information about present plans and future conditions as they are determined by present plans; and the pricing system fails to provide this.[1] Hence the belief that there is need either for centralized investment planning or for some additional communication system to supplement the pricing system as a signalling device.

It must be added that the argument of this section applies with especial force to underdeveloped countries. The plant capacity most economical to build and operate is not very different in different countries; but, as a percentage of an industry's total capacity, it is very much greater in underdeveloped than in fully industrialized economies. In underdeveloped countries, therefore, investment is likely to have a greater impact on prices, give rise to greater pecuniary external economies, and thus cause a greater divergence between private profit and social benefit.

(c) I propose to consider yet another reason for divergence between the profitability of an investment and its desirability from the community's point of view; but this is very different from those discussed in the last two sections and has to do with the difference between the national and international points of view. In appraising the social desirability of an economic action from the international point of view, all repercussions of that action must be fully taken into account, whereas, from the national point of view, the welfare of domestic nationals alone is relevant and the losses suffered and benefits gained by foreigners are ignored. The two points of view need not necessarily lead to different appraisals; but they usually do when the economic action considered is the allocation of investment funds among purely domestic, import-competing, and export industries. From the international point of view, all external economies and diseconomies must be taken into consideration; from the national point of view, one must count only the external economies and diseconomies that accrue to domestic nationals and leave out of account the pecuniary external economies accruing to foreign buyers from the expansion of export industries and the dis-

---

[1] Professor Kenneth Arrow pointed out to me, however, that, in a formal sense, future markets and future prices could provide exactly such a signalling device.

economies inflicted on foreign competitors by the expansion of import-competing industries. Accordingly, investment in export industries is always less, and that in import-competing industries is always more, desirable from the national, than from the international, point of view.

In discussions on investment policy this difference between the national and international points of view usually appears in the guise of a difference between the criteria of social benefit and private profit. For social benefit, when considered explicitly, is usually identified with national benefit in our society, whereas private profit, although an imperfect index of social desirability, accounts or fails to account for external economies and diseconomies without national bias and therefore probably comes closer to registering the social welfare of the world as a whole than that of a single nation. Hence, investment tends to be more profitable in export industries and less profitable in import-competing industries than would be desirable from a narrow nationalistic point of view.

It is worth noting that this argument is in some respects the reverse of the argument of Section II*b* above. There it was the failure of profit calculations to take into account pecuniary external economies that caused the divergence between private profit and social benefit; here the divergence is caused by the entry into the profit criterion of pecuniary external economies and diseconomies that accrue to foreigners and should therefore be excluded from social accounting concerned with national, rather than world, welfare. The argument is well known as the 'terms-of-trade argument' and has been used to explain the failure of foreign investments in colonial areas to benefit fully the borrowing countries.[1] The divergence between national welfare and private profit depends on the foreigners' import-demand and export-supply elasticities; and it can be offset by an appropriate set of import and export duties. This has been shown by Mr J. de V. Graaff, in his 'Optimum Tariff Structures'.[2] De Graaff presents his optimum tariff structure as one that will bring about that flow of goods and services which optimizes[3] the nation's welfare; but the

[1] Cf. H. W. Singer, 'The Distribution of Gains between Investing and Borrowing Countries', *American Economic Review (Proceedings)*, XL (1950), 473-85.
[2] *Review of Economic Studies*, XVII (1949-50), 47-59.
[3] In Pareto's sense.

same tariff structure will also bring about the allocation of investment funds that is optimal from the national point of view.

A REPLY[1]

In my 'Two Concepts of External Economies' I argued that the pricing system as a signalling device is likely to transmit less than the full available information relevant to investment decisions and that it may therefore need supplementing by some additional system of communication if the use and allocation of investment funds is to be efficient. With this Professor Stockfisch seems to agree. But he then goes on to compare the relative merits of the co-ordinated central planning of investment, on the one hand, and the pricing system supplemented by those nonmarket channels of information usually available to businessmen, on the other hand, arguing the superiority of the latter and attributing to me a preference for the former. I am aware neither of having expressed such a preference nor, indeed, of having dealt with the issue; but I agree that it is an important issue well worth discussing and am prepared to defend at least part of the position attributed to me.

Stockfisch maintains that a businessman who contemplates making an investment is likely to foresee and take into account its stimulating effect on complementary investments, as well as the latter's effect on the future demand for the output of the capacity he contemplates installing. With this I fully agree. But the trouble is that such anticipations are bound to be heavily discounted for uncertainty and that this uncertainty cannot be eliminated or even very much diminished by acquiring information on these other investment plans, since some or all of these will be contingent on our businessman's plans and will be formulated only *after* our businessman has made a definite and irrevocable decision on his own investment plan. In other words, unco-ordinated investment plans are likely to be made at different points of time; and the mere difference in timing causes them (or at least some of them) to be based on less information than would be available if the same investment decisions were co-ordinated and taken simultaneously. The better information, therefore, of the planners

[1] To a comment on the above essay by J. A. Stockfisch in *The Journal of Political Economy*, LXIII (1955), 446-49.

—that is, of the people who co-ordinate simultaneous investment decisions—depends not on their better foresight or superior intelligence but solely on the simultaneity of interrelated decisions. One might add perhaps that, quite apart from the difference in timing, more information is likely to be exchanged around a conference table than if each businessman tries to find out about the others' plans without disclosing his own.

But while I am confident that the co-ordinated and simultaneous planning of interrelated investments is subject to less uncertainty, I doubt if this fact always yields a benefit; and, accordingly, I would not draw the far-reaching policy conclusions that Stockfisch says should be drawn. For it seems, at least on the basis of the rough-and-ready argument I advanced, that the internalization of external economies through co-ordinated investment planning would generally raise the marginal efficiency of capital and hence lead to investment in larger productive units than would be built in the absence of co-ordination. In other words, the difference between co-ordinated and unco-ordinated investment planning would seem to be that the former leads to expansion in the form of the building of a few large plants, whereas the latter leads to expansion of a more tentative nature, proceeding by smaller steps but on more fronts.

Now it is by no means a foregone conclusion that the first of these alternatives is better than the second. It is better only if there are economies of scale whose exploitation depends on the difference in plant size between the two alternatives. If no such economies exist, no saving in production costs can be achieved by the co-ordination of investment decisions and the consequent building of large (instead of small) plants. In this case, therefore, economic considerations do not favour centrally planned investment; and political and social considerations are, of course, against it. This is why I feel that the case for the co-ordination of interrelated investment decisions is largely confined to the underdeveloped countries. In the United States of today, investment, though unco-ordinated, seems usually to make full use of the economies of scale; and this was probably also true during the industrial revolution, when both the scale of individual investments and the scope for economies of scale were very much smaller.

Chapter 4

MONOPOLY AND COMPETITION
IN EUROPE AND AMERICA

1955

Monopoly and competition have been a much discussed topic among economists ever since the publication in 1933 of Professor Chamberlin's and Mrs Robinson's well-known works on the subject. They provided the analytical tools and theoretical framework of the subject; and it is since then that most of us think of the two concepts as merely limiting cases and constituent elements of a more general type of market behaviour. In the intervening two decades most of the ideas contained in these works have been further developed, valuable new ideas have been added, and much empirical research has been done; nevertheless, our understanding of the subject has not advanced very much. This, to some extent, is a tribute to the early work on the subject; but it also reflects unfavourably on the work done since then. For one thing, the literature of the subject is very diffuse, replete with competing approaches, terminologies and classifications; many of them good and useful but creating, all together, a bewildering effect of redundancy and unnecessary variety, and rendering an integration of the various results almost impossible. For another, much of the recent work has tended to stay in accustomed grooves and accept traditional value judgments, without bothering to re-examine their validity. This is not to imply that the originators of the new approach made wrong value judgments and cut grooves leading the wrong direction; but the last twenty years has brought a shift in the economist's interests and emphasis, to which, I suspect, few of the contemporary writers in this field have paid enough attention. It would be desirable, therefore, to review and reappraise our entire approach to the problems of monopoly and competition, and to try and develop whatever modifications or additions to accepted theory seem to be called for in view of past experience and of the change in the economist's interests and emphasis. It is gratifying to find that a first preliminary step in this direction has recently been taken.

In 1951 the International Economic Association held a round-table conference on 'Monopoly, Competition and their Regulation' at Talloires, France; and the papers presented, complete with a summary of their discussion, have now been published.[1] Books of this kind are seldom very successful; but this is a welcome exception. Indeed, it is one of the few multi-authored books worth buying, even on budgets constrained by academic salaries. Much credit is due to the chairman of the Programme Committee, Professor Chamberlin, and to the members of his committee, for an excellent selection of authors and topics, and a happy matching of authors with topics.

This is not to say, however, that the papers are uniform in quality. For one thing, the eight papers that describe the state of competition in eight different countries are as varied as is the relevant statistical information available in these countries. For another, of the analytical papers (which form two-thirds of the remaining sixteen) a few make important original contributions, others do little more than restate or summarize positions already known. But the value of the book lies not so much in the new ideas it contains as in the survey of the entire field it affords. It is very useful to have within the same volume, a statement of the issues involved, accounts of the empirical information available, appraisals of various attempts to deal with the monopoly problem, restatements of most of the important approaches and ideas in the field, and a 'Summary Record of the Debate' to which all these were subjected during the conference. Much can be learned from the juxtaposition of competing theories, from the discussion of practical problems, and last but not least, from the failure of the conferees to resolve some of the problems discussed. The book might have been more constructive had the papers been written after and not before the conference; as it is, it provides

[1] *Monopoly and Competition and Their Regulation.* Papers and Proceedings of a Conference held by the International Economic Association, ed. E. H. Chamberlin (London: Macmillan Co. Ltd; New York: St Martin's Press; 1954).

the discerning reader both with a good survey and criticism of the accepted body of theory and with many of the elements that would have to go into an amendment of that theory.

It is not surprising perhaps that several of the papers condemn competition, both as a form of market organization and as a theoretical standard by which to judge the performance of an actual economy. Mrs Robinson leads the attack by arguing 'The Impossibility of Competition', mainly on the basis of the cobweb theorem, which she applies to the problem of investment. She is seconded by Mr Rothschild, who presents an imposing if mostly familiar catalogue of 'The Wastes of Competition' under both ideal and monopolistic conditions; and these theoretical strictures on competition are well supported by Mme Aubert-Krier's empirical study of 'Monopolistic and Imperfect Competition in Retail Trade' in France.

Criticism, however, is meted out impartially; and the attack on monopoly and other forms of market restriction is just as heavy if not quite as effective. Professor Schneider attacks cartels for their failure to promote research and product development, and on the grounds that they aim to maximize profits, not efficiency, and that, to judge by their frequent failure to raise the profits of the participants, they seldom achieve efficiency even as a by-product. He has a bad word to say also for monopoly: 'the widely held assumption that the ownership and control of plural production by single corporate enterprises contributes to efficiency would seem to rest upon an overwhelming absence of support' (p. 210). Professor Lombardini, in his examination of 'Monopoly and Rigidities in the Economic System' adds an interesting new kink (the uncertainty kink) to the familiar oligopoly kink, to explain the rigidity of monopoly price; and Professor Machlup condemns this rigidity—even when disguised as stability—by arguing that 'artificial stability of particular prices aggravates the instability of general incomes' (p. 394), and that even general wage stability, due to 'the exercise of monopoly power by trade unions may be extremely unstabilizing at times' (p. 393). Professor Hennipman, in an excellent paper on 'Monopoly: Impediment or Stimulus to Economic Progress?', warns against too ready an acceptance of the view ascribed to Schumpeter that 'the tendency of monopoly in general is conducive to progress' (p. 451); and Professor Lewis, discussing the 'Recent British Experience in Nationalization', is sceptical about the efficiency of nationalized enterprises, and cautions against pinning high hopes to them as an alternative to private monopoly. Professor Jeanneney draws somewhat less gloomy conclusions from the experience of 'Nationalization in France'.

Needless to say, all these views were not held by each of the persons mentioned; but there seems to have prevailed among the European members of the conference a general feeling of pessimism concerning the performance of competitive industry, the performance of monopoly, both private and public, and the possibility of controlling monopoly. Hence Mrs Robinson's prayer for a 'third way between a choice of two evils' (p. 513), which must have been shared by many other European members of the conference. The only hopeful note came from Sweden, as though in answer to Mrs Robinson's prayer, in Professor Svennilson's discussion of the successful Swedish experience with 'market therapeutics'—*ad hoc* measures aimed at improving the organization and efficiency of particular industries, based on the recommendations of study groups appointed by the government or formed by the industry itself.

In striking contrast to the Europeans' pessimism was the confidence of the Americans concerning the competitiveness and efficiency of their own economy. Professor Heflebower, reporting on 'Monopoly and Competition in the United States of America', maintained that competition in the United States, while wanting by theoretical standards, was nevertheless workable and adequate in some deeper sense of the word. Similarly, Professor Chamberlin felt that 'monopolistic competition may, in practice, contain more and stronger elements of competition than the unrealistic model of pure competition' (p. 508); and Professor Clark, in 'Competition and the Objectives of Government Policy', argued that if the US economy was not more competitive, this was due not to our inability to check monopoly but to the American public's not wanting more competition. The Canadians seemed to share much of this optimism, at least to judge by Mr McGregor's report on 'Preventing Monopoly—Canadian Techniques'.

The difference in spirit between the European and American members, and the underlying difference in performance be-

tween European and American economies, was much debated
and commented upon during the conference. There were
arguments that America is 'full of pushful immigrants' (p. 534),
stress was laid on the difference in man's aspirations between
Europe's old and America's new civilization (pp. 57-8), pleas
were made for research into American institutions that might
explain the difference between American and European competition, American and European monopoly (p. 495); but there
is no evidence in Mrs Henderson's excellent 'Summary Record
of the Debate' of any explanation of the difference with the
aid and within the framework of economic theory. Indeed,
she says explicitly that the problem remained unresolved (p.
495); and this, I feel, is a serious indictment of the traditional
theories of monopoly and competition. For it seems obvious
that the superior performance of the American economy must
have something to do with its having these 'more and stronger
elements of competition', whose existence most American
members of the conference asserted, but whose nature and
significance none explained. And yet, most elements of an
explanation seemed to be there, like the pieces of a jig-saw
puzzle, waiting to be assembled and to have the missing pieces
supplied. The problem is challenging and important enough to
be pursued a little further, if only as an illustration of the
thoughts aroused by, if not always contained in, the book
under review.

The difference between American and European efficiency
is a difference primarily in technological efficiency, which has
to do with the entrepreneur's choice among alternative
methods of production, with his success or failure in keeping
up with scientific progress, and with specialization among
different members of an industry. Efficiency in this sense is
coming more and more to the forefront of the economist's
interests, owing to its relevance to many contemporary economic problems, among them the problem of economic growth.
Let us remember, however, that this shift in interest and
emphasis is a recent development, to which many branches
of economic theory have not yet had a chance to adapt themselves.

At the time when the theories of monopolistic and of imperfect competition were developed, the economic effects of
competition that received the most attention were income

distribution, resource allocation among firms and industries, the utilization of existing capacity, and the managerial efficiency with which the entrepreneur runs his business. All these effects hinge on (1) the relation of price to the marginal cost of products or the marginal value of factors, and (2) the tendency (through the entry of newcomers) towards the competitive elimination of monopoly profit. These two categories stand in the centre of much of the recent work on monopolistic and imperfect competition, which explains its success in dealing with the problems of competition and monopoly as they relate to the above-mentioned effects.

As Professor Svennilson points out in 'Monopoly, Efficiency, and the Structure of Industry', today most of the above effects have ceased to be regarded as very important. Interest in the effect of market structure on income distribution has waned, because in a ' "world of monopolies" . . . different monopolies partly neutralize each other's efforts to exploit the rest of society' (p. 272), and also because taxation and social security policy have become effective tools for mitigating inequities of income distribution. As to the other effects mentioned above, I still think they are important, but they have certainly been overshadowed by the problem of technological efficiency as defined above. Efficiency in this sense may be measured by the relation of the firm's actual cost to the socially necessary minimum cost of production, as this is determined by the technical knowledge of the time and the factor availabilities of the place; and this relation, while known in the theoretical literature in the shape of Chamberlin's long-run cost curve, has not yet become an operating concept in the empirical work.[1] Moreover, the technological efficiency of the firm, the method of production it adopts, its ability or failure to keep up with technological progress, all have very much to do with the firm's scale of investment and operations, whence it follows that any theory trying to explain the influence of market structure on the firm's performance in the above sense must also concern itself with the relation between market structure and the scale of investment and output. The traditional theories, however, are ill-equipped for this task, primarily because their main concern is with current production, not with investment, and also because they tend, on the

[1] See, however, the reference to Bain on p. 95 below.

whole, to abstract from (long-run) problems of scale.[1] Their primary purpose, after all, was partly to explore the implications for static equilibrium theory of the relaxation of one of its simplifying assumptions, pure competition; and partly to enable equilibrium theory to deal with the problems raised by product differentiation and nonprice competition. This purpose, I believe, was pretty well accomplished. What remains yet to be done is to explore the consequences of the relaxation of yet another simplifying assumption, perfect divisibility and irrelevance of scale. This might best be done in the framework of a theory of investment under monopoly and competition, which could then be regarded as a new chapter added to accepted theory.

To explain the difference between American and European efficiency one must explain why American and European entrepreneurs pursued different investment policies and invested in different types of plant and equipment. When one realizes that, as a rule, the more efficient a method of production, the larger the scale on which it must be operated to make it profitable, one is tempted to explain everything by the large scale of the American economy. This, however, would be a very incomplete explanation. To begin with, Professor Robinson pointed out that in most industries the size of the average manufacturing plant, when measured in terms of manpower, is not significantly smaller in Europe than it is in America (p. 503). It is true that manpower is a singularly unfortunate index for measuring size when one is trying to explain differences in labour productivity,[2] since equality of size in terms of manpower would imply, in terms of the more relevant index, output, a disparity in size between America and Europe of the order of two to one or even three to one. Nevertheless, I doubt if such disparities in size are the main explanation, especially when experience suggests that there are also other, equally valid and equally important explana-

---

[1] The only exception I know of is E. H. Chamberlin's 'Proportionality, Divisibility and Economies of Scale' (*Quarterly Journal of Economics*, February 1948), reprinted as Appendix B in the sixth edition of his *Theory of Monopolistic Competition*.

It is also worth noting in this connection that all the customary measures of the degree of competition—demand elasticities, concentration ratios, Gini indexes, etc.—are not only independent, but designed to be independent, of scale.

[2] It is, of course, the only one available.

tions. For example, one would expect a plant *designed* to employ 500 workers to be more efficient than one that has *grown* to the same size (however measured) from small beginnings, by the addition here of a new workshop, there of a few machine tools—even if each and every addition was as efficient as could be. Indeed, what seems relevant from the point of view of technological efficiency is the scale, not of the plant, but of the individual investment or investments that created the plant. In other words, it is the firm's rate of growth, or rather the size of the discrete steps by which it grows that determines what method of production is chosen as being the most profitable one.

This suggests the growth rate of the economy or of the market in which the firm operates as an important factor—although this again is by no means the only or the main factor. For national differences in rates of growth would not be very important if each firm were restricted to its proportionate share of the market. In other words, whether the firm's market grew at 3 or at 10 per cent per annum would probably make little difference to its scope for modernization and the adoption of mass-production methods. More important is the firm's ability (and inducement) to expand at a faster rate than the market in which it operates, by arrogating to itself more than its proportionate share of the market's expansion and by encroaching upon its competitors' markets. This, however, depends on the nature and degree of competition, which determine the cost to the firm of expanding its market at a faster rate than the market as a whole expands; and the degree of competition and cost of expansion may well be significantly different on the two sides of the Atlantic.

In other words, when an entrepreneur invests in new productive capacity, the method of production that will appear the most profitable to him depends on the size of the market to which the new capacity will cater; and this in turn depends partly on the natural accretion to his market, partly on its further expansion through competition. It seemed right to define the natural accretion to the firm's market as its proportionate share in the expansion of the market as a whole; and it must be noted that the absolute size of this proportionate share depends on the firm's size (in terms of output) as well as on the rate of growth of the whole market. Hence, with the size

of the average firm larger in America than in Europe,[1] and
with the rate of expansion of the American economy also
greater, we already have two factors that would make for
greater technological progress in America. In addition, I shall
argue presently that competition is yet another factor biased
in America's favour.

The meaning of competition in this context is slightly
different from that customarily attributed to it. For one thing,
competition in the above sense is very much a long-run concept, while the preoccupation with price competition in so
much of the current literature naturally puts the emphasis on
the short-run. For another, the customary preoccupation with
income distribution and static welfare concepts makes one
think of competition as a restraining force, which limits the
would-be monopolist's control over supply, influence on price,
and ability to enjoy a quiet life; whereas here, competition
means the entrepreneur's opportunity to encroach upon the
potential[2] and actual markets of his competitors, and—if they
have similar opportunities—his inducement to encroach upon
their markets before they encroach upon his. Competition
always has to do with one firm's encroachment upon another's
market; but in much of the past literature attention is centred
on the behaviour of the firm whose market is being threatened
or encroached upon; whereas here our interest is focused on
the firm that does the encroaching and on the effects of its
encroaching on its own investment opportunities and decisions.[3]

A third difference between competition in the two senses
is the following. Most of the beneficial effects of competition
on income distribution, resource allocation and managerial
efficiency can be brought about by the mere threat (or rather
fear) of market encroachment; and this threat may forever
remain a threat and need never be carried out. In the realm of

---

[1] The size of the firm is relevant also for another reason. Expansion usually
goes hand-in-hand with the replacement of existing capacity; and part of
the market for the new capacity is created by the scrapping of old capacity.
Hence, the more old capacity the firm has for scrapping, the less expansion
is needed for providing the new capacity with an adequate market.

[2] By a firm's potential market we mean its proportionate share in the expansion of the whole market.

[3] For a statement of this difference in a slightly different context, see M.
Abramovitz, 'Monopolistic Selling in a Changing Economy', *Quarterly
Journal of Economics*, February 1938.

current production, therefore, competition may enforce the firm's good behaviour in a way not unlike that of the sword that hung above Damocles' head. By contrast, the technological progress of the firm, if conditional upon a substantial expansion of output, depends on the firm's really encroaching upon its competitors' potential or actual markets. These distinctions suggest that the competition relevant to the firm's investment decisions is essentially aggressive and may diminish both the number of competitors and the degree of competition. Indeed, it is closely related to the conception of competition as a struggle to establish a monopoly position.[1]

Returning now to the comparison between American and European economies, there is, unfortunately, no comparative study of degrees of competition and, to judge by the information contained or cited in the eight 'country papers', none is possible at present. A comparison between the United States and the United Kingdom has been made and shows a higher concentration ratio in the latter than in the former;[2] but one cannot generalize from this to a higher degree of concentration in Europe as a whole.[3] In contrast, however, to the lack of statistical information, institutional information is available, and it suggests that there may be a significant difference between American and European industry, with the representative American businessman facing lower costs and lesser difficulties than his European counterpart when he tries to expand his market sufficiently to render modern mass-production methods profitable.

To begin with, the American system of distribution, whereby the individual manufacturer markets relatively few products through a large network of retailers, probably makes for lower costs of market expansion than the European system

[1] Schumpeter assumed—unnecessarily, I think, and mainly for the sake of paradox—that the entrepreneur needs a monopoly position to render innovation worth his while; I am arguing that he needs a market that exceeds a certain minimum size, which is largely determined by the engineering characteristics of the new facility he contemplates installing, and which may or may not imply a monopoly position.

[2] Cf. Gideon Rosenbluth: 'Measures of Concentration', in *Business Concentration and Price Policy*, A Conference of the Universities-National Bureau Committee for Economic Research (Princeton: Princeton University Press, 1955).

[3] Whether concentration ratios are a suitable index for measuring competition in the sense here used is another matter; but with this we need not be concerned here.

of marketing a large variety of products through few but exclusive retail outlets. (Indeed, the mere fact that marketing as an activity is so much more specialized and highly developed in America than in Europe suggests that market expansion may well be cheaper and more easily accomplished in America.) Secondly, the American consumer's preference and expenditure pattern is probably more flexible and more easily swayed than the European's, partly perhaps because he is less conservative in such matters, and partly because his higher standard of living gives him more scope for flexibility.[1] Thirdly, the scope for expansion by encroaching upon the markets of inefficient firms is probably greater in America than in Europe, where the inefficient firms are usually the small family businesses, whose staying power and ability to sustain losses is much enhanced by the fact that their value to their owners consists not only in the profits they yield but also in the independent position and secure employment opportunities they provide.[2] A fourth and related factor is that family business, still preponderant in Europe, probably has less easy access to the capital and entrepreneurial talent needed for expansion if the owners are determined, as they often are, to keep the business a strictly family affair.

Such and similar factors seem to be important determinants of the cost of expansion and hence of the firm's ability and inducement[3] to adopt new methods of production whose profitability hinges on a high rate of output. They do not seem to have been discussed at the conference; as indeed there seems to have been little explicit analysis of the influence of competition on the nature of the firm's investment. By implication, however, and in slightly different guises, the subject was very much in the foreground. To begin with, Professor

[1] The pronounced positive correlation between the variance and the mean of family expenditures does not prove, but suggests strongly, that there is such a difference. Cf. M. Friedman, 'The Use of Ranks to Avoid the Assumption of Normality Implicit in the Analysis of Variance', *Journal of the American Statistical Association*, vol. 32, p. 675; D. S. Brady, 'Variations in Family Living Expenditures', *op. cit.*, vol. 33, p. 385; S. J. Prais & H. S. Houthakker, *The Analysis of Family Budgets* (Cambridge University Press, 1955), p. 56.

[2] Cf. J. Steindl, *Small and Big Business* (Oxford: Blackwell, 1945), Chapter 6, for an analysis of the small firm's staying power.

[3] One entrepreneur's ability to adopt new methods of production is his competitors' inducement to do likewise.

Hennipman's discussion of innovations follows lines that tie in with those sketched above. Secondly, there is evident, in several of the papers, a general trend towards the use of long-term concepts in dealing with problems of competition. Professor Chamberlin warns against relying exclusively on the elasticity concept for 'Measuring the Degree of Monopoly and Competition'; and Professor Bain, in his very interesting paper on 'Conditions of Entry and the Emergence of Monopoly', develops a complete long-run theory of price determination. He relates the firm's price not to its own costs but to the minimal average cost of the most-favoured firm and explains the margin between long-run price and minimal average cost in terms of the cost of entry. These concepts, which resemble closely our cost of expansion and socially necessary minimum cost, are used by Bain solely to explain prices, profits, and profit margins; but their relevance for the firm's investment policy is obvious.

Thirdly, there was much talk at the conference, both in the papers presented and in the ensuing discussion, of the importance of distinguishing between different kinds of competition. Mr Corwin Edwards, opening the conference with a statement of the 'Issues in the Monopoly Problem', clearly defined a variety of meanings of the term competition. But the interest of the conference in these matters was aroused only much later, by which time Edwards's clear-cut definitions seem to have been forgotten and the discussion revolved around the more intriguing but less clearly defined concepts of active competition and workable competition. There seems to have been a consensus that these concepts are important; and that active or workable competition may be present or absent independently or whether competition in the traditional sense is present or absent. But this, unfortunately, is about as far as the subject was pursued at the conference. To judge by internal evidence, by the fine display of winemanship in the illustrative examples, and by my own independent knowledge of the mellow charm and three-star restaurant of Talloires, the conferees were in no mood to use their considerable analytic powers for a rigorous definition and analysis of these concepts. There are definitions, but none too clear. Sometimes active competition seems to mean the entrepreneur's ability to expand his market and thus render profitable the use of a better method of production—this meaning is implied, for example, in Professor Clark's interesting discussion of the time element in competition (pp. 326-8). At other times, however, active competition seems to mean, not the market conditions that render innovation profitable, but the entrepreneur's innovating activity itself. This latter, of course, is the *desideratum*; but the former concept is the tool needed for analysing the conditions that hamper or promote the latter's advent.

It may seem unfair to the book under review to discuss at such length a problem it fails to solve. There are, indeed, many other subjects fully and satisfactorily treated in the volume; but its main value, at least in this reviewer's opinion, is the background and stimulus it provides for the solution, by its readers, of some of the unsettled problems of monopoly and competition.

Chapter 5

GROWTH—
BALANCED OR UNBALANCED?

1959

One of the questions most often asked by economists now-adays concerns the conditions most favourable to economic growth. This can lead one far afield, away from economics; but among the economic factors conducive to growth, two have received much attention: economic interdependence, which favours balanced growth, and economies of scale, which call for growth by large steps. Since growth by large steps often requires concentrated growth, there is something of a contradiction between these two factors. In addition, there are a number of other factors as well that also call for concentrated growth. The nature of these conflicting factors and of the conflict they involve is the subject matter of this paper.

THE EARLY ARGUMENT
FOR CONCENTRATED GROWTH

Historically, and that means both in economic history and in the history of economic thought, unbalanced or concentrated growth came first. An early example of concentrated growth is England's industrial revolution; its early theory is contained in Ricardo's doctrine of comparative advantage, as becomes apparent when one restates the classical doctrine in terms of growth theory and from the point of view, not of the world as a whole, but of one country—England. The problem, in terms of growth theory, is how to organize an economy whose different industries have different productivities; and Ricardo's doctrine of comparative advantage provides a solution to this problem.

In long-run equilibrium, of course, differences in value

G

productivity tend to disappear; but the problem must be placed in a dynamic setting and arises when technical change greatly raises the productivity and profitability of some industries but not of others. Assuming that productivity in the other industries cannot be increased, the question arises what would be better in such a situation, the balanced growth of all industries or expansion confined to the now more productive industries?

This was more or less England's problem at the time of her industrial revolution, which consisted in a tremendous increase in labour productivity and reduction in cost, but only in a relatively few industries: spinning and weaving of cotton and woollen textiles, coal mining, iron manufacture, and heavy engineering. In such a situation, the resources saved through the increase in productivity in these industries can either be used to expand the output of these selfsame industries; or they can be transferred to those other industries whose productivity has not risen and used to expand their output. It is obvious that the additional physical output will be greater in the first case than in the second—and so will be the increase in the *value* of output if relative prices do not change much. In other words, a given technological improvement, if used to expand the output of the industries in which the improvement has occurred, will lead to a very different and very much greater increase in output and, possibly, welfare than if it is used to release resources to other industries and increase their output.

The above argument, however simple, is so important for what follows that we shall illustrate it with a numerical example at the risk of boring some (we hope not all) readers with it. Assume that the industries destined to be affected by the industrial revolution employ half the economy's resources and produce half its national product. Assume further that the industrial revolution lowers costs of production in these industries to one quarter of what they used to be.[1] On these

---

[1] This example is not too extreme. Cf. the following quotation from Maurice Dobb, *Studies in the Development of Capitalism*, p. 303: 'D. A. Wells, writing in the late '80s and speaking both of USA and of Britain, estimated that the saving in time and effort involved in production in recent years had amounted to as much as 70 or 80 per cent "in a few" industries, "in not a few" to more than 50 per cent and between one-third and two-fifths as a minimum average for production as a whole. It is possible that over manufacturing industry in general in this country [Great Britain] the real cost in labour of producing commodities fell by 40 per cent between 1850 and 1880.' It is true

assumptions, the complete displacement of the old by the new methods of production in the industries affected would enable the economy to produce its pre-revolutionary output with the aid of only five-eighths of the resources previously needed; and the remaining three-eighths could be used to produce additional output. If these freed resources were entirely re-absorbed in the now more efficient industries, the latter's output would be quadrupled and, *assuming no change in relative prices*, the national product would increase by 150 per cent. If they were used to expand the output of all industries in equal proportions, the increase in national product would be 60 per cent; if they were entirely diverted from the revolutionary industries and used to expand the output of the other industries only, the increase in national product would be a mere 37½ per cent.

These three examples were chosen for their simplicity rather than for their importance; and it is well to bear in mind that the first and the last are not *extreme* limiting cases. In particular, a reduction in the costs of production of an industry to $\frac{1}{p}$th of their original level may well (and often does) lead to a more than p-fold expansion of demand for its output, in which case it will not only reabsorb the resources freed but divert additional resources from other industries as well. (We are now leaving open the question of what happens to prices.) As to the last case, it implies (with unchanged prices) a zero income elasticity of demand for the output of the now more efficient industries. Negative income elasticities of demand, however, are not an impossibility; and they would lead (again with unchanged prices) to a greater diversion of resources to other industries than that which would merely absorb the resources freed in the now more efficient industries. In short, the cost reduction of our example could raise the national product by any figure within an even wider range than the 37½ to 150 per cent suggested above. Here, then, is a most persuasive argument in favour of concentrating growth as much as possible in the now more efficient industries.

Concentrated growth, however, creates the problem of a changed and unbalanced composition of output; and the time-

---

that labour is not the only cost of production; on the other hand, these estimates refer to a relatively short period and purport to show the change in the overall average costs of entire industries.

honoured method of solving this problem is foreign trade. Ricardo advocated that each country concentrate its resources into its most efficient industries and use foreign trade to convert the resulting unbalanced pattern of output into a pattern of product availabilities that is more balanced in the sense of conforming more closely to the pattern of consumers' preferences and producers' needs. Concerned primarily with the point of view of the world as a whole, the classical economists showed how the unbalanced composition of two countries' national products can be mutually offsetting, and how each can, by trading with the other, convert its unbalanced pattern of output into a balanced pattern of product availabilities. From one country's—England's—point of view, the problem is how she can use world markets to convert her unbalanced pattern of output into a balanced pattern of product availabilities without turning the terms of trade against herself to such an extent as to offset the advantage of unbalanced over balanced growth. I do not know if the classical economists ever asked this question in this form; but somehow or other England solved the problem, and this may be an important reason for her rapid development and great prosperity in the nineteenth century.

The statistical picture is very striking. The expansion of Britain's industrial production was very largely based on foreign trade, the proportion of which to total national income rose from 16.6 per cent at the beginning of the nineteenth century to 66 per cent in 1910-13.[1] The proportion and rise in the proportion of exports in the total output of Britain's new and revolutionary industries was greater still, rising in some cases to as much as 89 per cent.[2] The increased importance of Britain's foreign trade testifies to the increasing divergence between the pattern of her output and the pattern of her demand, as well as to her increasing reliance on foreign trade for converting the one into the other. One would expect this trend to have worsened Britain's terms of trade; but the statistical evidence shows that the terms of trade, while they turned against Britain, did not change very much. Schlote's

---

[1] Cf. Werner Schlote, *British Overseas Trade from 1700 to the 1930s*, Blackwell, Oxford, 1952.
[2] This was the percentage of exports in the total output of Britain's cotton piece goods industry in the decade before the First World War.

index of Britain's terms of trade fell by barely a third from the 1810s to the 1880s and rose slightly thereafter. It seems, therefore, as though Britain had retained most of the benefit from her unbalanced growth; accomplishing this half by design, half by accident, through the opening up of under-developed countries, the construction of their transportation systems, and the export of British capital that implemented these development; for all this must have raised the demand for Britain's exports, lowered the cost of her imports, and thus helped to prevent the terms of trade turning more sharply against her.

THE PRINCIPLES OF BALANCED GROWTH

Unbalanced growth on these principles and for these reasons is out of fashion today. For one thing, political uncertainty, balance-of-payment difficulties, and high competition in world markets have rendered export markets very precarious; for another, we live in an age of mass production, which is feasible and profitable only if it caters to a highly stable and homo-geneous market. All of these factors have rendered dangerous and undesirable a great divergence between the patterns of output and consumption and the consequent great dependence on foreign trade and other countries' policies. This was first pointed out almost 100 years ago by Friedrich List, who advocated economic self-sufficiency and, in analysing the means of achieving it, developed a rudimentary argument in favour of balanced growth. His harmony of interests could be an early statement of economic interdependence, and his general argument a precursor of the modern case for balanced growth.

Today, we take it for granted that a fair degree of self-sufficiency is desirable and base the argument for balanced growth on the recognition of economic interdependence. To analyse this, it is convenient to distinguish between inter-dependence in production and interdependence in consump-tion, and to deal with each of them in turn.

To produce a good and to invest in capacity for producing a good are the more profitable, the greater the availability (1) of the goods that serve as factors of production in its manu-facture, (2) of the goods with which it is combined in the manufacture of other goods, and (3) of the capacity for producing goods in whose manufacture it serves as a factor of production. Since this statement holds true of all goods, it is generally desirable and profitable to expand simultaneously, and in the proportions determined by technological production coefficients, the production and productive capacity of all goods whose relation to each other is that of factor to product or common factors to the same product. These relations are called interdependence in production; and the effects of such interdependence on the profitability of investment are usually discussed in the literature under the name of pecuniary external economies.[1]

Very similar are the meaning and effects of interdependence in consumption. Production generates income, which gives rise to consumers' demand for an entire range of goods. Hence, an increase in output increases demand *in a given pattern* for a whole range of goods; and the profitability of output expansion will be maximized if the pattern of output expansion conforms to the pattern of demand expansion created by the additional income paid out in producing the additional output. The effects of this type of interdependence on the *aggregate volume* of income, output, and employment are discussed in Kahn's theory of the multiplier; its effects on the *pattern and geographical distribution* of demand and output are usually subsumed in discussions of pecuniary external economies, often without a clear distinction between interdependence in production and interdependence in consumption.

All of these ideas, however simple they may be, have for a long time remained alien to orthodox economic thought, even though the gist of them was already contained in List's writings. One reason for this may be that Britain's own economic development, following by and large Ricardo's doctrine, depended singularly little on these principles; another reason may be that List did not formulate his ideas very clearly and combined them with political ideas that were repugnant to the liberal and idealistic spirit of the nineteenth-century British economists—and let us remember that orthodox economic theory is largely British in origin. A further reason may be that traditional economic theory deals mainly with the problems of developed economies, where these prob-

---

[1] Cf. H. W. Arndt, 'External Economies in the Economic Growth', *Economic Record* (1955), 192-214. See also Chapter 3 above.

lems hardly arise. For, in the developed economy, where additions to output and income made by a single investment are usually a small fraction of the total, interdependence in production and consumption can mostly be ignored with impunity.

The situation is very different in underdeveloped economies. There, a single investment can make a big addition both to the total marketable output of a product and to total money income, and this means that considerations of interdependence and the principles of balanced growth assume great importance. For in such cases, estimates of the profitability and desirability of investment and of the optimum size of investment become very different when interdependence is taken into account from what they are when interdependence is ignored. It is obvious that the estimates which ignore interdependence are the wrong ones; and it can be and has been shown that the private entrepreneur makes estimates close to these when he bases his judgment on market information alone. Hence the desirability in underdeveloped countries of recognizing economic interdependence and of influencing investment planning or investment decisions accordingly. This favours balanced growth, which means a simultaneous advance on all fronts, a many-sided expansion of productive capacity that maintains the product mix in conformity both with consumers' preferences (interdependence in consumption) and with the technical requirements of the productive system (interdependence in production). The advantages of such growth all have to do with effective demand. In discussions of external economies, all the stress is usually put on the greater profitability of each individual investment that balanced growth assures. Equally or even more important advantages, however, are the avoidance of bottlenecks, of special shortages, and special excess capacities; and the minimization of inflationary pressures and dangers that the avoidance of special shortages achieves. To judge by the experience of some of the countries now in the process of development, this last-mentioned may well be the main argument in favour of balanced growth.

All this has been much stressed in recent discussions of the problems of economic development; and rightly so, considering the almost complete neglect of the subject in the earlier theory of economics. There are also obstacles to and arguments against growth; and they too must be expounded now that the case for balanced growth is becoming so widely known and accepted.

In presenting the modern argument for concentrated growth, we do not want to imply that the early argument is not valid. The gain to be had from concentrating on the production of goods in whose manufacture one has a comparative advantage is a genuine gain; and if we stressed the fact that this gain is obtained at a cost—the uncertainty that dependence on foreign trade involves—we still believe that *within limits* the gain is worth the cost. If the extent to which Britain's textile industries relied on export markets at the turn of the century seems excessive and highly precarious by today's standards, we would also regard as excessive and prohibitively expensive any attempts to render an economy completely self-contained and independent of foreign trade. In other words, the problem here is to weigh the benefits of the higher income to be had from concentrated growth against the disadvantage of the greater uncertainty that it involves, and to push the degree of concentration to the point and no further than the point at which the two are equated on the margin.

In contrast to the above, all the modern arguments in favour of concentrated growth are based on technological considerations, and they raise the problem of weighing these technological advantages of concentrated growth against the economic benefits of balanced growth. The first of these arguments has to do with economies of scale.

Economies of scale render production cheaper and investment more profitable above a certain minimum level of output and productive capacity. The desire, however, to secure these economies and to keep every investment above this minimum level may well conflict with the principles of balanced output and balanced growth. The simple and obvious reasons for such conflict are (1) insufficient effective demand to render profitable, and (2) insufficient savings to render possible, the construction of productive capacity of optimum size and design whenever total effective demand and/or total available savings are too thinly spread over a wide range of industries. One might also distinguish here between an economy that is too small to provide a market for the output even of one optimum-sized plant in every industry and an economy that is growing too slowly for the *accretion* of demand to justify or for the rate of capital accumulation to finance the simultaneous building of *additional* capacity of optimum size in every industry.

Such conflicts can be resolved by sacrificing economies of scale for the sake of balance, by sacrificing balance—at least temporarily—in order to secure the economies of scale, or by striking a compromise between the two. In the first case, investment will be less efficient, output smaller, and growth slower than they could be; whence it follows that it is always desirable to sacrifice balanced output or balanced growth, at least to some extent. This, indeed, is what usually happens.

Countries too small to secure the advantages both of large-scale production and of a balanced economy usually have much more liberal foreign-trade policies than do large countries; and this is explained not by ideological differences but by the above conflict and the small countries' willingness to resolve this conflict by accepting the uncertainties of great dependence on foreign trade for the sake of obtaining economies of large-scale production in at least some industries.[1]

Countries in the process of development face a slightly different conflict but usually resolve it in a similar way. This is certainly true of planned economies, and of economies that plan their investment; and their several-year investment plans, of which one hears so much nowadays, may be regarded as plans for unbalanced growth, extending to several years so as to restore balance by the end of the period for which the plans are made. In the interim, imbalance manifests itself by the completion of productive capacity before the demand for its full utilization has arisen, or by the creation of consumers' or producers' demand before the capacity to fill this demand is completed. The temporary excess capacity may have to be accepted in most cases as an inevitable cost of (temporarily) unbalanced growth for the sake of securing economies of

---

[1] The conflict can be eliminated, of course, by forming larger economic units; and it is no accident that the countries most in favour of Western European integration are the small ones.

scale; the temporary excess demand may be filled by imports, which is one reason why the availability of foreign loans or foreign exchange is so strategic a factor in investment planning.[1] Such dependence on foreign trade, however, is very different from that which accompanies unbalanced growth concentrated on industries with a comparative advantage. For one thing, this is a temporary dependence, while that is permanent; for another, the dependence here is primarily on foreign import supplies, there on foreign export markets.

This way of securing the economies of scale at the cost of a temporary imbalance comes about also in the unplanned market economy. There have been instances, especially in the smaller European countries, of productive units being built in industries new for the country but with capacities larger than the domestic market, in the hope of capturing an export market, but yet with a view to relying ultimately on the expanding domestic market. Too often, however, the economies of scale are sacrificed in the market economy because effective demand, or capital funds, or both, are insufficient for the building of efficient large-scale productive capacity. This, then, is the case where balanced growth is secured at the high cost of having less efficient investment and a slower rate of growth than the best methods of production known would have made feasible.

Indeed, something like this can happen even when the economy is large enough and its rate of growth and capital accumulation high enough to enable all industries simultaneously to add new optimum-sized plants to their already existing equipment. Technical progress may render large-scale mass production the most economical in an industry that consists of many firms, all of them smaller than the new optimum-sized plant. In such a case, and there may be many such cases, it can happen that none of the firms has access to enough capital and can capture enough of the new accretion of demand to be able to build an optimum-sized plant—with the result that traditional methods of production are retained in the industry's expansion and the new economies of scale are left unutilized. We have discussed this case in detail elsewhere, and there blamed this kind of situation on the lack—or the

---

[1] The other reason, of course, is that underdeveloped countries usually have to buy much of their productive equipment abroad.

wrong kind—of competition.[1] For, we argued, if only competition were great enough, the firm able to lower its costs of production could also capture a substantial part of the new market, and the prospect of its doing this would enable it to obtain the requisite amount of capital.

Here, too, however, there is a conflict. It is different from that discussed earlier and arises because securing the economies of scale is incompatible, not indeed with balanced growth, but with retaining the existing pattern of competition. If efficiency calls for mass production and large-scale plants in an industry hitherto composed of small firms and small plants, either the relative size of the members of the industry will become more unequal or the number of independent firms will be reduced, and competition is likely to suffer in either case. Hence, when we advocate the kind of competition that renders possible the building of bigger productive units, we may be advocating the kind of competition that will destroy itself in the long run—but this problem, however serious, is not strictly relevant to the subject matter of this paper and is mentioned here only because of its affinity to the earlier problem.

So far, all of our arguments and analyses were based on the tacit assumption that the state and rate of change of technical knowledge are given and independent of economic considerations. This assumption, however, is clearly unrealistic. The development of technical knowledge depends very much on economic factors; indeed, many of the major technical inventions have been sparked by shortages created by an unbalanced pattern of growth or resource availability in the face of rigid interdependence and complementarity in production. Hence, when we drop the assumption of given technology, we find further arguments in favour of concentrated growth.

The analysis of long-run trends in output and employment in individual US industries has shown a close correlation between total output and labour productivity (output per worker).[2] The rise in an industry's labour productivity is the fastest during periods of fast rise in its total output. From this

[1] Cf. my 'Economies of Scale, Competition, and European Integration', *American Economic Review*, XLVI (1956), 71-91, and also Chapter 4 above.
[2] The National Bureau of Economic Research has done, and I believe is still doing, work on this subject. E.g. F. C. Mills, 'Productivity and Economic Progress'. Occasional Paper No. 38, National Bureau of Economic Research.

it need not follow that by promoting a rise in output one can also promote a rise in productivity; but there are independent reasons for believing that this, indeed, will happen. For one thing, the faster the rate of expansion, the higher the proportion of new as against replacement investment; and new investment provides much more scope for innovation and technical improvement than does the replacement of worn-out capacity. For another thing, the faster an industry expands, the more easily can newcomers with new ideas enter the industry, and the greater becomes the industry's general receptivity to new methods and experiments.

These are arguments in favour of fast growth, by which in this context is meant an annual expansion of from 15 to 20 per cent or more. Such fast expansion of an individual industry would be compatible with balanced growth only if the economy as a whole were expanding at a comparable rate; but outside of some of the planned economies this condition is not likely to be fulfilled. In the market economy the overall rate of growth is always very much slower; and the fast growth therefore of some industries can be obtained only at the cost of no or slow growth in other industries. Unbalanced growth appears, therefore, as the price of the fast growth that in a variety of ways stimulates technical progress. In addition, however, unbalanced growth itself may also be a stimulus to technical invention and innovation, for the fast expansion of output in one field or at one stage of production is likely to create bottlenecks and shortages of specialized resources in closely related fields or at other stages of production within the same field; and the desire either to eliminate such shortages or to find new methods that economize the resources in short supply is known to be among the most powerful stimulants of technological progress.[1] An example of the former is provided by the development of England's textile industry during the industrial revolution. Kay's invention of the flying shuttle expanded weaving capacity and thus created the shortage of spinning capacity that led to the inventions of Paul and Wyatt, Hargreaves, Crompton, Kelly, and Arkwright, which revolu-

---

[1] This seems to be generally accepted today. Most historical studies of the great inventions of the eighteenth and nineteenth centuries stress the fact that these were not fortuitous events but came about in response to an economic need. For a short summary, see Maurice Dobb's essay on 'The Industrial Revolution and the Nineteenth Century' (1).

tionized spinning. The resulting great expansion of spinning capacity, in its turn, created the shortage of weaving capacity that led to Cartwright's invention of the power-loom. An example of the latter (i.e. of the stimulating influence on invention of the need to economize resources in short supply) is the early development of mass production methods in the United States. This occurred largely in response to the shortage of skilled labour; for the idea of subdividing a complex manufacturing process into relatively simple constituent parts was conceived of primarily in order to economize skilled labour.

Having enumerated and discussed the arguments both for balanced and for unbalanced or concentrated growth, we may well ask what conclusions can be drawn from all this for practical policy. To answer this question, let us recall, first of all, that most arguments for concentrated growth are, in reality, arguments for fast growth or growth by large steps —tantamount to arguments for concentrated growth only when the economy's overall growth rate is slow. Second, let us also recall that foreign trade, by converting an unbalanced pattern of output into a balanced pattern of availabilities, can always secure the advantages of balance for an unbalanced economy. What emerges from these considerations is an argument in favour of large size. In a large economy, mere geographical extent and diversity of climates and natural resources automatically assure some degree of self-sufficiency and balance, while allowing plenty of scope for concentrated growth on a regional or functional basis. The United States and the Soviet Union furnish examples of both types of development. The approximately 3 per cent annual rate of expansion of the American economy has in the recent past been the average of a much faster growth rate in the South and Far West and a virtual standstill in New England. Similarly, the expansion of the Soviet economy has for many years past been concentrated in its Far Eastern regions. In some cases and during some periods, such regionally concentrated growth was balanced within the region; more often it was concentrated in a few industries and the resulting unbalanced pattern of the region's output converted into a balanced pattern of availabilities through interregional trade.

The economic advantages of large size and the fact that

they are compounded from the advantages of balanced and those of concentrated growth are being increasingly realized —witness the trend toward, and arguments in favour of, integration and the formation of large economic areas, not only in Western Europe but in many other parts of the world as well. In a sense, this is merely a modern and perhaps more realistic and promising attempt at realizing that old ideal of the economist: free trade; but the modern argument for this limited form of free trade has become very different from the classical (and especially from the neo-classical) argument and much closer to the arguments advanced in this paper.

Chapter 6

INTERNATIONAL TRADE AND ECONOMIC INTEGRATION AS A MEANS OF OVER-COMING THE DISADVANTAGES OF A SMALL NATION

1960

THE SMALL ECONOMY

I propose in this paper to attempt a theoretical discussion, first of some of the factors that inhibit efficiency and growth in too small an economy, and second of the influence international trade and economic integration are likely to exert on these factors. Strictly speaking, the task I have been asked to undertake comprises only the second of these two. But to discuss the influence of trade and integration on the inhibiting factors, these latter must first be analysed; also, the discussion of these factors and their influencing must be closely co-ordinated; and at the time of writing I have no way of knowing the coverage and approach of the other papers. I can only hope, therefore, that this paper will not repeat too much of what has already been said and discussed at an earlier stage, and that whatever repetition it contains may not be too boring.

In discussing the sub-optimal nature of too small an economy and the factors that render it sub-optimal, it is useful to distinguish between technological and economic factors. Technologically an economy can be too small if its market is too small to provide an adequate outlet for the full-capacity output of the most efficient productive plant in a given industry. From this point of view, then, the minimum size of an economy is generally different for different industries; and if we have an economy which is too small from the point of

view of some but not of other industries, we have here right
away a simple technological determinant of the composition
of foreign trade that is completely neglected in the classical
theory of international values. One must also note in this
connection the complexities introduced by the existence of
intermediate products and industries. An economy, for
example, that is large enough to provide adequate domestic
market outlets for the output of at least one optimum-sized
plant in all industries producing final products may still be sub-
optimal if some of these plants need equipment, servicing, or
other intermediate products, but provide too small a market
for some of these.[1] The technological optimum-size for an
economy therefore may be very much larger than one might
think at first.

In contrast to the technological factors stand the economic
ones, all of which have to do with competition and its influence
on efficiency. Economically, therefore, an economy is too
small if it fails to provide the competitive conditions necessary
to spur to utmost efficiency and to lead to the establishment of
the technically most efficient plants. An economy large
enough to absorb the output of at least one optimum-sized
plant in all industries may still not be large enough to provide
the incentive for the building of such plants. Thus, the technological optimum size of an economy is a necessary but not a
sufficient condition to ensure the utilization of the most efficient means of production. In other words, the technological
optimum is probably reached very much sooner than the
economic optimum; and this accounts for the often-held
belief that small economies are more in need of central planning, while large economies, having more competition, can
rely more easily on the working of the profit motive. There
is some truth in this belief; but it must also be remembered
that the competition referred to here is a broader concept than
mere market competition and therefore is not confined to an
economy governed by the profit motive. This will be discussed in more detail later on, when I deal with the ways in

[1] This point and, generally, the fact that industrial interdependence renders
very much larger the scale of output necessary for the full exploitation of
economies of scale than would appear at first thought has been discussed in
detail a few years ago in the pages of the *American Economic Review*
('Economies of Scale, Competition and European Integration', *American
Economic Review*, March 1956, pp. 71 ff.).

which international trade and economic union stimulate competition and thus encourage efficiency and economic growth.

SOME CHARACTERISTICS OF EXPORT TRADE

Let us turn now to the ways in which international trade and economic union can offset the disadvantages of smallness in the purely technological sense. The days when international trade was believed to be just as good as domestic trade are long past. Today, the condition of efficient production is very often the large-scale production at a stable rate of relatively few varieties of the product. In other words, mass-production methods to become profitable require a market outlet that is large, homogeneous, and stable over time; and these requirements rule out reliance on export markets, except to a very limited extent. For export markets these days are regarded as highly precarious—liable to be closed off suddenly for political reasons or as a result of balance-of-payments difficulties; and they are also the markets in which competition has highly undesirable characteristics, in the sense that competitors' behaviour is unpredictable on the basis of rational economic considerations alone, being governed by political motivation as well. In England—traditionally an important export producer—today's rule of thumb seems to be that it is not prudent to rely on exports for more than 20-25 per cent of a company's total market outlet.

There are means, of course, of eliminating or insuring against these disadvantages of export trade. International commodity agreements, long-term contracts between contractors and subcontractors are means of introducing long-term stability into international trade relations; but the range of products to which they are suited is limited. It is no accident that commodity agreements are usually confined to staple foods and primary products; long-term contracts between producer and distributor concerning industrial products are seldom feasible. Also, long-term agreements may be able to stabilize a situation already established; but when it is a matter of a producer investing in mass-production equipment in the hope of *expanding* or *creating* a *stable* market, then the disadvantages and precariousness of export markets cannot be guarded against—this, I suspect, is the really important case.

We may conclude, therefore, that if an economy is too small technologically—in the sense of providing insufficient market outlets for the output even of a single modern and efficient plant—then international trade is of little avail. Economic union would be better, provided it guarantees not only free and unrestricted trade but also complete stability of exchange rates among members of the union.

EXPORT TRADE AS AN ESCAPE FOR
THE SMALL ECONOMY

Let us now investigate the way in which international trade and/or economic union can offset the disadvantages of smallness in the economic sense. First of all, what are the disadvantages? They all have to do with competition. Competition encourages economic efficiency and progress if the economic unit is large enough. It will fail to do this, however, when the economy is too small and competition in consequence is too personal and too weak.

There are several ways in which increasing the size of the economic unit or increasing contacts between different economic units leads to efficiency. One way—and one almost too simple to mention—has to do with differences in temperament and custom. There are tremendous national differences in temperament, work habits, commercial and industrial practices, economic imagination, awareness of opportunities to increase manufacturing efficiency and to exploit market possibilities; and more contact and freer trade would be almost certain to effect not only a levelling of these differences but an upward levelling in the direction of greater industrial and commercial efficiency. Not only the more efficient but the economically and technically more imaginative, more pushing, and more ruthless would be bound to prevail over their more easy-going competitors and force these to imitate their customs and methods. That there is much scope, and unexploited scope, for such development is obvious; and the great uniformity of economic temperament and practice in the United States, achieved despite great racial, climatic, and dietary differences, indicates the possibility of exploiting this scope —although, of course, such uniformity in the United States was achieved by more intimate interchange and intermingling than mere social contact and economic competition.

I am not at all certain that in purely human terms I would welcome such levelling and the elimination of national differences; but its effects on economic productivity and output, as shown in the customary statistics of these quantities, are almost certain to be salutary. Let me add that these effects of competition are likely to be achieved by freer trade and economic union alike, provided they promote economic, social, and intellectual contact to a significant extent.

FREER TRADE AND THE INTENSITY OF COMPETITION

A second way in which freer trade or economic union can promote economic and technical efficiency is by rendering competition less personal and thereby more effective. There is far too great a tendency among some economists to regard the existence of many small firms in an industry as proof of atomistic competition and to identify this latter with the kind of competition that promotes technical efficiency and progress. This, however, is often wrong, and competition among many small firms is seldom of such a kind as to encourage efficiency and growth. For one thing, relations among the small producers composing an industry are often so close and friendly as to keep each of them from engaging in competitive actions that would hurt the rest. For another, in an industry composed of many small firms the problem who among them is to build a modern large-scale plant may be an insoluble one. To begin with, each firm may be too small to possess or have access to enough capital with which to build such a plant; secondly, to operate a large-scale plant efficiently and profitably, it might be necessary to encroach upon competitors' markets; and each of the existing firms may shrink back from so ungentlemanly an action. Indeed, it is typical of many European industries that the first efficient, modern, large-scale plant often is built to cater to the export market—not because the internal market is not large enough to provide an adequate market outlet but because this is already being catered for by old-established small manufacturers whom it would be ungentlemanly to push out of the market. It can also happen, however (and probably often does), that the efficient large-scale plant is not built at all, because considerations of business ethics stand in the way of creating (by diverting from competitors) an adequate domestic market for it, and because the export market may be considered too precarious to serve as the main basis of mass production.

To what extent these problems would be solved by freer trade or economic union is difficult to tell. My feeling is that international trade, however free, would usually be considered too precarious to serve as the main basis for mass production, and that thorough-going economic integration would be required to solve these problems of too small an economy.

PROFIT MARGINS

A third way in which free trade or economic union might promote technical progress has to do with profit margins and turnover. An economy can be too small in terms not only of area or population but also of purchasing power. In many European countries it is said, especially of consumers' durables, that they cannot be mass-produced cheaply because low incomes preclude a mass market—on the other hand, the lower cost *and price* of such goods would by itself raise real incomes and thus go some way towards creating the mass market on which their cheap mass production hinges. In other words, there is here a *circulus vitiosus*, which may in some instances be quite important, and which may well be broken by increased competition brought about by freer trade or economic union.

How is this vicious circle brought about in the first place? One of its causes may be, in the case of consumers' durables, inadequate facilities for hire purchase or its rejection on ethical or religious grounds (the Thomist condemnation of interest is still upheld by many Catholics in the case of consumer credit). In this connection, the above-mentioned spreading of the most successful commercial practices through more economic and social contact may do much to break the circle. Another possible cause, and the one I propose to discuss in more detail, is the policy of high margins and low turnover.

It is a frequent comment of American businessmen viewing the European scene that both European economies and European businessmen would be better off if the latter tried to expand their markets by a lowering of profit margins and prices. Needless to say, this argument assumes that the price reduction would so much increase turnover as to yield new economies of scale and reduce unit costs of production (implying that prices could be reduced to a greater extent than profit margins), and that the higher rate of turnover would compensate or more than compensate businessmen for the lower rate of profit per unit of output. Let us for argument's sake accept this view as correct and explore some of its implications.

The argument has often been advanced to European businessmen; and they have—most of them—rejected it. For one thing, high margins, low turnover, and catering for a small and intimately known market probably offer the businessman a quieter and easier life and more security and stability than a large and impersonal market with small profit margins, where he must ever be on the alert to keep his position and preserve his profits. For another thing, some manufacturers reject the principle of low margins and high turnover, because they realize that the adoption of mass-production methods usually involves a sacrifice of quality, workmanship, and finish; and they are reluctant to make this sacrifice. To some extent such reluctance may be a simple value judgment and a rational choice; to some extent it may also stem from a lack of realization that high quality can also be achieved (and in the United States is in the process of being achieved) with the use and through the perfection of mass-production methods. Also, European businessmen often feel that they owe part of their market—especially their export market—to quality production; and they may be reluctant to sacrifice this part of their market even if the additional market to be gained through price reduction promises to be larger and more profitable. This is a matter of preferring one bird in the hand to two in the bush. Furthermore, some European businessmen may be reluctant to lower price for fear that the resulting rise in turnover would not be sufficient to justify the adoption of new and cheaper methods of production and would not recoup their profits. In this expectation they may be right or wrong —this, after all, is a matter of correctly estimating the price elasticity of demand.

There are a few conspicuous and well-publicized instances of highly successful attempts to introduce a cheap mass-product and create a mass market; and they certainly seem to prove that businessmen often underestimate the elasticity of demand of the market facing them. The success of cheap mass holidays in England, of a cheap refrigerator in Germany, of a washing machine in France, and of paper-bound pocket books all over the world, are the first examples that come to mind. But this is a small sample and presumably a biased one (for success always gets more publicity than failure) from which no general conclusions should be drawn, For all I know, European businessmen may often, perhaps mostly, be right when they insist that a price reduction would not stimulate turnover sufficiently to render the economies of scale of mass production feasible and profitable. I shall argue, however, that even in this case there may be truth in the American business-man's contention.

Assume an economy in which the average consumer's consumption pattern is fairly rigidly fixed by tradition or by his aspiration to emulate the consumption pattern of the upper classes, which in turn is largely independent of cost considerations. In other words, we are assuming an economy in which the average consumer's elasticity of substitution between different consumers' goods is low. In such an economy, a reduction in the price of a single consumers' good would not raise its sales very much, partly because the income effect of a single price reduction (the reduction, that is, in the price of a single good) is likely to be small, and partly because its substitution effect is—by assumption—also small. In such an economy, therefore, rational profit calculations might well prevent businessmen abandoning a high-margin low-turnover policy, since a price reduction would probably fail to stimulate turnover sufficiently to render mass production feasible and profitable.

In this same economy, however, concerted action by many businessmen and the simultaneous reduction of the prices of a large number of consumers' goods could have a very different effect. For such a price reduction *would* have a sizeable income effect and thus lead to a much larger increase in consumers' demand and hence sale of consumers' goods; and this increase in turnover might well be sufficient to render price reduction and the transition to cheaper mass-production methods profitable.

Here, then, is an argument based on the simple notion of interdependence in consumption (or rather of pecuniary external economies due to interdependence in consumption) that shows the possibility of *profitably* expanding the domestic market and introducing mass-production methods through concerted action (central planning if you like) in a situation in which the same would not be feasible and profitable under atomistic conditions. The argument, of course, stands or falls with the assumption of a low elasticity of substitution in consumption; and the realism of this assumption can only be ascertained by empirical investigation.

But whether or not this last assumption is realistic, the point is this. I have cited several possible reasons—and there may be many more—why entrepreneurs may retain their traditional policy of high margins, low turnover, and small-scale production under circumstances where the opposite policy would be not only socially more desirable but—in the sense and under the conditions just described—also more or at least equally profitable. I do not feel competent to appraise the relative importance of these different reasons; but I do think that they merit attention and that some might be quite important. If this is so, then the increase in competition brought about by freer trade or economic union might well break the *impasse* and bring about a change in producers' thinking and policies. For increased competition would force prices down; and a forced price reduction would be likely to eliminate *all* the above-cited reasons for the undue retention of the traditional policy of high margins, low turnover, and small-scale production. To begin with, a forcible price reduction would deprive entrepreneurs of their freedom of choice between high profits on the one hand, and pride of workmanship and quality or a quiet life and financial security on the other hand. For it would impose lower profit margins, and entrepreneurs, if they are to avoid losses, would be forced into a mass-production policy, the exploration of potentialities of market expansion, and the abandonment of the high technical standards and easy way of life that small-scale production with high margins so often entails. Secondly, economic union or a general freeing of trade would bring about the all-round reduction of prices that would be necessary, according to our last argument, to create a mass market for certain consumers' goods (primarily consumers' durables and semi-luxuries) through a raising of real incomes.

COMPETITION AND SECURITY

The above were a few examples—probably a very incomplete list—of the various ways in which competition may affect economic efficiency and technical progress—its absence inhibiting, its presence encouraging the adoption of the best methods known and a general staying alert and keeping up with changing conditions and requirements. In the traditional theory of competition it is customary barely to mention these aspects and to concentrate instead on matters of income distribution and static efficiency. These aspects, however, are important; they would be among the most valuable consequences of freer trade or economic union—they would certainly be no less and perhaps more important than the latter's purely technological effects of the kind discussed at the beginning of this paper.

At the same time it must also be realized that if competition favours efficiency and progress, it does so at a cost. For these results of competition are achieved through the greater rewards it offers to those who have, and the worse punishment it metes out to those who lack, success—whether this is due to efficiency, alertness, and resourcefulness, or to adventurousness, ruthlessness, and luck. Such conditions undoubtedly make for the greater insecurity and precariousness of the economic position of the individual; and it was partly to guard against such insecurity that competition was restricted. Freer trade and economic union, if they are to encourage efficiency, would tend to remove or offset these restrictions; and I doubt if one can have their beneficial effects without paying for them the price of lesser stability and greater insecurity. Whether the advantages of greater efficiency and faster progress can also be had in other ways and at a lesser price is a subject that lies beyond the scope of this paper.

B

THEORETICAL WELFARE
ECONOMICS

Chapter 7

A NOTE ON WELFARE PROPOSITIONS
IN ECONOMICS

1941

Modern economic theory draws a sharp distinction between positive economics, which explains the working of the economic system, and welfare economics, which prescribes policy. In the domain of welfare economics the impossibility of interpersonal utility comparisons has for a long time been believed to impose strict limitations on the economist, which kept this branch of economic theory in the background. Recently, however, there has been a reawakening of interest in welfare problems, following assertions that these limitations are less restrictive than they were hitherto supposed to be.[1] The present note attempts to analyse the problem in detail.

I

The aim of welfare economics is to test the efficiency of economic institutions in making use of the productive resources of a community. For analytical and historical reasons it is useful to distinguish between welfare propositions based on the assumption of a fixed quantity of employed resources and those that regard that quantity as variable.

The former are concerned with the allocating efficiency of

[1] Cf. N. Kaldor: 'Welfare Propositions of Economics and Interpersonal Comparisons of Utility', *Economic Journal*, vol. 49 (1939), p. 549; J. R. Hicks: 'Foundations of Welfare Economics', *Economic Journal*, vol. 49 (1939), p. 696. See also N. Kaldor: 'Note on Tariffs and the Terms of Trade', *Economica* (NS), vol. 7 (1940), p. 377; and J. R. Hicks: 'The Rehabilitation of Consumers' Surplus', *Review of Economic Studies*, vol. 8 (1941), p. 108. The present note is a criticism of the principle enunciated in Mr Kaldor's first-quoted article and underlying the argument of the others. It is not presented in polemic form, in order to enable the reader not acquainted with the articles here quoted to follow its argument.

the system;[1] i.e. with its ability of best allocating a given quantity of utilized resources among their various uses in consumption and production. They can be conceived of as criteria for judging institutions and policy in a closed community whose potential resources are fixed and can be trusted to be fully employed either because of the automatism of the system or because of the existence of a governmental policy aiming at full employment.

The latter, which may be called welfare propositions in the wider sense, are in addition to the above problems concerned also with the total quantity of resources available to an open group and the degree of utilization of those resources. They are therefore relevant, first of all, to problems of international trade from the point of view of a single country; and secondly, to the general problem of employment.

II

All the welfare propositions of the classical economists—viz., perfect competition, free trade, and direct taxation—belong in the first category; a fact which has not always been realized. They are all based on the principle that given the total quantity of utilized resources, they will be best distributed among different uses if their rates of substitution are everywhere and for every person equal; for only in such a situation will each person's satisfaction be carried to that maximum beyond which it cannot be increased without diminishing someone else's. Perfect competition, free trade, and direct taxation are one (probably the simplest) among the many ways of achieving this aim.

By limiting our universe of discourse to two commodities and two persons, we can illustrate this principle on a simple diagram. Let us draw the indifference maps of the two individuals superposed on each other, one of them reversed, with the axes parallel and in such a position that their intersection gives the quantities of the two goods jointly possessed by the two people. Every point of the rectangle enclosed by the axes corresponds to a given distribution of the two goods between the two persons, and the two indifference curves going

---

[1] This expression was suggested to me by Mr George Jaszi to whom I am also indebted for reading the manuscript and making valuable suggestions.

through that point show their respective welfare positions. At some points, indifference curves do not cut but are tangential one to another. At these points the rate of substitution of the two goods is equal for the two persons, and they represent optimum situations, because once such a point has been reached no redistribution of the two goods can increase the welfare of either person without diminishing that of the other. The locus of all optimum points gives the contract curve.

We judge the allocating efficiency of economic institutions by the criterion whether or not they enable people so to redistribute goods and services among themselves (irrespective of their initial position) as to arrive on the contract curve. That perfect competition or, from the point of view of the universe, free trade are efficient in the above sense can be proved by showing that all pairs of offer (reciprocal demand) curves drawn from any point within the rectangle intersect on the contract curve. Similarly, excise taxes and, from the point of view of the universe, import and export duties are inefficient, because they can be represented as distortions of offer curves that make them intersect outside the contract curve. The arguments based on this diagram can be generalized for any number of persons and commodities.[1] It implies only one limitation: the quantities of goods available to the community as a whole must be fixed; for they determine the points of intersection of the axes and the position of the contract curve. This shows that the propositions illustrated by the diagram are allocative welfare propositions; and it also appears to limit their applicability to the problem of exchange of goods whose quantities coming on to the market are given. It can be proved, however, that our arguments are equally valid when instead of these quantities those of the factors utilized in their production are considered to be fixed. For the formal proof of the geometrical arguments and their generalizations the reader is referred to the original sources and to textbooks dealing with the subject.[2]

[1] This holds good for all arguments based on other diagrams in this note.
[2] Cf. F. Y. Edgeworth: *Mathematical Psychics*, London, 1881, and 'The Pure Theory of International Trade', *Economic Journal*, vol. 4 (1894); Alfred Marshall: *The Pure Theory of Foreign Trade* (1879), London School reprint, 1930; and his *Principles of Economics*, Bk. V, Chap. II. Note on Barter and Mathematical Note XII; A. P. Lerner: 'The Symmetry between Export and Import Taxes', *Economica* (NS), vol. 3 (1936); J. R. Hicks: *Value and Capital*,

III

We have seen above that allocative welfare propositions are based on the criterion of economic efficiency. They state that of alternative situations, brought about by different institutions or courses of policy, one is superior to the other in the sense that it would make everybody better off for every distribution of welfare, *if* that were the same in the two situations. This is different from saying that one situation is actually better than the other from everybody's point of view, because a change in institutions or policy almost always redistributes welfare sufficiently not to have a uniform effect on everybody but to favour some people and prejudice others. It follows from this that economic welfare propositions cannot as a rule be made independently of interpersonal comparisons of utility.

It would hardly be satisfactory, however, to confine the economist's value judgments to cases where one situation is superior to the other from the point of view of everybody affected. It is doubtful if in practice any choice comes within this category; besides, there would not be much point in soliciting the economist's expert opinion when everybody is unanimous, except in order to enlighten people as to their true interest.

Favouring an improvement in the organization of production and exchange *only* when it is accompanied by a corrective redistribution of income fully compensating those prejudiced by it might seem to be a way out of the difficulty, because such a change would make some people better off without making anyone worse off. For instance, it might be argued that the abolition of the Corn Laws should not have been advocated by economists without advocating at the same time the full compensation of landowners out of taxes levied on those favoured by the cheapening of corn. Yet, in a sense, and regarded from a long-run point of view, such propositions are not interdependent of value judgments between alternative income distributions either. For, going out of their way to preserve the existing distribution of income, they imply a preference for the *status quo*.

There seem to be two solutions of the problem. First of

Oxford, 1939, etc. For the best analysis of the nature of this kind of diagram see A. L. Bowley: *The Mathematical Groundwork of Economics*, Oxford, 1924.

all, in addition to admitting his inability to compare different people's satisfaction, the economist may postulate that such comparisons are impossible, and that therefore there is nothing to choose between one distribution of income and another. He may then make value judgments on the sole criterion of efficiency without bothering about concomitant shifts in the distribution of income, since he considers one income distribution as good as any other.[1] In this case, however, he cannot claim that his value judgments are independent of interpersonal utility comparisons, because they depend on the assumption of their impossibility.

Secondly, the economist may put forward his welfare propositions with due emphasis on their limitations, as being based on the sole criterion of efficiency. He may then point out the nature of eventual redistributions of income likely to accompany a given change, and stress the necessity of basing economic policy on considerations both of economic efficiency and of social justice.[2] Such an attitude, which I think is the only correct one, may diminish the force of the economist's welfare propositions but does not make them less useful. The above considerations qualify also the welfare propositions to be discussed below.

IV

When we come to the problem of welfare propositions in the wider sense, we can no longer illustrate a change in economic institutions or policy on a single diagram. For such a change will no longer mean a mere redistribution of income and alteration of the rules of production and exchange; but may also involve a change both in the total quantity of resources available to the community, and in their degree of utilization.

---

[1] This, I think, was the attitude of the classical economists; at least of those who did not, like Bastiat, impute ethical values to the distribution of income under perfect competition. It seems to be the correct interpretation of that fairly representative statement of Cairnes's: '. . . standards of abstract justice . . . are inefficacious as means of solving the actual problems of . . . distribution. . . . If our present system of industry (perfect competition) is to be justified, it must . . . find its justification . . . in the fact that it secures for the mass of mankind a greater amount of material and moral well-being, and provides more effectively for its progress in civilization than any other plan.'
[2] Or, of course, he may also renounce his claim to purity and base his own recommendations on both criteria.

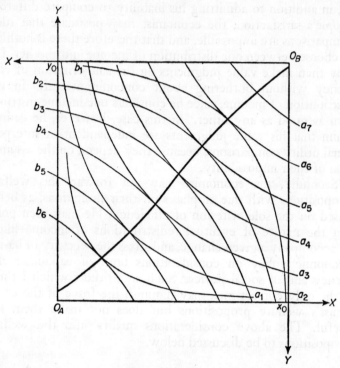

Fig. 1. Diagram 1

The former may be due to the imposition of a duty on international trade, which from the point of view of an individual country alters the quantities of imports and retained exports available for home consumption; while the latter may be caused by this or any other change if it affects the propensity to save or the inducement to invest and thereby changes employment. Analytically there is no difference between the two cases. In both, the quantities of resources available for consumption are changed, hence the relative position of the indifference maps is altered; whence it follows that welfare propositions in the wider sense must involve the comparison of two diagrams. Since these are constructed from the identical two indifference maps and differ only in the latter's relative position to each other, such comparisons are not the hopeless task they might seem at first sight. For we can represent some (not all) welfare positions on both diagrams; and it is possible to

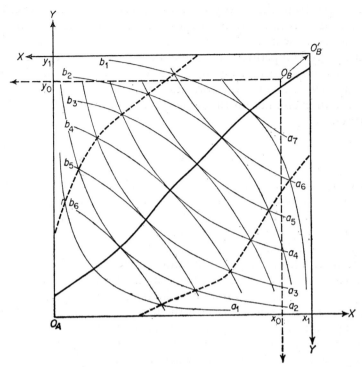

Fig. 1. Diagram 2

represent on one diagram the welfare positions corresponding to all those points of the other diagram's contract curve that are inferior to its 'own' contract curve. This follows from the fact that our diagrams admit the representation of all welfare situations that are inferior (worse from the point of view of at least one of the two persons) to their contract curve, while welfare positions superior to the contract curve cannot be represented on them.

Our welfare propositions may necessitate the comparison of points on the contract curves of the two diagrams, or of points suboptimal to them, or of a point on one contract curve with a point suboptimal to the other contract curve. The first case is that where the system's allocating efficiency is at an optimum both before and after the given change; the second, where it is suboptimal both before and after the change; the third, where the change affects allocating efficiency. Taking an

I

example from the theory of international trade, the first case may be illustrated by the imposition of an import duty by a country in which taxation is direct and domestic markets are perfectly competitive;[1] the second case can be represented by a duty imposed in a monopolistic world; and the third by a duty which favours the formation of monopolies or is linked with an excise tax on the home production of import substitutes.

V

Let us draw two diagrams (fig. 1), both consisting of the superposed indifference maps of individuals A and B, but with the difference that in the second, B's map has been shifted by $o_B o_B$; so that the joint possessions of A and B have increased by $x_0 x_1$ of X and $y_0 y_1$ of Y compared with what they were in the first. This shift will bring into a position of tangency indifference curves that in the first diagram have neither touched nor intersected, and will thus make the second diagram's contract curve superior to that of the first diagram throughout its range. This follows from that fundamental postulate of economic theory that indifference curves can never have a positive slope, and it will be the case whenever the shift in the relative position of the indifference maps represents an increase in the quantity of at least one of the two commodities without a diminution in that of the other. From the fact that the second diagram's contract curve is superior to that of the first, it follows that the latter can be represented on the second diagram by tracing the locus of the points of intersection of all the indifference curves that in the first diagram are tangential to each other. This will give us a curve on each side of the second diagram's contract curve, and the area between them represents welfare positions that are superior to the first diagram's contract curve. Hence, a change that brings the

[1] A tariff on foreign trade is not incompatible with the tariff imposing country's domestic trade and production being of optimum allocating efficiency. The reader must not let himself be confused by the fact that similar diagrams have been used for illustrating the waste caused by tariffs from the point of view of the universe as a whole. We are here solely concerned with the effects of a tariff on the welfare of a single country, consequently the indifference maps that constitute our diagrams belong to inhabitants of the same country.

welfare of our groups from a point of the first diagram's contract curve on to a point of the second diagram's contract curve (or at least within the area between the broken lines), can be said to be desirable with the same generality and significance with which perfect competition or direct taxation are said to be desirable on the ground of their allocating efficiency. In other words, while it need not actually improve everybody's position, it would do so for every possible distribution of welfare if the change were to leave that distribution unaffected.

The above argument is an explicit formulation of the statement that getting more of some (or all) commodities at no cost of foregoing others is a good thing. This may be considered as overpedantic, since that statement seems to be obvious; on the other hand, it is subject to the same limitations that qualify allocative welfare propositions (cf. Section III above); and besides, it is not even always true. Increased plenty is a good thing only if it is not linked with a redistribution of welfare, too retrogressive from the point of view of social justice; and if it does not lead to a serious deterioration of the allocating efficiency of the economic system. For the former there exists no objective criterion, but there is a simple test for the latter. To test whether a diminution in allocating efficiency has not obviated the advantages of increased plenty, we must see if after the change, it is possible fully to compensate people prejudiced by it out of funds levied on those favoured by the change, without thereby completely eliminating the latter's gain. From the geometrical argument above it follows that if this test is fulfilled for one initial income distribution, it will be fulfilled for all possible initial income distributions, and *vice versa*. Our test is completely general also in the sense that it is applicable whether or not the initial situation is of optimum allocating efficiency. (I.e. whether or not it lies on the contract curve.)

VI

The kind of change contemplated above, where the quantity of some or all goods is increased without a diminution in others, is likely to occur as a result of increased employment, capital accumulation, technical progress, better utilization of strategic advantages in international trade (by putting a duty on the export of goods for which foreign demand is inelastic), and the like. Another kind of change, especially important in international trade, is that where the quantity of some resources is increased and that of others diminished.[1] In fig. 2 this is represented by a parallel displacement of one of the two indifference maps in the negative direction; so that the

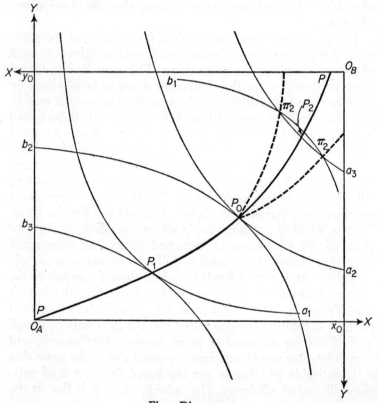

Fig. 2. Diagram 1

quantity of X is diminished by $x_0 x_1$ and that of Y increased by $y_0 y_1$. Nothing general can be said about the relationship of the two contract curves in this case without detailed knowledge of the shape of the indifference maps. It is possible that

[1] This is the effect of import and export duties whenever the foreigners' reciprocal demand for exports is not inelastic and employment is given.

the change will result in superior welfare positions throughout the whole range of the contract curve, in the same way as was depicted in fig. 1. This is especially likely to happen when the increase is large and the diminution small. When on the other hand, the diminution is large and the increase

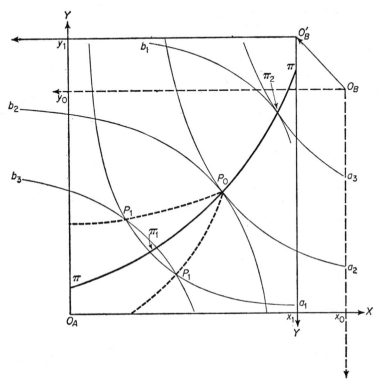

Fig. 2. Diagram 2

small, the change may result in inferior positions throughout the contract curve; a situation which can be visualized by thinking of diagram 2 of fig. 1 as showing the initial, and diagram 1 the new, position. Between these two extremes lies the more general case in which some sectors of the new contract curve are superior to the old one, while others are inferior to it. Its simplest example is illustrated in fig. 2, where P_0 is a common point of the two contract curves, to the left of which the new contract curve, $\pi\pi$, represents welfare positions superior to the corresponding welfare positions of the old contract curve, *PP;* while to the right of P_0, the old contract curve is superior to the new one. In each diagram the broken lines show the welfare positions corresponding to the other diagram's contract curve wherever that is inferior to the diagram's own contract curve.

The economic meaning of this is that the identical change in the composition of the national income would improve general welfare for some hypothetical welfare distributions and worsen it for others. Imagine members of a community divided into two groups according to their preference for goods Y and X respectively.[1] Then assume a change that increases the quantity of Y and diminishes that of X, but leaves the distribution of money income between our two groups unaffected. From the point of view of individuals, the change will appear as a shift in relative prices; which, given the distribution of income, will be likely to make those with a special preference for Y better off, and those with a liking for X worse off, than they were before. Assume next that the members of our first group are rich and those of the second poor. Then the gain of the first group expressed in money (or in terms of any single commodity) will be greater than the money equivalent of the loss suffered by the second group. Therefore, if we so redistributed income as to restore approximately the initial distribution of welfare, there would be a net gain, making members of both groups better off than they were before. Conversely, if the people favoured by the change were poor and those prejudiced by it were rich, the money equivalent of the former's gain would be insufficient fully to compensate the latter's loss, so that a redistribution of income tending to restore the initial distribution of welfare would result in a net loss of satisfaction for everybody.

What significance are we to attach to this case? To refrain altogether, as the classical economists did, from making welfare propositions relating to it, seems unduly restrictive. It is true that, as we have seen, such a change would improve general welfare for some welfare distributions and worsen it for others; on the other hand, we are not interested in all

[1] The term 'preference' is used in a loose sense. It denotes the whole shape of indifference surfaces and not only their slope at the relevant point, which in equilibrium conditions is the same for everybody.

possible welfare distributions. There are only two distributions of welfare that really matter. Those actually obtaining immediately before and after the change contemplated.[1] It seems therefore sufficient to concentrate on these and to investigate how the change would affect general welfare if it were to leave the distribution of welfare unaffected and if that were both before and after it, first what it actually is before, secondly what it actually is after, the change, Whenever these two comparisons yield identical results, we can make welfare propositions of almost the same generality and significance as the allocative welfare propositions of the classical economists; especially since the identical results of the two welfare distributions imply a strong presumption in favour of the same result holding for all intermediate welfare distributions as well.

We propose, therefore, to make welfare propositions on the following principle. We must first see whether it is possible in the new situation so to redistribute income as to make everybody better off than he was in the initial situation; secondly, we must see whether starting from the initial situation it is not possible by a mere redistribution of income to reach a position superior to the new situation, again from everybody's point of view. If the first is possible and the second impossible, we shall say that the new situation is better than the old was. If the first is impossible but the second possible, we shall say that the new situation is worse; whereas if both are possible or both are impossible, we shall refrain from making a welfare proposition.[2]

We can illustrate this procedure in fig. 2 for the special case when allocating efficiency is at its optimum both before and after the change. Each situation can then be represented by a point on its respective contract curve and compared with the corresponding point on the other contract curve. If both points lie to the left of P_0 on their respective contract curves,

---

[1] The reader's attention is called to the fact that in reality the distribution of income is not *given* as we have assumed in the argument above. As a rule, the change will affect the distribution of welfare not only by shifting relative prices but also by boosting some industries and depressing others, and thereby redistributing money income.

[2] It need hardly be recalled that in the situation discussed in Section *v*—that is, when the quantities of goods and services all change in the same direction —this last case can never occur, and we can always make welfare propositions.

the change will increase general welfare, because starting from the new situation on the second diagram's contract curve it is always possible to travel along that curve by redistributing income and arrive at a point which is superior to the initial situation from everybody's point of view; whereas starting from the initial situation on the first diagram's contract curve, it is impossible by travelling along that curve to reach a position superior to the new situation. If on the other hand, both points lie to the right of the common point P_0, the change can be said to diminish general welfare on the same reasoning; while if one point lies to the left and the other to the right, we can make no welfare propositions relative to our group.

VII

Our two criteria for making welfare propositions bear a close resemblance to Paasche's and Laspeyres' formulae in the theory of cost of living index numbers. There, just as here, the difficulty lies in comparing averages whose weighting is different;[1] and the solution is sought in comparing the two real situations not one with another, but each with a hypothetical situation, which resembles it in weighting but is otherwise identical with the other real situation. In the theory of index numbers, budgets of different dates or places are compared each with the cost of the identical bundle of commodities at the prices of the other date or place; and these two comparisons, expressed as ratios (Paasche's and Laspeyres' formulae), are the limits within which the true difference in the cost of living must lie.[2] In welfare problems, of course, we can aim neither at a 'true' answer nor at its quantitative expression without measuring satisfaction and comparing different people's. But our two criteria are exactly analogous to Paasche's and Laspeyres' formulae. For we compare the first welfare situation with what general welfare would be if the satisfaction yielded by the physical income of the second situation were distributed as it was in the first; and contrast the second situation with the welfare that the first situation's

---

[1] Because the general welfare can be conceived of as average welfare.
[2] Cf. Henry Schultz: 'A Misunderstanding in Index Number Theory', *Econometrica*, vol. 7 (1939), p. 1; and A. A. Konüs: 'The Problem of the True Index of the Cost of Living', *Econometrica*, vol. 7 (1939), p. 10.

physical income would yield to each person if it were so distributed as to make the distribution of welfare similar to that of the second situation.[1]

Mr Kaldor and Professor Hicks have asserted that it is *always* possible to tell whether a given change improves general welfare, even if not all people gain by it and some lose. The test suggested by them: to see whether it is possible after the change fully to compensate the losers at a cost to those favoured that falls short of their total gain, is fundamentally identical with the first of our two criteria. The objection to using this criterion by itself is that it is asymmetrical, because it attributes undue importance to the particular distribution of welfare obtaining before the contemplated change. If the government had a special attachment to the *status quo* before the change and would actually undertake to reproduce that welfare distribution by differential taxation after the change, then Mr Kaldor's test would be sufficient. For then, the economist could regard that particular welfare distribution as the only relevant one and would be entitled to use it as his sole standard of reference. But in the absence of such a governmental policy there can be no justification in attaching greater importance to the welfare distribution as it was before than as it is after the change.

To illustrate the pitfalls of this one-sided criterion, imagine a change, say the imposition of a duty on imports, that brings the welfare of A and B from P_1 (fig. 2) on the contract curve of diagram 1 on to π_2 on the contract curve of diagram 2. According to Mr Kaldor's test this change is desirable, because by redistributing income we could travel from π_2 along the $\pi\pi$ curve to π_1, which is superior to P_1. But once the tariff has been imposed and situation π_2 established, it will be free trade and the resulting (original) situation P_1 that will appear preferable *by the same test*, because starting from P_1, income could be so redistributed (travelling along the PP curve in the

---

[1] We say that the distribution of welfare is similar in two situations if every member of the community prefers the same situation. A more exact definition would be unnecessary for our purposes; besides, it is also impossible, since welfare cannot be measured.

first diagram this time) as to reach P_2, which is superior to π_2. So the two situations can be shown each to be preferable to the other by the indentical criterion: an absurd result, which can only be avoided by using our double criterion.

N.B.—Since the above paper was written, there was much discussion and criticism of the double criterion here proposed. For the best treatment of its significance, see Martin J. Bailey, 'The Interpretation and Application of the Compensation Principle', *Economic Journal*, vol. LXIV (1954), pp. 39-52.

Chapter 8

A RECONSIDERATION OF
THE THEORY OF TARIFFS[1]

1942

The theory of tariffs, the most fertile field of economic speculation in the days of the classical economists, has for sime time
lain barren. Historically, it was the origin of the modern
subjective theory of value (in the doctrine of comparative
costs), it was earliest in emphasizing the importance of demand
in determining relative prices (J. S. Mill's reciprocal demand),
and it has provided the analytical tools, Marshall's offer curves,
from whose application to the problem of exchange between
persons the general theory of perfect competition has been
developed. Unfortunately, however, the analogy between
countries and persons was considered irreversible. Our theory
of the individual's rational economic behaviour was not
applied to problems of international trade because of our supposed inability to draw community indifference curves.
Hence, we have no theory of the rational behaviour of a single
country, and even less do we know what would be the result
of such behaviour on the part of all countries.

Free trade can be shown to be beneficial to the universe as
a whole but has never been proved to be the best policy also
for a single country. That, however, is not always realized;
and 'strange to say, a confusion between ideas so different as
part and whole pervades many of the arguments in favour of
Free Trade'. Edgeworth, who made the above remark, was

---

[1] I propose to give this name to that part of the theory of international trade
which deals with the problem of tariffs and the gain from trade. We shall
not be concerned here with the problem of international capital transfer.

I am indebted to Miss Anne A. Aickelin for her valuable suggestions concerning the presentation of this article and for much of the reasoning and
results of sections VI and VII.

conscious of the need for remedying the shortcomings of the theory of tariffs, and took a step in the right direction when he made use of indifference curves in his 'Pure Theory of International Trade'.[1] But either he was unaware of the difficulties attending the use of community indifference curves, or he did not deign to justify what to him may have seemed a perfectly legitimate commonsense approach, treating countries as individuals. In any case, his approach was abandoned and condemned as inadmissible. Later economists either persisted in the error pilloried by Edgeworth or adopted the following somewhat defeatist attitude. They declared that owing to the impossibility of interpersonal utility comparisons it was impossible to choose among alternative trade policies from the point of view of a single country. Since, therefore, national interest gave no directives concerning international trade, and because free trade was known to be beneficial for the world as a whole, it was concluded that free trade was the most rational policy (for want of a better one, so to speak) also from the point of view of single countries.

It is the aim of this article to attempt to get out of this *impasse*. To that purpose we shall have to modify somewhat the meaning of the classical welfare propositions. That will enable us to draw community indifference curves to serve as a standard of reference, against which we can compare the national welfare to be gained from various trade policies. These welfare propositions, however, assume full (or a given level of) employment and, as will be seen below, only appraise a country's efficiency at making use of its strategic advantages in exploiting the foreigner. Since welfare also depends on the degree of utilization of resources, we shall also have to consider the effect of tariffs on employment. Which of these two considerations was more important in swaying international trade policies in the past I do not feel competent to decide. In the future, welfare considerations in the classical sense may well acquire predominance. For it is likely that after the war governments will generally have to assume responsibility for maintaining employment and the stability of economic life, which would render the classical assumption of full employment legitimate. Finally, we shall analyse the infant industry

---

[1] *Economic Journal*, vol. 4 (1894); reprinted in F. Y. Edgeworth, *Papers Relating to Political Economy*, London, 1925, vol. ii.

argument and try to give it a more exact interpretation than it has hitherto received.

I

A tariff usually favours some and prejudices other inhabitants of the country imposing it. Hence, its appraisal from the point of view of that country must, among other considerations, include a value judgment of the redistribution of welfare occasioned by it. That, being a question of social justice, is outside the economist's domain; which is the reason economists give when they refrain from appraising tariffs from the point of view of a single country. In so doing, however, they seem to ignore that the classical economists' welfare propositions also have to share with considerations of social justice when serving as a guide to economic policy—a fact which does not diminish their usefulness.[1,2]

The classical argument in favour of perfect competition and free trade is not that they would improve everybody's and every country's welfare, but only that they create a situation in which it would be impossible to increase anybody's welfare without diminishing someone else's. Perfect competition and free trade are economically more efficient than imperfect competition and tariff-ridden trade respectively, because they would make everybody and every country better off for any distribution of welfare among them *if* that were the same in the alternative situations. Actually, the transition from one situation to the other generally redistributes income so as to make some better off and others worse off than they were before. This fact may raise problems of equity, which cannot be ignored, but it does not render the criterion of economic efficiency nugatory.

The classical welfare propositions appraise the efficiency of a closed system. They state that a given change increases or diminishes the economic efficiency of a community that com-

[1] Cf., however, N. Kaldor: 'Welfare Propositions of Economics and Interpersonal Comparisons of Utility', *Economic Journal*, vol. 49 (1939), p. 549; J. R. Hicks: 'Foundations of Welfare Economics', *Economic Journal*, vol. 49, p. 696; and N. Kaldor: 'A Note on Tariffs and the Terms of Trade', *Economica* (NS), vol. 7 (1940), p. 377.
[2] Cf. the preceding chapter for a more detailed statement of the following argument.

prises *all* the people affected by the change. But just as we can say that, considerations of equity apart, free trade is beneficial to the universe as a whole; so we should also be able to tell whether free trade or protection is better from the point of view of a single country, ignoring the fact that some of its inhabitants may prefer the former and others the latter situation. We do not suggest that considerations of equity should be disregarded. On the contrary, they should always be weighed against considerations of efficiency. But for purposes of analysis they must be kept strictly apart.

In the following we shall only be concerned with problems of efficiency. We propose to apply the criterion of efficiency underlying the classical welfare propositions—or rather a slight modification of it—to the problems of an open economy; and we shall appraise the efficiency or inefficiency of tariffs from the point of view of the country imposing them. In this way we shall be able to make fairly general statements, which must be qualified by considerations of equity in particular instances. Equity is a matter of ethics and has nothing to do with economics; hence we shall not be concerned with it any further. But the reader is reminded once more that all our statements concerning national welfare are subject to modification by considerations of social justice.

It is well known that when the foreigners' reciprocal demand for a country's exports is inelastic, a suitable tariff will increase the quantities available for home consumption both of imports and of exportable goods. Hence, such a tariff will improve the welfare of the country imposing it in exactly the same sense in which perfect competition improves that of a closed community. For, although it may actually make some people better and others worse off than they were before, it *could* make everybody better off for any given distribution of welfare.[1]

When the elasticity of the foreigners' reciprocal demand is greater than unity, a tariff will increase the quantity of retained exportable goods but diminish that of imports. The first will increase, the second diminish welfare; the question is which of the two opposing tendencies is the stronger and the one to prevail. To answer this question, one would like to follow

[1] Because if there is more of some goods without there being less of others, everybody can be given more and made better off, whatever the initial distribution of income.

Edgeworth's example and set the foreigners' reciprocal demand curve against the home country's indifference map, as shown in fig. 1. Indifference maps for a whole community can indeed be constructed; but they have serious limitations.[1] Through each point of the map, representing a given combination of commodities, not one but an infinity of community indifference curves can be drawn, corresponding to different distributions of the given quantities of the two commodities among members of the community. A proposal to choose from this infinity of distributions the one considered optimal and use as one's reference system the community indifference map corresponding to this optimal distribution seems like cutting the Gordian knot;[2] but it is not satisfactory either. To know what tariff policy would be best if income distribution were optimal is no more interesting than to know what political institutions would be best if human beings were perfect. We want to find the tariff policy best for the actual world, imperfect as this may be; and this is why the actual rather than the optimal income distribution is the one relevant for our purposes. However, distribution among members of a community depends partly on the tariff policy of that community; and this means that the community indifference curve going through each point of the foreigners' reciprocal demand curve must correspond to the distribution created by the tariff policy that brought the community to that point of the demand curve. This rule assigns a unique community indifference curve to each point on the foreigners' offer curve (which are the only points we are interested in);[3] but since each of these curves corresponds to a different distribution, there is no guarantee that they will not intersect. And indifference curves lose much of their usefulness if they cannot be trusted to intersect.

In the original version of this paper, I tried to meet this difficulty by qualifying every statement with the proviso: 'if

[1] The reader interested in the construction of community indifference curves is referred to Section II of the original version of this paper (*Review of Economic Studies*, vol. IX (1942), pp. 93-5) or to W. J. Baumol: 'The Community Indifference Map: A Construction', *Review of Economic Studies*, vol. XVII, pp. 189-97.

[2] Cf. P. A. Samuelson: 'Social Indifference Curves', *Quarterly Journal of Economics*, vol. LXX (1956), pp. 1-22.

[3] On the assumption that there is a unique tariff policy that would bring the community to a particular point on the offer curve.

the relevant community indifference curves do not intersect in the relevant range'. Since then, Graaff has proved that this qualification and weakening of the argument was unnecessary, because the superiority, from a single country's point of view, of the optimum tariff over free trade can be shown with the same generality as the superiority of perfect over imperfect competition in a closed economy.[1] In the following, therefore, I shall try to present a simplified version of Graaff's proof and then proceed with the argument in terms of community indifference curves, which still seem to me the best suited for treating this subject.

II

Fig. 1 represents the Marshallian reciprocal demand or offer curves. With exports measured on the horizontal, imports on the vertical axis, the lower curve shows the home country's,

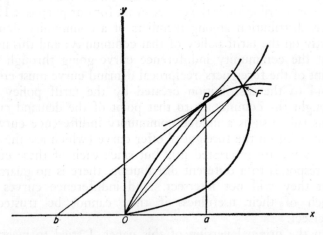

Fig. 1.

the upper the foreigners' offer curve. F is the trading point under free trade; and the home country can, by imposing an appropriate tariff, push back the trading point to any other point on the foreigners' offer curve. One of these points, P, shows trade under the optimum tariff, since at this point the

[1] Cf. J. de V. Graaff: 'On Optimum Tariff Structures', *Review of Economic Studies*, vol. XVII (1949), pp. 47-59.

foreigners' offer curve touches the home country's highest community indifference curve. Since the indifference curves through points F and P generally belong to different income distributions, we cannot be certain that they do not intersect and represent unambiguously different levels of the home country's welfare. Hence the need to prove the superiority of P over F without reference to the relative position of the two indifference curves. We shall do this by showing that P is while F is not a position of Pareto optimum.

Under free trade, the slope of the line OF shows the ratio of the prices of exports and imports in the home country; and if competition is perfect, it also shows the ratios of the two commodities' marginal costs of production in the home country (in case there is an industry producing import substitutes) as well as the marginal rate of substitution of every consumer of the two commodities. Indeed, the consumers' uniform marginal rates of substitution are represented by the slope of the community indifference curve through F, which at this point is tangential to OF.

Nevertheless, from the home country's point of view, the Pareto conditions of optimality are *not* fulfilled at this point of free trade and perfect competition. For, while the consumer's marginal rate of substitution equals all other consumers' marginal rates of substitution and also the marginal rate of transformation (ratio of marginal costs) within the domestic economy, it does *not* equal the marginal rate of transformation of exports into imports through foreign trade. The latter is represented by the slope of the foreigners' curve, since this is the locus of trade points the home country can reach by adopting different tariffs. The slope of this curve is obviously different from that of the line OF (the ratio of import to export prices) whenever it is not a straight line through the origin (i.e. less than infinitely elastic). The economic meaning of this is that the cost, in terms of exports, of an additional unit of imports exceeds the ratio of import to export prices, because to obtain an additional unit of imports, it is not enough to surrender a quantity of exports equal in value, it is also necessary to persuade foreigners to buy these additional exports. The cost of so persuading them is the excess cost, which accounts for the higher marginal cost of obtaining imports through foreign trade than through the

K

transfer of resources within the home economy from export to import-competing industries. Point F therefore represents a suboptimal situation, in which some of the marginal conditions of a Pareto optimum are not fulfilled.

The foregoing argument also suggests the way in which the situation can be improved and a true Pareto optimum achieved. By imposing an import duty equal in value to the above-mentioned cost of persuasion, the ratio of the domestic price of imports (which includes the duty) to the price of exports can be made equal to the marginal rate of transformation through foreign trade; and perfect competition inside the home country can be trusted to equate to this price ratio both consumers' marginal rates of substitution and the marginal rate of transforming exports into imports through shifting resources within the home economy. This is the situation illustrated by the tangency of offer curve and indifference curve at point P in the diagram. It is a Pareto optimum situation, in which all the marginal conditions of optimality are fulfilled; hence it is superior in a welfare sense to the free trade point F, where these conditions are not fulfilled. From the home country's point of view therefore the difference between points P and F is the same as that between a point on the contract curve and one off it. Accordingly, we can rest assured that the community indifference curve through P represents a level of welfare truly and unambiguously higher than that represented by the community indifference curve through point F.[1]

III

At this stage of the argument, two questions are likely to arise in one's mind. One may ask first, why it is that the duty is not disruptive of the Pareto optimum; when after all, import duties are rather like excise taxes, which usually interfere with

[1] At the optimum point P (fig. 1), the ratio of export to import prices within the home country (where the import price includes the duty) is shown by the slope of the tangent at P, or by Pa/ba; the same ratio from the foreigners' point of view (which excludes the duty) is given by the slope of OP, or by Pa/Oa; and the height of the duty as a proportion of the import price is given by the expression:

$$\frac{ba/Pa - Oa/Pa}{Oa/Pa} = Ob/Oa$$

Pareto optima. Excise taxes do this, because they cause different members of the community to face different prices of the same commodity. A cigarette tax, for example, confronts smokers with a higher cigarette price than that received by cigarette manufacturers. Similarly, an import duty causes domestic consumers of imports to pay higher prices than those received by their foreign manufacturers; but it creates no price disparities within the home country, since it does not render unequal the price paid by domestic consumers and that received by domestic producers of import substitutes. This explains why, from the home country's point of view, the duty does not disrupt the Pareto optimum.

The second question we have to answer is how and why a duty can *bring about* a Pareto optimum. We are dealing here with a world of perfect competition. In such a world, one would expect free trade to be the best policy—and it would be that, if achieving Pareto optimum for the world as a whole were the aim. From the narrow nationalist point of view of the home country, however, the situation is different. While every firm and household within the country is a perfect competitor, the country as a whole, facing the outside world as an entity and wielding the power to impose duties, is not; and it can exploit its imperfectly competitive position for the sake of raising its inhabitants' welfare by an appropriate tariff policy.

Indeed, no one trained in general economic theory can fail to be struck by the perfect parellelism between tariffs and monopolistic price determination when he first examines the literature of the theory of tariffs. That this obvious analogy, which has been emphasized before,[1] has not yet gained general acceptance may be due, partly to the historical accident that duties are usually imposed on imports and not on exports,[2] and partly to the convention in the theory of production that

[1] Cf. A. P. Lerner: 'The Diagrammatical Representation of Demand Conditions in International Trade', *Economica* (NS), vol. 1 (1934); and N. Kaldor: 'A Note on Tariffs and the Terms of Trade', *Economica* (NS), vol. 7 (1940). In fact, the argument of this section is little more than a repetition of what they, and especially Mr Kaldor, already said more succinctly. Nevertheless, this was necessary because of the incomplete nature of their definition of community indifference curves.

[2] Cf. A. P. Lerner: 'The Symmetry between Import and Export Taxes', *Economica* (NS), vol. 3 (1936), for a proof that the economic effects of export and import duties are identical.

imagines the monopolist as restricting his output and then letting the price to be determined by demand. In reality, producers exploit their monopolistic position by adding to their costs a monopolistic profit margin, which is an obvious and exact parallel to an export duty.

According to the traditional theory of production, the producer aims at maximizing his money profits, and in this he differs from the tariff-imposing government, which aims, or should aim, at maximizing not the total tariff revenue, but the welfare of the country as a whole. But to represent the entrepreneur as maximizing his money profits is to give an inaccurate though simplified interpretation of rational behaviour. To the extent that he is the owner of productive

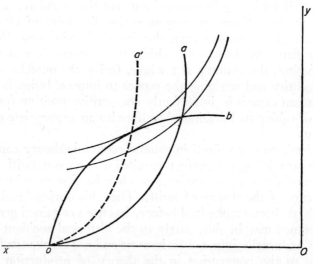

Fig. 2.

resources, for whose use he pays himself wages, rent and/or interest, the entrepreneur's most rational behaviour would be not to maximize profits but to equate his marginal net revenue to the marginal cost of the use of his own productive factors.

This argument can be illustrated with the aid of the entrepreneur's indifference map (fig. 2), showing his relative valuation of his own productive services (x) on the one hand, and of money income (y) on the other. In this indifference map we can draw as an independent datum the entrepreneur's total net revenue curve, *ob*, which is derived from the total demand curve confronting his firm, and which can also be interpreted as the community's total demand curve for his services. The offer curve or total cost curve, *oa*, of the entrepreneur's own factors can be derived geometrically from the indifference map. The entrepreneur will maximize his welfare by producing the output and utilizing his private resources to the extent that brings him to the point of tangency of the total net revenue curve (*ob*) with one of his indifference curves. He will achieve this aim by adding to the cost of his services a monopolistic profit margin that so distorts his offer curve as to make it intersect the total net revenue curve at that point. The magnitude of this margin depends on the elasticity of demand for his services, and becomes zero as that approaches infinity.

This, as the reader will have noted, is just the application of Marshall's and Edgeworth's foreign trade diagrams to illustrate the behaviour of the entrepreneur or of any other owner of productive resources. The argument remains the same when we reinterpret the axes as measuring imports and exports, and the Marshallian curves as showing the foreigners' reciprocal demand for and the country's offer of exports in terms of imports. The monopolistic profit margin will now be called protective tariff, whose rate determines the point on the foreigners' reciprocal demand curve at which international trade takes place. The indifference curves will now show the country's collective appraisal of the relative advantages of exports and imports; and since that depends on the distribution of welfare—itself a function of the degree of protection—we must be careful to draw the requisite community indifference curves through each point of the foreigners' offer curve.[1] The optimum tariff will be that to which the community indifference curve tangential to the foreigners' demand curve belongs. If the foreigners' reciprocal demand is infinitely elastic, free

[1] I.e. the indifference curve representing that distribution of welfare which corresponds to the degree of protection bringing trade to that point.

trade will be the optimum policy on this criterion.[1, 2]

Economists sometimes assert that tariffs are always erected without regard to national welfare, solely on the instigation of sectional interests directly profiting by them. It cannot of course be denied that people who stand to gain most from a given change will be its most ardent advocates. But that in itself is no proof that the change will not increase national welfare. In fact, sectional interests, representing an industry or group of industries, are unlikely to achieve their aim unless they succeed in convincing public opinion that their interest coincides with the national interest. Their frequent appeal to the terms of trade argument shows that public opinion *is* concerned with national welfare as defined above, and that such considerations do play an important part in determining international trade policy. For the terms of trade argument can be regarded as a rough-and-ready way of presenting our welfare argument. If the imposition of a tariff affects the terms of trade very much, that is a sign of the foreigners' reciprocal demand not being very elastic. That, in its turn, makes it plausible that the tariff has brought the trading point[3] on to a higher community indifference curve.

IV

So far we have been concerned with a problem of partial equilibrium: the rational behaviour of a single country trying

---

[1] It is not always realized that the (terms of trade) elasticity of the reciprocal demand curve would be equivalent to the price-elasticity of the foreigners' demand for exports, *only* if imports were the *numéraire*. Otherwise, the elasticity of reciprocal demand, τ, is given by the expression:

$$\tau = \frac{\epsilon\eta + \eta}{\epsilon + \eta}$$

where ϵ is the price-elasticity of the foreign supply of imports, and η is the (absolute value of the) price-elasticity of the foreigners' demand for exports. It is evident from the formula that if ϵ is positive (upward sloping supply curve), $\tau \gtreqless 1$ as $\eta \gtreqless 1$, independently of the value of ϵ. The condition for τ tending to infinity, is that both ϵ and η should tend to infinity. For, if $\epsilon \to \infty$, $\tau \to \eta$; and if $\eta \to \infty$, $\tau \to (\epsilon + 1)$. Thus, τ cannot exceed the value of the expressions: η and $(\epsilon + 1)$; and will generally be smaller than either of them.

[2] Cf. Edgeworth, Collected Papers, vol. II, p. 39; and Kaldor, *op. cit.*

[3] By trading point we mean the point in the diagram at which trade actually takes place.

to maximize its national welfare. We now propose to consider a problem of general equilibrium: the mechanism of the interaction of various countries' trade policies.

Let us draw a pair of Marshallian offer curves and call the countries whose trading terms they represent A and B (fig. 3). Free trade would result in the exchange of the two countries' produce at p_0, the point of intersection of the two curves. That would be a situation most advantageous from the point of view of the two countries taken together, because their community indifference curves going through that point and corresponding to their distributions of welfare under conditions of free trade are tangential one to another.

From the point of view of each country separately, however, it would be more advantageous to impose a tariff that brings it to a higher indifference curve of its own. That will be possible for either country, if the other country's offer curve is not a straight line (i.e. infinitely elastic). Which of the two countries will reap this advantage (which is not open to both of them simultaneously!) depends on the promptness of their actions. Assume that country A is more alert and imposes an optimum tariff, which so distorts its offer curve as to make it intersect B's offer curve at p_1. Country B will now have forfeited its own opportunity of imposing an optimum tariff which would have brought it to p_b), and it will also be worse off than it was under free trade; facing the new less favourable terms on which country A is now willing to do trade, and which are represented by oa_2, A's new tariff-distorted offer curve. Nevertheless, B will be able to recover some of its lost advantages by imposing a tariff of its own that so distorts its offer curve as to bring its point of intersection with oa_2, on to a higher one of its (B's) community indifference curves. Then it will be country A that will face new, less favourable trading terms, represented by B's distorted offer curve, ob_2; but also A may be able to regain some of its lost advantages by revising its tariff and further distorting its offer curve to, say, oa_3.

At each successive step, the welfare of the two countries taken together will have diminished. Nevertheless, each time one country has raised its tariff, the other country may be able somewhat to improve *its* welfare by further raising its own tariff, if it can thereby reach a higher one of its community indifference curves. That is always possible after the first tariff has been imposed[1] and may be possible after several subsequent tariff raises. The 'competitive' raising of tariffs will continue until equilibrium is reached at the point where the two tariff-ridden offer curves are both tangential, each to one of the other country's community indifference curves. At that point, which need not be unique, neither country can hope to increase its national welfare by further raising its tariff. The number of successive tariff raises necessary to reach it depend on the shape and relative position of the two countries' community indifference curves.[2]

Fig. 3 has been drawn in such a way that the equilibrium point, p_3, should be reached in three steps of optimum tariff raises. It is likely, however, that in general the number of steps would be greater; and in no case can they be under two.

Exception may be taken to our above argument on the ground that long before they have reached equilibrium, the two countries will have recognized the causal connection between the raising of their own tariff and retaliation by the other country, and come to some agreement. In other words, it may be argued that if protection is the monopolistic behaviour of a collectivity, two countries raising tariffs against each other are bilateral monopolists—and we know that bilateral monopoly results in the two parties coming to some working agreement, whose terms depend on their bargaining skill and are analytically indeterminate.

[1] This follows from the rule for the derivation of offer curves. B's relevant community indifference curve at p_1 must be tangential to the straight line connecting p_1 with the origin. A's tariff-distorted offer curve, oa_2, is bound to have a greater slope at p_1 whence it follows that country B can reach a higher community indifference curve by imposing a tariff that makes its offer curve intersect oa_2 somewhere below p_1.

[2] Since the above was written, Harry G. Johnson, in his 'Optimum Tariffs and Retaliation' (*Review of Economic Studies*, vol. 21, pp. 142-53), has shown that this sequence of events is not the general case but only a special (though to my mind a likely) one. In particular, he has shown (1) that the point of equilibrium is always one with some trade, (2) that if the elasticities of the two countries' offer curves are sufficiently different, one country may, even in the final equilibrium position, end up better off than it was under free trade, and (3) that after the initial imposition of tariffs by the two countries, further tariff readjustments need not be increases but may be reductions. This last is especially likely in cases where a great asymmetry between the two offer curves enables one country to gain by protection despite retaliation by the other. Johnson has also shown that the adjustment process may converge not only to an equilibrium point but also to a tariff cycle.

That, indeed, would be the case if there were two countries only. When, however, there is a large number of countries, and each trades with many of the others, any single country will be justified in neglecting the danger of retaliation to its own tariff policy. We must, therefore, reinterpret our diagram so that one of the Marshallian curves should stand for the offer curve of the several single countries in succession, and the other represent the reciprocal demand for that country's exports of the rest of the universe; i.e. of all other countries taken together. No single country will have scruples in establishing or raising its tariff; knowing that its own reciprocal

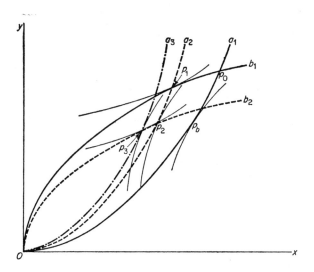

Fig. 3.

demand for foreign produce contains only a negligible fraction of the total foreign demand facing any other single country, and that therefore changes in it are unlikely to influence the latter's policy. As all countries act on this principle and raise their tariffs, the universe's reciprocal demand curve facing each of them will get distorted just as much as if tariffs had been raised against it by the rest of the world acting in unison. To call the raising of tariffs on these assumptions irrational, would be similar to calling competitive behaviour irrational. There, each producer's quest for higher profits tends to eliminate the profits of all; here, the attempt by each country to increase its own advantage from trade diminishes the advantage of all. The theory of perfect competition and the above argument, which may be named the theory of heterogeneous competition (polypoly), are based on identical assumptions in that they both assume a sufficiently large number of independent economic units for each of them to neglect the reaction of others to his own actions. They differ in so far that perfect competition does while our above argument does not assume that the produce of various units is perfectly interchangeable. That the two assumptions have nothing to do with each other is well known; and the importance of keeping them strictly apart has recently been emphasized.[1] The difference—real and supposed!—between a country's produce and its foreign substitutes determines the elasticity of the foreigners' reciprocal demand, and hence the size of the optimum initial tariff and of subsequent tariff raises. The more perfectly identical are in the estimation of foreigners their substitutes for our country's produce, the more elastic will be their demand for its exports, and the smaller will be the tariff it can profitably impose upon foreign trade. If foreigners produced perfect substitutes, their reciprocal demand would be perfectly elastic[2] and the optimum tariff rate would be zero, and would remain zero even after other countries have imposed tariffs of their own. Perfect competition refers to this limiting case alone.

At this stage we may attempt to sketch a long-period theory of international trade. Imagine an initial situation where trade is free, or at least tariffs are low and the most-favoured-nation clause is in vogue; and where each country trades with most of the others, and there is some triangular trade. Countries that believe themselves to be sufficiently small to erect or raise tariffs unpunished will do so as soon as they discover that they can thereby increase their national welfare. When a number of countries have followed this course, those still on a free trade basis will find themselves monopolistically exploited and may be perfectly justified in saying that they are being

[1] Cf. Robert Triffin: *Monopolistic Competition and General Equilibrium Theory*, Cambridge, Mass., 1940.

[2] We assume that the price-elasticity of the world's supply of any single country's imports approaches infinity.

forced into erecting tariff walls too. That they can thereby often improve their position we have shown above; and this should be as obvious as that a monopolistically exploited consumer can improve his position by charging monopolistic prices in his capacity of producer.

When tariff walls have been erected all round, those who started the process will find some of their initial advantage gone; but they are also likely to find that they can improve their position by raising tariffs further, even if initially they made full use of their monopolistic position. As tariff walls rise, conferences on international trade may be called to arrest the process, which is obviously harmful to all concerned. Yet, as long as it remains in the individual interest of each country separately to raise tariffs, such collective attempts are bound to be ineffectual if not backed by international sanctions; just as cartel agreements are ineffectual if there is not a large producer with enough authority to enforce them.

As tariff walls mount and international trade dwindles, the number of countries each country trades with will diminish. That will tend to destroy the atomistic nature of international trade and lend increasing reality to the danger of retaliation. In other words, it will lead to the realization of the interdependence of the various countries' tariff policies. That may cause the most-favoured-nation clause to fall into disuse and tariffs to be determined by bargaining, before equilibrium had been reached. If, on the other hand, equilibrium is reached, so that no country can improve its welfare by raising tariffs further, in that case also bargaining will appear as the only way in which national welfare can still be increased. So in either case, heterogeneous competition leads through the rational behaviour of each competitor to 'paucilateral' and bilateral monopoly; and tariff autonomy will, in time, give way to tariff clubs and bilateral trade agreements.

V

Bilateral trade agreements are a matter of higgling and bargaining and have little interest for the economist. Nevertheless, it may be worth our while to make a short digression and discuss barter agreements, a special form of them, which has recently acquired some importance. Barter trade agreements not only set the terms on which indefinite amounts of goods are to be traded for each other, but also fix the exact amounts to be exchanged. They have been introduced by Nazi Germany in her trade with South American and South-East European countries, and declared by a Nazi spokesman to be the principle on which trade in Hitler's 'New Order' would be based. Since by their very nature they overrule all existing tariffs, it is to be expected that they should be able both to improve and to worsen the situation they replace. We set out to prove that barter agreements may be to the mutual advantage of countries whose trade was previously conducted across tariff walls; but that at the same time they are a convenient way of exacting tribute from conquered or intimidated countries.

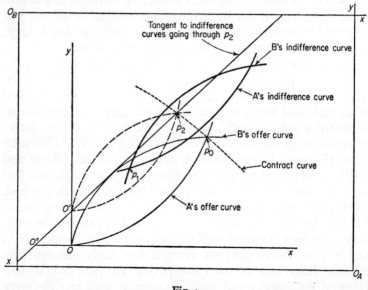

Fig. 4.

Let us draw a pair of Marshallian offer curves belonging to countries A and B, and assume that owing to the existence of trade barriers between them, their trading point is not at the intersection of the offer curves but, say, at point p_1 (fig. 4). We shall not bother to draw the two tariff-distorted offer curves that intersect at that point. The two countries' community indifference curves going through p_1 and corresponding to their distributions of income brought about by this particular set of tariffs intersect one another, as shown in the figure, since they could not be tangential under any combination of tariffs. That means, however, that a new trade agreement bringing the trading point within the area enclosed by the two indifferent curves would be beneficial to both countries.

We know that no further raising of tariffs could bring the trading point within the area between the indifference curves, since that could only move it leftwards and downwards; that is, away from the contract curve, which we can now draw into our diagram. An agreement between the two countries mutually to lower their tariffs could improve both their welfare; but only to a limited extent. For no combination of tariffs could bring them on to the contract curve,[1] while free trade would take them to p_0, the intersection of the offer curves, which in our particular example lies outside the indifference curves going through p_1. The two countries can, however, reach a point on the contract curve within the indifference curves going through p_1 by concluding a barter trade agreement that overrides all existing tariffs and directly fixes the physical quantities to be exchanged in such a way as to bring them to, say, p_2.[2]

From the definition of the contract curve it follows that there must be at least one initial distribution of resources between A and B wherefrom free trade would lead to p_2.[3] Anyone acquainted with the derivation of offer curves from indifference maps will see at once that the tangent to the two indifference curves going through p_2 is the locus of all such initial situations; for it is the locus of the origin of all pairs of offer curves that intersect in p_2. It follows from this that the barter agreement leading to p_2 is equivalent in its effect to free trade between the two countries, after the payment of a tribute from A to B that brings them from the origin of the barter diagram to any point of the tangent drawn through p_2.

[1] Ruling out 'negative tariffs'.
[2] It has been pointed out to me by Mr Kaldor that the same result could also be reached by having additional trade duty free.
[3] In fig. 4 the intersection of the axes of the two indifference maps gives the total quantity of the two goods jointly possessed by A and B, while the origin of the barter diagram itself shows their initial distribution between A and B. Cf. A. L. Bowley: *Mathematical Groundwork of Economics*, Oxford, 1924, for the best description of such a diagram.

In the figure, the new offer curves are drawn (broken line) from o' as origin, assuming that the tribute is paid in terms of y. But the tribute could just as well be paid in terms of x, bringing the origin of the offer curves—still intersecting in p_2—to o''; or it could be paid in any combination of x and y, as long as the rate of transformation between them remained equal to the slope of the indifference curves tangential to each other in p_2. Barter trade agreements, therefore, represent the exploitation of one country by the other, just as tariffs do; but with the difference that to the extent that they bring the trading point nearer the contract curve, they are more efficient.

So far we have only considered barter trade agreements that are voluntarily entered into and therefore do not increase the exploitation of one country by the other but only render existing exploitation more efficient. If, however, one of the countries can bring political or military pressure to bear on the other country, it can force it into a barter agreement that brings them on to a trading point outside the area enclosed by the indifference curves going through the point reached under existing trading conditions (p_1). In an extreme case, a barter agreement may bring the trading point outside the indifference curves going through the origin of the barter diagram (not drawn in the figure), indicating that trade under such circumstances would be worse for the exploited country than no trade at all.[1] Barter agreements, of course, need not necessarily be efficient in the sense of leading to the contract curve. They do, if after their conclusion the relative prices of the bartered goods are the same in the two countries;[2] and *the conformity of that price ratio in the two countries is an index of the efficiency of the agreement.*

To sum up the above argument, barter trade agreements are a method for one country to exploit another, more efficient potentially than tariffs. They are equivalent to free trade *plus* the payment of a tribute from one country to another, if efficient.[3] A barter agreement may be to mutual advantage if it supersedes protective tariffs, provided that it does not increase

---

[1] In a happier age, Edgeworth and Marshall have not even drawn the contract curve beyond these limits.

[2] We are referring to the ratio of market prices and not to that of the purely fictitious prices that usually figure in such agreements.

[3] If inefficient, they can be represented by the payment of a tribute *plus* trade under a tariff.

already existing exploitation but merely makes it more efficient. To the extent that it increases the degree of exploitation, it may be regarded as a method of turning political ascendancy to economic account by exacting tribute from defeated, conquered or intimidated countries. As such it is more efficient than, say, the reparations imposed in the Versailles treaties were, because it presents no transfer problem. On the other hand it imposes tribute in a veiled form, and is therefore less open to the critical scrutiny of public opinion.

VI

So far we have been concerned with the theory of tariffs on the classical assumption of full (or a given level of) employment. We now proceed to consider the effect of tariffs on employment; such effect to be added to or subtracted from the effects of tariffs on national welfare hitherto discussed. For an increase in employment increases national welfare in exactly the same way as a tariff does when the foreigners' reciprocal demand is inelastic. It increases the quantity of all goods except that of involuntary idleness, and thus makes it possible for everybody to be better off than he was before, whatever the distribution of welfare. Before examining how tariffs affect employment, however, it will be necessary shortly to recapitulate the theory of employment in a closed community.

It is generally agreed today among economists that it is most convenient to think of the level of employment as being determined by the equality of investment and saving. If we consider investment activity in the short period as a datum—a convention based on the consideration that capital equipment, having the longest gestation period, is the commodity whose rate of production is least dependent on present and most irrevocably determined by past decisions—employment and income must be such as to make saving equal to investment. The function showing the proportion of income the community saves out of each level of income is called the propensity to save function. If its form is approximately linear, the process by which additional investment generates additional income can be illustrated by an infinite geometric progression, well known as the theory of the multiplier.

In a closed community saving must equal investment in

short-period equilibrium, because that is the condition for the equality of anticipated and realized receipts in current production. In an open economy, the condition for short-period equilibrium is still the equality of anticipated and realized receipts in domestic current production. But since in the latter case there are two alternatives to spending on home produced goods: saving, and spending on imported goods; and the receipts of domestic producers originate not only in domestic expenditure but also in exports, it follows that, in an open economy, the condition for short-period equilibrium is the equality between the sum of imports and saving and the sum of exports and investment. In other words, an open economy has no inherent short-run tendency to equate either saving with investment or exports with imports; but only to make the discrepancies in these two equal to each other.[1] Only to the extent that the central bank allows changes in its reserves (caused by the export or import surplus) to influence its interest rate policy, and to the extent that this affects investment activity, will there be a tendency towards the equality of saving and investment and of exports and imports separately.

After this digression we can conveniently list the factors through which a change in trade policy can influence the level of employment. They are: (1) the value of imports net of tariffs; (2) the value of exports; (3) the shape of the propensity to save function; and the two determinants of the level of investment activity: (4) the rate of interest; and (5) the marginal efficiency of investment.

(1) The imposition or raising of tariffs always diminishes the *net* value of imports, and on that count *always* increases employment and income. It increases them to the extent that is needed to raise the community's saving and expenditure on imports (net of the tariff), by the amount of the initial fall of imports. The ratio between the value of additional income and the primary fall of imports may be called the foreign multiplier. Its value is equal to that of the investment multiplier in the same economy.

(2) The impact effect of tariffs to create an export surplus is sometimes said to be of short duration only. If it is based

[1] Cf. M. Bronfenbrenner: 'The Keynesian Equations and the Balance of Payments', *Review of Economic Studies*, vol. 7 (1939-40).

on the belief that exports automatically tend to be equal to imports, that statement is wrong, as has been shown above. While trade is relatively free, that statement is also wrong if it is based on the consideration that one country's export surplus is the import surplus of other countries, who may retaliate. For the argument of section IV about the danger of retaliation holds good here just as much as it did there. If during a world depression a country imposes tariffs to diminish its imports, and if subsequently its export surplus is eliminated by a diminution of its exports, that may be due not so much to retaliation as to the existence abroad of the same motive to diminish imports (i.e. other countries, also suffering from depression, might have thought of the same way of relieving it). This argument also shows that our long-period theory of tariffs is not dependent on the assumption that trade policies are determined by welfare considerations of the kind discussed in section I. If the desire to increase employment and to stop import surpluses and resulting depression were the sole motive force behind rising tariff walls, it would still be true that the rational behaviour of each country, aiming at full employment and greater internal prosperity, tends to defeat that aim and only results in ever-mounting tariffs.

(3) The form of the propensity to save function depends on the distribution of income; for rich people generally save a larger proportion of their income than the poor. Hence, we can say that the more unequal is its distribution, the greater the proportion of the national income which will be saved. A change in trade policy, therefore, will on this account tend to raise or to lower the level of employment according as it makes the distribution of income less or more unequal. This is a purely economic argument in favour of trade policies that tend to make the distribution of income more equal.

(4) Since tariffs always diminish the value of imports and do not directly affect that of exports, they always enhance the liquidity of the banking system—or at least alleviate the drain on its reserves. Increased protection, therefore, will always lead to lower interest rates, provided that the banking system allows its interest rate policy to be at all influenced by its liquidity. But too much importance should not be attached to this as a factor stimulating employment. Our preoccupation

L

with the rate of interest is probably explained by the fact that for a long time in the past it was the only lever through which our economic system could be controlled; and that it was a powerful tool then is probably due more to its influence on short-term international capital movements than to its effect on industrial investment.[1]

(5) The marginal efficiency of investment is defined as the ratio of the flow of expected net receipts from operating capital equipment to the latter's cost of construction. It is therefore an increasing function of the price of the industry's output, and a diminishing function of the price of capital equipment and co-operating factors. Tariffs will affect the marginal efficiency of investment if they alter the relationship of these prices. The prices relevant here are those including the tariff. Hence, an import duty raises the prices of the goods on which it is imposed. To a lesser extent, it also raises those of their substitutes and lowers the prices of their complements. An import duty, therefore, will increase the marginal efficiency of investment in industries producing goods identical with or similar to those hit by the duty; it will diminish the marginal efficiency of investment in industries that *make use* of such goods and that produce goods complementary to them. This argument, therefore, together with that of paragraph (3) of this section, does not enable us to make *general* statements about the effect of tariffs on national welfare, though it is very important in considering the effects of *particular* tariffs.

VII

The preceding argument, concerning the effect of duties on the marginal efficiency of investment, has an important bearing also on the secular aspects of the free trade *versus* protection controversy. First of all, it provides an economic explanation of why England was for such a long time the champion of free trade. In eighteenth- and nineteenth-century England free trade, by lowering the price of labour[2] and raw materials, meant a higher rate of profit in industry, greater investment opportunities, more prosperity, and fuller employ-

---

[1] Cf. P. B. Whale: 'The Working of the Pre-War Gold Standard', *Economica* (NS), vol. 4 (1937).
[2] *Via* cheapening foodstuffs, the primary wage good.

ment. It depressed agricultural production; but possibilities of expansion being more restricted there, it increased national prosperity and income on balance. In all other countries the situation was the reverse during the same period: it was protection that raised the marginal efficiency of investment in industry and, maybe, depressed agricultural production.[1] This is so because free trade favours whichever line of activity is already best established in a country. If we believed that the division of labour among nations is the outcome of inherent and unalterable national and geographical characteristics, that would be an argument in favour of free trade. If, however, we recognize, as I think we should, that specialization among countries is to a large extent a matter of historical accident, we would have to draw a different conclusion.

Since the progress of our material welfare depends mainly on technical advance, our civilization offers the greatest rewards to industrial skill and technical ingenuity, and the nations specializing in these fields will inevitably lead, and agricultural nations lag behind. Hence, the best long-run policy a nation can pursue is to create an atmosphere favourable to industry and technical progress. But, it may be asked, if industry is more profitable than agriculture, why does it need special stimulus? The answer to that question can best be put in the language of external economies. The produce of industry consists of goods and services sold for money, and of benefits for whose use no charge can be made by their very nature, but which nevertheless contribute to the social product. These benefits are called external economies from the point of view of those benefited: they consist in the training of workers, the creation of a labour market and of markets for by-products, the stimulus given to transport facilities, the arousing of interest in science and engineering, and the like. In an industrial community, a new firm or industry will not

[1] I am doubtful about this last statement, because historically, the transition from agricultural to industrial production was invariably accompanied by drastic institutional changes, which probably gave a stimulus to agricultural production more important than the depressing effect taken account of by more formal analysis. Such a stimulant, for instance, must have been the transition from barter to a money economy. By introducing the new habit of expressing welfare in terms of money, and thereby minimizing the importance of those elements of welfare that cannot be so expressed (leisure, a comfortable life, etc.), it must have stimulated farmers to produce more for the market.

only contribute to, but also benefit by, the external economies already in existence. The free benefits he makes use of *repay*, so to speak, the entrepreneur for his free contribution to the community's welfare. No free benefits compensate the first firm or industry to be established in an agricultural community for the advantages it confers on the firms and industries to follow. Yet, those advantages may be very important and valuable from society's point of view, and should be accounted for when calculating the firm's or industry's marginal productivity. A firm's or industry's economic right to live, therefore, should be based not on its private but its social marginal productivity, which takes account of intangible factors[1] and products. In an industrial community these two are likely to cancel each other out, making private and social marginal productivity approximately equal. In an agricultural economy the difficulties of beginning may make an industrial firm's private marginal productivity significantly lower than its social marginal productivity; and to make up for the difference, protection or the payment of subsidies is economically justified.

This is, I think, what writers like Carey, List and Schüller really meant. The above argument shows that to extend public assistance to infant industries is economically fair and proper, provided it does no more than equate private to social marginal productivity. Tariffs are the cheapest way of giving such assistance from the point of view of the country imposing them, which adds yet another rational reason for imposing tariffs, at least in the special case of industrially backward countries. This, of course, is not incompatible with the fact that from the universe's point of view, direct subsidies, paid out of general taxation, would be more efficient.

Protection, in this restricted and true sense of the word, was probably the main factor motivating the first tariffs of capitalism. One gains that impression not only when perusing the writings of early Continental and American writers on the subject; but also from the fact that the export duties of the mercantilist era should have been replaced by import duties. For these are more suitable for affording protection in the above defined sense; while those would have been more natural and more efficient had the monopolistic exploitation of

[1] Only those that have an opportunity cost.

foreigners been the primary aim.[1] In more recent times, changing the terms of trade and creating employment were probably more important considerations with public opinion and legislative bodies in determining tariff policy.

VIII

We have tried to show in the foregoing that to impose tariffs on international trade is generally in the rational interest of single countries for more than one reason. This does not conflict with the fact that free trade is the best policy for the universe as a whole. For just as each entrepreneur's competitive behaviour diminishes the profits of all entrepreneurs, so each single country's effort to increase its national welfare tends to diminish the welfare of all.

Free trade leads to the best allocation (most efficient utilization) of the world's resources, provided that full employment is somehow ensured. It leads to a distribution of welfare among nations that, if ethically neutral, is at least based on historically and geographically determined inequalities and not on inequalities of political and military power. Any corrections of this distribution that may be considered necessary or just, are better made openly (preferably in kind), in the form of payments of tribute or assistance, than surreptitiously, under the cloak of tariffs or barter agreements. That is a better guarantee of economic efficiency and justice.

But it is not enough to declare the desirability of free trade and trust that enlightenment will bring it about: nor is it enough to create initial conditions favourable to it: it must be imposed and enforced. Whether this should be done with the aid of the more effective sanctions of a new League of Nations, or through the political prestige of a British Empire, or in any other way, is beyond the economist's competence to decide. We can only tell that some form of compulsion is necessary to ensure free trade. The truth of this statement is attested by the past history of international trade as much as by our rationalization of it. Both show that independent states,

---

[1] This is in apparent contradiction with footnote 2, p. 147. But Mr Lerner's demonstration that the effects of import and export duties are identical in all respects only holds good of duties that are levied at a uniform rate on all commodities.

in possession of their full sovereignty, will keep on erecting and raising tariffs in order to increase their share of the world's resources, to achieve fuller employment, and to protect their growing industries. Of these three aims only the last is likely to be realized; the second will generally defeat itself as tariffs are erected all round; whereas the first will not only defeat itself but every country will actually be impoverished as they all raise their tariffs. It is to guard against this general impoverishment that free trade must be enforced and each country kept from seeking more than its share of the world's resources. Employment can be maintained and infant industries subsidized by other means than protection. This, from a single country's point of view, is probably the cheapest way of achieving those aims; but it is against the general interest to let one country do what would be detrimental to all if generally practised.

The enforcement of free trade, of course, would not in itself solve all problems of international economic co-operation: on the contrary. Since freer trade means more trade, problems of a satisfactory international standard, of international co-operation in maintaining a stable level of employment, and the like, would become greater in proportion. I believe, however, that post-war reconstruction would lead to better and more stable results if free trade were enforced and a constructive attempt made at solving attending problems, than if undue faith in the principle of *laisser faire* resulted in a repetition of past mistakes.

Chapter 9

A NOTE ON PROFIT MAXIMIZATION
AND ITS IMPLICATIONS

1943

That the entrepreneur aims at maximizing his profits is one of the most fundamental assumptions of economic theory. So much so that it has almost come to be regarded as equivalent to rational behaviour, and as an axiom, which is self-evident and needs no proof or justification. Doubts have been raised by several writers whether maximizing his profits is always the entrepreneur's best policy.[1] But such doubts were few and have died away without reverberation; mainly, I think, because it has never been made clear what exactly profit maximization implies; and perhaps also because we have a vested interest in maintaining this assumption—it makes economic analysis so much simpler. In the following we set out to show that by attributing to the entrepreneur the desire to maximize his profits we also attribute to him a particular psychology, which, though very plausible, is rather special.

Let us draw the entrepreneur's indifference map between money income, m, and entrepreneurial inactivity, i (fig. 1).[2] Entrepreneurial activity is the negative of i and is measured from right to left along the horizontal axis. Assume next that entrepreneurial activity is a limitational factor in the manufacture of the entrepreneur's produce and can, therefore, be

---

[1] Cf. J. R. Hicks: 'Annual Survey of Economic Theory: The Theory of Monopoly', *Econometrica*, vol. 3 (1935), p. 8; B. Higgins: 'Elements of Indeterminancy in the Theory of Non-Perfect Competition', *American Economic Review*, vol. 29 (1939), pp. 468-79. See also E. S. Lynch's comment on the latter article and Professor Higgins's reply in *American Economic Review*, vol. 30 (1940), pp. 347-50.

[2] This term is somewhat inelegant but it is more accurate than the usual term, leisure.

[3] I am indebted to Mr D. E. McCoy for drawing the diagrams.

measured in terms of output.[1] Point w represents zero output or total entrepreneurial inactivity.

Since the unit of measurement along the horizontal axis is the unit of output, we can draw the entrepreneur's total receipts curve and total outlays curve in this diagram. The vertical difference of the two curves shows, for each level of output, the entrepreneur's total net income from operating his firm. Taking these differences as ordinates we can draw the entrepreneur's net income curve (fig. 2). The point at which the net income curve is tangential to an indifference curve is the

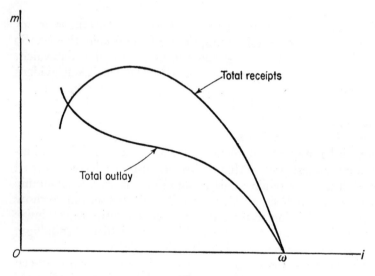

Fig. 1.

entrepreneur's point of maximum satisfaction and determines his optimum rate of output. This optimum rate of output may or may not maximize his profits; and our problem is to find out under what conditions (i.e. for what shape of the indifference map) it does.

The entrepreneur's net income would be highest at point h. But for an indifference curve to be tangential to the income curve at this point, it would have to be horizontal or even upward-sloping over part of its range. This is very unlikely

[1] A limitational factor is a factor of production whose quantity per unit of output is fixed and cannot be varied.

and conflicts with our general notions of the shape of indifference curves.

We must bear in mind, however, that what the entrepreneur
is supposed to maximize is not his total net income. He is
assumed to maximize the difference between his total receipts
and his total costs; and total costs are always assumed to com-
prise, not only the entrepreneur's outlays, but also the wages
of routine management and supervision, which he is supposed
to pay to himself and include in his regular cost calculations. In
other words, the entrepreneur's income consists of two elements. The wages of routine management, which form part

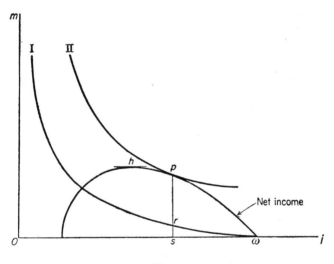

Fig. 2.

of costs; and the profits of entrepreneurship proper, which are
his residual income. Marshall called both elements profits:
the one normal, the other extraordinary, profits. For our
purposes it will be more convenient to refer to the former as
the entrepreneur's wages, and to apply the term profit only
to his residual income. But irrespectively of terminology, it is
always his residual income only that the entrepreneur is supposed to maximize. That this dichotomy of the entrepreneur's
income is always implied in the orthodox theory will become
plain to the reader when he recalls the full equilibrium conditions of perfect competition: the equality of price with

marginal and average costs. While the latter condition elimi-
nates the entrepreneur's residual income completely, he is still
supposed to earn wages for supervision (normal profits) in this
situation. These must consequently be included in costs; and
they are supposed to represent the entrepreneur's minimum
(i.e. marginal) income. Profits, therefore, the entrepreneur's
residual income, are of the nature of a rent.[1]

In our diagram (fig. 2) we can separate the two elements of
the entrepreneur's income by drawing the indifference curve
that goes through the point w. This indifference curve represents the minimum satisfaction that will keep the entrepreneur
in his profession. If his satisfaction were to fall below this level
he would cease being an entrepreneur and do something else.
That part of his income, therefore, which brings the entrepreneur to this level of satisfaction is his minimum income, the
wage of routine management.[2] Only the part of his income
that brings his satisfaction above the indifference curve I can
be regarded as profit proper. In fig. 2, therefore, of ps, the
entrepreneur's total net income, pr is profit, and rs is wages.

We are now in a position to answer the question, under what
conditions does the maximizing of profits lead to the maximization of the entrepreneur's satisfaction? Profit, the vertical
distance between the net income curve and the indifference
curve I, is greatest at the level of output where the tangents to
the two curves are parallel. The entrepreneur's satisfaction is
greatest at the level of output where the net income curve is
tangential to an indifference curve. It is clear that the two
levels of output need not coincide. For we used one indifference curve to determine maximum profits, another one for
determining maximum satisfaction: and as long as we make no
special assumption about the individual's psychology or behaviour, there is no definite relationship between the shape or
position of the various indifference curves in his indifference
map. In order, therefore, that maximum profits should maximize his satisfaction, the entrepreneur must have a special type

[1] Cf. Alfred Marshall: *Principles of Economics*, definitive edition, pp. 618-19;
Joan Robinson: *The Economics of Imperfect Competition*, London, 1933,
chapters 7, 8 and 9; B. Higgins: *op. cit.*
[2] Since this part of the entrepreneur's remuneration enters into cost, the indifference curve I must be added vertically to the total outlays curve (fig. 1)
to give the entrepreneur's total cost curve. We have not drawn this curve,
since it is not needed for our argument.

of psychology, and, corresponding to it, a special type of indifference map.

The geometrical nature of this condition will be immediately obvious to the reader. For the net income curve to be tangential to an indifference curve at the same level of output at which its slope equals that of indifference curve *I*, the tangents to the two indifference curves at that level of output must be parallel. In order that this condition may be satisfied for any and every kind of net income curve, *all* indifference curves must have the same slope for *each* abscissa. In other words, the several indifference curves must be vertical displacements of each other.

The economic meaning of the above geometrical condition is that the entrepreneur's choice between more and less activity —or between more income and more leisure—must be independent of his income. This is equivalent to Marshall's familiar assumption of a constant marginal utility of money; or, to use more up-to-date terminology, to a zero income elasticity of supply of entrepreneurship.

At first sight it may seem strange and unrealistic to attribute to the entrepreneur a type of behaviour that would fulfil this condition. For, if his aim is to make money, it seems natural that the amount he is already making should affect the ardour and energy with which he seeks to make more. But the assumption that the entrepreneur's willingness to work is independent of his income need not imply that he is not interested in the material rewards of his work. It may also mean that he is so keen on making money that his ambition cannot be damped by a rising income. The latter interpretation seems to be the more realistic one of the two. Businessmen regard the income they earn as an index of their success and efficiency; and their ambition of excelling in their profession manifests itself in the desire to make more money. We claim that a businessman's entrepreneurial activity will remain unaffected by a rise in his income if he makes money, not in order to have more to spend, but for its own sake, because it is an index and token of his success in life.

The man who aims at raising his standard of living tends to relax his efforts when they meet with success. This is so, not only because material demands are satiable, but also because leisure is an essential ingredient of a good life. He, however, who wants success for its own sake, and measures it in terms of money, is likely to keep working unabated even after his income has risen. This is likely to be the case, partly because the desire for success is more insatiable than the demand for material goods, and partly because it is not a high but a rising income that is a sign of business success.[1]

For the supply of entrepreneurship to be independent of income it is not necessary that the entrepreneur's psychology should be such that he save the total increment of a rise in his income. He may devote part or all of it to raising his standard of living, provided that he regards this as no more than a by-product of his business success and its outward manifestation. As long as raising his standard of living does not become the entrepreneur's primary aim, the amount of work and energy expended by him will remain independent of his income and be limited only by considerations of age and health, habit and temperament; by family and social obligations; by competing (e.g. political) ambitions; and the like. In such a case, therefore, the assumption of a zero income elasticity of supply of entrepreneurship will be perfectly justified, and it will be correct to ascribe to the entrepreneur the desire to maximize his profits. Only when he is more susceptible to the attractions of leisure than to those of his work and is consequently induced by a higher income to take life easier, will the entrepreneur's optimum behaviour be, not to maximize profits, but to keep his exertions and output below the point at which profits would be at a maximum.

The puritan psychology of valuing money for its own sake, and not for the enjoyments and comforts it might yield, is that of the ideal entrepreneur as he was conceived of in the early days of capitalism. The combination of frugality and industry, the entrepreneurial virtues, is calculated to ensure the independence of the entrepreneur's willingness to work from the level of his income. The classical economists, therefore, were perfectly justified in assuming that the entrepreneur aims at maximizing his profits. They were concerned with a type of businessman whose psychology happened to be such that for him maximizing profits was identical with maximizing satisfaction.

The entrepreneur of today may have lost some of the

[1] A high but constant level of income can be a sign of past business success.

frugality and industry of his forefathers; nevertheless, the assumption that he aims at maximizing his profits is still quite likely to apply to him—at least as a first approximation. For this assumption is patently untrue only about people who regard work as plain drudgery: a necessary evil, with which they have to put up in order to earn their living and the comforts of life. The person who derives satisfaction from his work—other than that yielded by the income he receives for it—will to a large extent be governed by ambition, a spirit of emulation and rivalry, pride in his work, and similar considerations, when he plans his activity. We believe that the entrepreneur usually belongs to this latter category.

However, we set out, not to justify or criticize the assumption that entrepreneurs aim at maximizing profits, but to make its implications explicit. Many of us have been in the habit of regarding this assumption as similar in every respect to the assumption that the individual maximizes his satisfaction. We have shown above that this is not so. For to say that the individual maximizes his satisfaction is a perfectly general statement. It says nothing about the individual's psychology or behaviour, is, therefore, devoid of empirical content, and is true by definition. As against this, the assumption that the entrepreneur maximizes his profits is based on observation and implies a special hypothesis concerning the businessman's psychology. It is, therefore, an empirical law, which need not apply to every businessman, and may conceivably be untrue even about the representative entrepreneur. Its justification lies in its usefulness, which should be enhanced by a better understanding of its exact meaning and limitations.

Chapter 10

THE STATE OF WELFARE
ECONOMICS[1]

1951

Welfare economics is that part of the general body of economic theory which is concerned primarily with policy. Some people would argue that all economics is or should be concerned with policy. Without welfare economics, however, economic theory would be a collection of techniques and the economist would be little more than a technician, a politician's handyman, who has to wait for the latter to state his aims and can merely advise him on how to go about achieving those aims. Welfare economics supplies the economist—and the politician—with standards, at least with some standards, by which to appraise and on the basis of which to formulate policy. Hence, whenever the economist advocates a policy, for example when he favours full employment or opposes governmental interference in economic affairs, he makes a welfare proposition.

In the days of the classical economists, the whole body of economics was 'political economy', centred around the welfare problem. Adam Smith defined political economy as a branch of the art of legislation.[2] The utilitarians, too, with their calculus of pleasure and pain, were interested mainly in the establishment of principles that can guide policy. Doubts whether the economist can establish such principles began, however, to arise at the beginning of this century, when we became aware of the insoluble difficulties that beset the economist when he tries to measure and compare different people's utility.

[1] Paper read in Chicago at a joint session of the American Economic Association and the Econometric Society on December 30, 1950.
[2] Cf. Adam Smith, *Wealth of Nations*, Book IV, Introduction.

The ordinal nature of utility and the impossibility of inter-personal utility comparisons soon became axioms generally accepted by most people who were concerned with such matters; but the full implications of all this for the usefulness of economics and of economists were not realized for a long time. The Cambridge economists, upholders of the classical tradition, duly noted these difficulties and promptly dismissed them as unimportant. They regarded the attempt to avoid cardinal utility with the use of indifference curves as an in-genious *tour de force* and a plaything of the purist; and they continued as before to accept the law of diminishing marginal utility and to make the commonsense assumption that by and large different people derive the same satisfaction out of the same income. In the words of Alfred Marshall, 'it would naturally be assumed that a shilling's worth of gratification to one Englishman might be taken as equivalent with a shilling's worth to another . . . until cause to the contrary were shown'.[1] Here the matter rested, and until about ten years ago most of the important publications on welfare economics, such as Pigou's *Economics of Welfare*, and Kahn's 'Ideal Output', continued to come from Cambridge, all based on the postulate of equality; that is, of the equal ability of different people to enjoy themselves.

In the United States, the situation was very similar. Here, the attack on the utility theory came not only along the lines already mentioned but also from those who, like Professor J. M. Clark, called for a theory more firmly based on a study of human psychology. Here too, however, there were a few eminent economists who shared the commonsense views of the Cambridge school and were willing to retain the old utility theory for the sake of its obvious usefulness. Irving Fisher persevered in trying to measure utility. Professor Frank Knight expressed the view that the arguments for progressive taxation and for a greater equality of incomes were too important to be dismissed merely because we had not yet found a way of proving the underlying assumptions.[2] I believe that also Profes-sor Chamberlin felt very much like Knight, at least to judge by his *Theory of Monopolistic Competition*, which was the only

[1] Alfred Marshall, *Principles of Economics*, 8th edition, p. 130.
[2] Frank H. Knight, 'Realism and Relevance in the Theory of Demand', *Jour. Pol. Econ.*, vol. LII, No. 4 (December 1944), pp. 289-318.

important work on welfare economics published on this side of the Atlantic during this period.

The majority of theoretical economists, however, in America, in England, and on the Continent of Europe alike, were fully convinced by the argument that the utility calculus is inadmissible. They were willing to reject the measurability of utility, to refrain from interpersonal comparisons of utility, and to take the consequences—although few of them realized what the full consequences were. These were pointed out in 1932 by Professor Robbins.[1] He maintained that if economics was to have the objectivity of a science, economists may not make interpersonal comparisons and may not, in their capacity as economists, argue for or against any policy or change of policy that would make some people better and others worse off than they were before. Considering that practically every economic change favours some and hurts others, Professor Robbins was, in effect, barring himself and his colleagues from any policy recommendations whatever.

There must have been many economists who disliked these conclusions; but they were unable to refute them. Accordingly, apart from the above-mentioned exceptions, welfare economics ceased to exist at this stage. Students were taught the behaviour of the firm under pure and under monopolistic competition; but they were rarely taught what in my opinion is the only justification of even mentioning pure competition, namely that it leads, or would lead, to an efficient allocation of resources and an efficient organization of production. It is highly paradoxical that the theory of allocation under pure competition, which used to be the justification of *laisser faire* in the days of the classical economists, ceased to be part of the curriculum in the '20s and '30s, and had to take refuge under a pseudonym, as the economic theory of socialism. As is well known, Barone's 'The Ministry of Production in the Collectivist State' and Lerner's and Lange's writings on the economic theory of socialism are our main sources for the modern theory of optimum welfare under pure competition; and a recent restatement of this theory by Professor Bergson was published in a paper entitled 'Socialist Economics'. The reason, of course, for this paradoxical state of affairs is that apart from

[1] Lionel Robbins, *An Essay on the Nature and Significance of Economic Science* (London, 1932).

the Cambridge economists, only the socialist writers and writers on socialism could accept, without further ado, the postulate that men are equal in their ability to enjoy life. Most other economists studiously avoided the subject of welfare economics as unscientific; and, for the sake of maintaining their status as scientists, they were willing to become technicians, concerned solely with observation, description, classification, and the collection of data. If most of them nevertheless continued to praise competition, to condemn tariffs, or to advocate a neutral monetary policy, they did so out of sheer habit, not realizing that if economists are to refrain from interpersonal comparisons of utility, they may not express a preference between monopoly and competition, protectionism and free trade, or inflation and price stability.

The reaction to this state of affairs came in the late '30s. Frustrated by their inability to answer the pressing questions posed by the depression, and realizing that Keynes's *General Theory* provided them with the answers, or at least with some of the answers sought, many economists seemed to throw scientific objectivity to the winds in their desire to render themselves useful. The choice between prosperity and depression, between a high and a low national output, seemed so obvious and so easy to make that few if any economists stopped to ask themselves whether they had made their choice on objective and purely scientific grounds. A whole new generation of economists, and many members of the old, wholeheartedly advocated full employment, full-employment output, and policies aimed at maintaining full employment. Here then, in a way, was a rebirth of welfare economics; and few of Keynes's pupils and followers worried over any possible loss in their status as scientists that their policy recommendations might involve.

It is well to remember, however, that there was such a loss, at least by the standards established by Professor Robbins. For a comparison of the relative merits of prosperity and depression does involve an interpersonal comparison of utilities. The overwhelming majority of people may be better off in times of prosperity; but there are some, however few, who live on fixed incomes or accumulated savings, and who, in depression, can 'pick up bargains', as one economist has put it, that are not available to them in times of prosperity. The economist, there-

M

fore, who favours prosperity and advocates a policy of full employment makes an implicit value judgment. He implies that the gain of those millions who benefit by prosperity is in some sense greater or more important than the loss of real income suffered by those few whose money incomes are fixed.

Strictly speaking, such an assumption is not objective and not scientific. Nevertheless, most people feel instinctively that it is right. This fact explains why most economists were undaunted in their advocacy of a high level of income and employment; and it also explains, I believe, the recent revival of interest in welfare economics and the re-examination of its foundations.

The new discussion of the basis of welfare economics was opened in 1938, significantly enough by a pupil of Keynes, Mr Harrod. He stated, and I quote, 'If the incomparability of utility to different individuals is strictly pressed, not only are the prescriptions of the welfare school ruled out, but all prescriptions whatever. The economist as an adviser is completely stultified, and . . . he had better be suppressed completely. No,' Harrod protests, 'some sort of postulate of equality has to be assumed. But it should be carefully framed and used with great caution.'[1] In other words, Harrod felt that without welfare economics, the economist would be completely useless and without function in society. He was willing therefore to follow in the path of the Cambridge school, to relinquish the economist's claim to scientific objectivity, and to let him assume the equality of man for the sake of maintaining his usefulness as an adviser and policy maker. I believe that the person who came the nearest to carrying out what Harrod advocated was Professor Abba Lerner. Standing very close to the Cambridge school, he maintained throughout an active interest in welfare economics; and he tried, in his *Economics of Control*, to justify the assumption of equality on a probability basis. Professor Friedman, however, in his review of Lerner's book,[2] has shown that this attempt was not altogether satisfactory.

At the same time that Harrod advocated a cautious return to the postulates of the classical and neo-classical economists,

[1] R. F. Harrod, 'Scope and Method of Economics', *Economic Journal*, vol. XLVIII, No. 191 (September 1938), p. 397.
[2] Cf. *Journal of Political Economy*, vol. LV, No. 5 (October 1947), pp. 409-11.

there arose two new schools of thought that tried, each independently of the other, to restore the economist to his position of policy maker without the necessity of assuming the equal ability of different people to enjoy life.

The first of these schools is associated with the names of Kaldor, Hicks, and Hotelling, and is generally called the new welfare economics. The second school, which is associated with the names of Bergson and Samuelson, has developed the concept of the social welfare function.

THE NEW WELFARE ECONOMICS

The new welfare economists, despite their name, actually said little that was new. They accepted the usual simplifying assumptions of Pareto and Barone: to wit, the independence of different people's satisfactions and the absence of external economies and diseconomies. On these assumptions, they were able to segregate the conditions of optimum welfare into two groups and deal with them separately under the headings of efficiency and equity. This device was already known to Pareto but was more fully developed and explicitly stated by Lange.[1] Since virtually all changes in economic policy or institutions affect both the efficiency of the economic system and the distribution of welfare it gives rise to, one would think that all economic changes ought to be judged by standards both of efficiency and of equity. The new welfare economists, however, maintained and set out to show that the economist is justified in making policy recommendations on the basis of efficiency considerations alone. Their critics, notably Professor Samuelson and Mr Little, argued that they failed in this attempt. In my opinion, this criticism is not wholly justified; and it will be well therefore to restate the arguments of the new welfare economists.

To prove their point, the new welfare economists have advanced two arguments, which are really separate and different from each other, although their authors do not seem to have been aware of this fact. One of these arguments does not, in my opinion, stand up under scrutiny; but the other is valid, at least if certain special institutional conditions are fulfilled.

[1] Oscar Lange. 'The Foundations of Welfare Economics', *Econometrica*, vol. 10 (July-October 1942), pp. 215-28.

The first argument is usually attributed to Dr Hicks, although it was first and most rigorously stated by Professor Hotelling. In a 1938 article in *Econometrica*, Professor Hotelling raised the question whether it would not be better to pay for the construction of bridges and tunnels, and for public utilities at large, out of general taxation rather than out of tolls and rates levied on the users of public utilities.[1] He recalled Pareto's definition of an efficient economic organization, under which no one could be made better off without making someone else worse off. Any change in policy or institutions, therefore, that improved efficiency could, if accompanied by an appropriate system of compensations and collections, render everyone better off than he was before. Hotelling believed that 'such adjustments would not in fact be made; that the general well-being would be purchased at the expense of sacrifices by some; and that it is unjust that some should gain at the expense of others, even when the gain is large and the cost small'.[2] Nevertheless, Hotelling felt that in the case he was considering, the economist was justified in making policy recommendations and basing these recommendations on the criterion of efficiency alone. For he conceived of economic policy in this field as a succession of many small changes, each of which would bring the system closer to perfect efficiency, and each of which would redistribute welfare in a random fashion. If this were so, the successive redistributions would cancel each other out and leave the improvement in efficiency as the net result, so that everybody would be better off in the end. Bearing in mind that Hotelling was concerned not with economic policy at large but with a rather restricted and special problem, his assumptions and conclusions can probably be accepted.

Doubts as to the validity of Hotelling's argument arise only when it is elevated into a general principle and made applicable to all economic policy recommendations. This is what Dr Hicks has done. His argument, in his own words, runs as follows: 'If a community were organized on the principle of making all alterations which were improvements [in the

---

[1] Harold Hotelling, 'The General Welfare in Relation to the Problems of Taxation and of Railway and Utility Rates', *Econometrica*, vol. 6 (July 1938), pp. 242-69.
[2] *Op. cit.*, p. 258.

efficiency sense], then, although we could not say that all the inhabitants of that community would be necessarily better off than they would have been if the community had been organized on some different principle, nevertheless there would be a strong probability that almost all of them would be better off after the lapse of a sufficient length of time."[1] On the strength of this argument, Hicks maintains that economists can and should make policy recommendations on the basis of efficiency considerations alone. This attitude has been criticized, correctly I believe, by Mr Little. He points out that some economic changes may occasion major changes in distribution, that we cannot prove the randomness of different redistributions; and that for both these reasons we cannot expect successive redistributions of welfare to cancel out and offset each other. Accordingly, Mr Little concludes that Hicks is wrong in urging the economist to ignore the problem of distribution and base his recommendations on efficiency considerations alone.[2]

Having examined and rejected one of the arguments of the new welfare economists, we can now turn to the second argument, which has been advanced by Mr Kaldor.[3] Kaldor believes, just like Hicks, though for different reasons, that the economist should favour all changes in economic policy that improve the efficiency of the economic system, even when they inflict losses upon some people and independently of whether or not these people are compensated for their losses out of the gainers' gains. Kaldor seems to think of every decision affecting economic policy as consisting of two parts: the economic decision whether or not to make the change itself, and the political decision whether or not to compensate the losers in case the change in policy is made and inflicts losses on some people. He advocates that the economist should take an active part in making the first part of this decision and base

[1] J. R. Hicks, 'The Rehabilitation of Consumer's Surplus', *Review of Economic Studies*, vol. VIII, No. 2 (February 1941), p. 111.
[2] I. M. D. Little, *A Critique of Welfare Economics* (Oxford 1950), Chap. VI.
[3] Nicholas Kaldor, 'Welfare Propositions of Economics and Interpersonal Comparisons of Utility', *Economic Journal*, vol. XLIX (September 1939), pp. 549-52. It is worth noting that Hicks has endorsed Kaldor's argument in his 'The Foundations of Welfare Economics', *Economic Journal*, vol. XLIX (December 1939), pp. 696-712. The position, however, that Hicks took in the latter article cited above suggests strongly that he was not aware of the difference between Kaldor's argument and his own.

his recommendations on efficiency considerations alone, because, according to Kaldor, the economist can rely on others to take care of the distributive aspects of the problem. If I interpret Kaldor correctly, he has in mind a community whose political representatives are fully conscious of the problem of distribution and are willing to take full responsibility for maintaining an equitable distribution of income. In such a community, the economist can make policy recommendations on the basis of efficiency considerations alone, because he can rest assured that if his recommendations are followed and result in a redistribution of income which the community considers undesirable, this will be corrected as a matter of course through a system of compensations. In other words, the economist can forget about the problem of distribution, provided that others are willing to take care of it.

This is likely to be the case in a socialist economy; and generally in an economy where the public regulation of economic affairs and public responsibility for a satisfactory distribution of income are the rule rather than the exception. It may well be that the England of today is such a community; and that in England, therefore, economists can concentrate on the improvement of efficiency and rely on Parliament to take care of the maintenance of equity. Kaldor's argument, however, has no universal validity. I doubt for example if it could be applied in the United States or in the England of the time when Kaldor's article was written. This is not to imply that Congress or Parliament in the free enterprise economy is not concerned with the equity of income distribution. Progressive taxation and social insurance testify to the contrary. Nevertheless, there is a presumption in the free enterprise economy against the State correcting the income distribution brought about by the market mechanism. This militates against any economic policy that would have to be accompanied by a payment of subsidies or compensations. In other words, the effects of an economic policy on efficiency on the one hand and on income distribution on the other hand cannot—as a rule—be separated in a free enterprise economy, because in such an economy compensation payments are not feasible politically. This implies that in the free enterprise economy all economic policies must be appraised by their effects on efficiency and equity simultaneously; and no recommendations can be made on the basis of one of these criteria alone. I would conclude, therefore, that while the new welfare economics has, in Kaldor's argument, provided the economist with a guide to policy in some communities, this guide has no universal validity and provides no basis on which, for example, we in the United States could make policy recommendations.

Before proceeding, I want to mention in passing another criticism that has been levelled against the new welfare economics. This criticism has to do with Kaldor's compensation principle. According to this principle, the test of increased efficiency is that the gainers from a change can more than compensate the losers. This is a very simple test; but there are two objections to its use. One is that the compensation principle makes use of the consumer's surplus concept. Professor Samuelson has argued that this is so treacherous a tool that it is better not to use it, especially since there exist other and more satisfactory tools that serve the same purpose.[1] The other objection is that in certain exceptional cases it is impossible to decide which of two alternative situations is more efficient; and one may get the paradoxical result that each situation is more efficient than the other. This objection, which I raised in 1941,[2] applies equally to the compensation principle and to any other test of efficiency; but it probably is not very important—certainly much less so than I and others have originally believed. In many important cases the paradoxical result cannot arise. I was aware but not fully aware of this when writing my 1941 *Note*; a good further discussion of it was published by Graaff and Bailey.[3] I believe that Bailey's article should have cleared up and put an end to this particular controversy.

THE SOCIAL WELFARE FUNCTION

Let us examine next the other new approach to welfare econ-

---

[1] Paul Samuelson, *The Foundations of Economic Analysis* (Cambridge, Mass., 1947), pp. 195 ff.
[2] In the paper reprinted as Chapter 7 above.
[3] J. de V. Graaff, 'On Optimum Tariff Structures', *Review of Economic Studies*, vol. XVII (1), No. 42 (1949-50), pp. 47-59; M. J. Bailey, 'The Interpretation and Application of the Compensation Principle', *Economic Journal*, vol. LXIV, No. 253 (1954), pp. 39-52.

omics, that of Professor Bergson,[1] which has been endorsed and further developed by Professors Samuelson and Tintner. Bergson defines a social welfare function, which may be regarded as a function either of the welfare of each member of the community or of the quantities of products consumed and services rendered by each member of the community. This social welfare function is completely general. It can take into account external economies and diseconomies as well as the dependence of one person's satisfaction on other people's welfare. In fact, the social welfare function, as Bergson defines it, is so completely general that it is impossible to tell, on the basis of internal evidence alone, what use Bergson wanted to make of it. It may be that he aimed merely at a formal and rigorous restatement of the main problems of welfare economics. If so, he certainly has clarified the issues and facilitated further work in the field. Bergson's work, however, has been hailed as a major contribution to welfare economics on the basis, I believe, of a more positive interpretation of it. Accordingly, I too shall put this interpretation on Bergson's social welfare function and appraise it on this basis.

The social welfare function can be thought of as a function of each individual's welfare, which in turn depends both on his personal well-being and on his appraisal of the distribution of welfare among all members of the community. It would seem therefore as though the social welfare function would solve the fundamental problem of welfare economics and make is unnecessary for the economist to decide what is a desirable distribution of welfare. For the social welfare function is a kind of collective utility function, which expresses everybody's preferences relating not only to his personal satisfaction but also to the state of the entire community and to the distribution of welfare among the members of the community. Hence, one might think that the economist could concentrate on stating the conditions that would maximize the social welfare function and on advocating the economic policy that would bring about these conditions; and that he could rest assured that this would bring about the economic system that conforms most closely and in every respect to the preferences of the community.

[1] A. Bergson, 'A Reformation of Certain Aspects of Welfare Economics', *Quarterly Journal of Economics*, vol. LII, No. 4 (February, 1938), pp. 310-34.

Unfortunately, however, the social welfare function so interpreted has not, or at least not yet, fulfilled the hopes that it seemed at first sight to have held out. For the construction of a social welfare function raises two very serious problems. One is the problem of specifying the shape of the social welfare function and its exact dependence on the welfare of each individual. At first sight, the use of the social welfare function would seem to relieve the economist from the necessity of making any value judgment at all. It looks as though he would not need to decide what is the most desirable distribution of welfare, because the social welfare function itself expresses the community's opinion on this subject. All that the economist would have to do therefore would be to see to it that the actual distribution of welfare conforms to society's preferences as expressed by the social welfare function.

The problem, however, is not quite so simple as this. For the shape of the social welfare function must somehow be determined; and this, to put it crudely, amounts to determining the relative weights attached to each individual's preferences when these are aggregated into the social preference function. Should everybody's preferences be given equal weight, or, if not, on what principle should different weights be allotted to different people's preferences? Most people would probably feel instinctively that everybody should be given an equal vote; but let us remember that it was the same instinct that led earlier generations of economists to give equal weights to different people's satisfactions. Do we stand on surer ground when we give people equal votes than did the classical economists when they assumed that everybody had the same ability to enjoy life? I doubt it. But even if we did, to determine the shape of the social welfare function would still involve a value judgment, which presumably would have to be made by the economist. It appears therefore that the introduction of the social welfare function has not really solved the economist's problem. It has indeed taken off his shoulders the responsibility for attaching weights to different people's satisfactions or welfare; but it has imposed upon him the new and very similar responsibility of attaching weights to different people's opinions and preferences.

Furthermore, there is also a second objection to the use of the social welfare function, which has been pointed out by

Professor Arrow.[1] He has shown that if a choice is to be made from among more than two alternatives, we cannot, in general, construct a social welfare function that could be regarded as a true representation of individual preferences and would at the same time lead to a consistent and non-contradictory social ordering of all available alternatives. By a true representation of individual preferences is meant, in this context, a social ordering that is positively correlated with individual preferences, one that is independent of the presence or absence of irrelevant alternatives, and one that is determined neither by the wishes of a dictator nor by mere convention or tradition alone. In short, Arrow shows that we cannot, in general, construct a social welfare function in a way that fulfills the above simple and reasonable requirements without getting involved in a contradiction.

It would take too long to reproduce Arrow's argument; but I will reproduce a simple example he gives. Imagine a community of three people, x, y, and z, who have to choose from among three alternative social policies, a, b, and c. x prefers a to b, b to c, and hence also a to c. y prefers b to c, c to a, and hence also b to a. z prefers c to a, a to b, and hence also c to b. If we then give each person's preferences equal weights, we can try to construct a social preference function on the basis of majority rule. Since two out of three people prefer a to b, we have a social preference for a over b. On the same basis there is a social preference also for b over c. From this it follows that there must also be a social preference for a over c. But two out of three people prefer c to a, so that there is a social preference also for c and a. Hence, majority rule in this example leads to a contradictory social preference function.

Arrow's objection does not rule out altogether the use of the social welfare function. It only demonstrates the limitations of the approach. His work can be regarded as a rigorous proof of a truth that has been known for a long time; namely, that democratic procedure does not always work. Further research in this field therefore will have to concentrate on

[1] Arrow's work on this subject has appeared in several forms and in several places. For the simplest formulation of his contribution see Kenneth Arrow, 'A Difficulty in the Concept of Social Welfare', *Journal of Political Economics*, vol. LVIII, No. 4 (August 1950), pp. 328-46.

finding the special conditions under which a non-contradictory and meaningful social welfare function can be constructed; or in other words, under which democratic procedure can function.

Some work along these lines has already been done in the field of political theory by Mr Duncan Black, of Glasgow University.[1] He has shown that the political preferences of a group, as expressed in the passing of a bill or the election of a candidate, can always be said to represent, in a meaningful sense, the preferences of the members of the group, provided that the alternatives from among which choice is made can be ordered along a (one-dimensional) scale from, say, left to right, and provided that all the members of the group, while they may differ in their preferences, agree on the order in which the alternatives are arranged from left to right.

These conditions, for instance, would rule out Arrow's example. Think of A as a leftist policy, B as a middle-of-the-road policy, and C as a rightist policy. Then X is a leftist, Y is a middle-of-the-roader; but there is something wrong with Z. His first choice indeed is the rightist policy C; but his second choice, A, violates Black's conditions. For Black would have a rightist person take the middle-of-the-road policy as his second choice; and in that case, of course, Arrow's contradictory result would not arise.

It so happens that in the political sphere the above condition is quite often satisfied, although there are some conspicuous instances in recent history when it was not satisfied. The obvious example is the 'tactical' alliance in Germany between communists and nazis shortly before Hitler's accession to power, with its disastrous results.

In the economic field, the available alternatives cannot as a rule be reduced to one-dimensional ordering; and in this field therefore the restriction to be imposed for ensuring the existence of a meaningful social welfare function will probably have to be of an entirely different nature. As far as I am aware, no work has been done as yet to discover what these minimum restrictions are. One can only guess that some mini-

---

[1] Duncan Black, 'The Rationale of Group Decision-Making', *Journal of Political Economics*, vol. LVI, No. 1 (February 1948), pp. 23-34; and also his 'The Decisions of a Committee Using a Special Majority', *Econometrica*, vol. 16, No. 3 (July 1948), pp. 245-61.

mum degree of agreement and uniformity of preferences will be required to ensure the existence of a social welfare function in the economic sphere.

THE EMERGENCE OF A CONSTRUCTIVE THEORY OF WELFARE ECONOMICS

So far, then, the outlook seems rather bleak. Neither the new welfare economics nor the social welfare function has provided the economist with an answer to his dilemma. But the situation is not quite so bad. Arrow's criticism of the social welfare function and Black's work in the political sphere have at least pointed the way along which constructive work in this field will have to be done. As to the new welfare economics, its discussion by sympathetic critics and by critical sympathizers has already yielded some constructive results. Most of these have to be found in reading between the lines; but some of them are contained in Little's *Critique of Welfare Economics.*

One definite conclusion that has emerged from the welfare controversy is that while in some cases and in some communities the economist can make policy recommendations on efficiency grounds alone, in our society he cannot usually do so but must take into account also considerations of distribution and equity. When he does so, the economist introduces a value judgment into his recommendations. In our society, therefore, the economist must make a choice. If he wants to maintain strict objectivity, he becomes a technician; if he wants to advise on policy, he must in most cases relinquish his claim to the objectivity of a natural scientist.

My feeling is that most economists who choose the latter rôle are not unduly disturbed by the price they have to pay for their position as advisers. After all, it is the function of social science to make judgments and recommendations on the distribution of welfare; and not only is the economist a social scientist, he is probably the best qualified among social scientists to deal with this subject.

But if the economist takes it upon himself to make policy recommendations, and does so, as indeed he must, on the basis of both efficiency and equity considerations, it is essential that he should be fully conscious of this fact, and that when he makes his recommendations he should make it absolutely clear and explicit on what basis he has arrived at them.

Needless to say, if the economist's recommendations are to command assent, his judgment on equity must conform to the judgment of public opinion. For example, when economists advocate the maintenance of full employment or of price stability, their recommendations carry weight, because their implied judgment on equity coincides with that of public opinion. Nevertheless, the economist cannot disclaim responsibility for having made a value judgment on the ground that he was only interpreting the preferences of society as a whole. For to begin with, in so arguing he would make the implicit value judgment that the majority opinion fully represents and should determine society's preferences. Secondly, as Arrow has shown, society's preferences may be inconsistent and contradictory; and in such cases they can certainly not serve as a guide for the economist to follow. Thirdly, there probably exist wide areas of choice where a judgment must be made but where the majority of people are unable to make a judgment because they are ill-equipped for it.

For all these reasons, the economist must make his own judgment and assume full responsibility for it. He may not be able to go against public opinion; but he must lead rather than interpret it. This, I am afraid, is a very commonplace conclusion to end with; but it is, I believe, the only conclusion to be drawn from the current controversy on welfare economics.

C

PRACTICAL WELFARE ECONOMICS

Chapter 11

SOME CONSEQUENCES OF THE HABIT OF JUDGING QUALITY BY PRICE[1]

1944

The economic theory of consumers' choice is based on the assumption that the consumer knows what he buys. He is presumed to be an expert buyer who can appraise the quality of the various goods offered for sale and chooses between them by contrasting, one against the other, the price and quality of each good. This assumption was probably a reasonable one in the early days of industrial capitalism when modern economic theory began. The range of consumers' goods was limited and confined to staple commodities; and housekeeping was a skilled craft requiring and imparting a thorough knowledge of its tools and raw materials. It was natural for the average housewife to be an expert in the markets where she did her shopping.

Today, the consumer is no longer an expert shopper. The rise in the standard of living has greatly expanded the range and variety of consumers' goods and increased the share of complex technical commodities in the consumer's budget. Housekeeping has been rendered simple by complicated machinery replacing the humble household implements of old, and processed foodstuffs and other ready-made articles taking the place of staple foodstuffs and materials. As a result of these changes the average consumer of today has become a layman not only when it comes to buying a motor-car or a wireless set but also with respect to prime necessities and household implements. Few of us can appraise the qualities of an electric iron or toothpaste, and the frequent introduction of new models and improvements prevents us from relying on

[1] Based on a Paper read before the Marshall Society at Cambridge on March 2, 1945.

N

experience. Since the discovery of vitamins we dare not rely entirely on our palate even for judging the quality of food. To make matters worse, the consumer's bewilderment is artificially fostered by the partiality of advertisers for technical terms, for complicated names of chemical ingredients, and for impressive descriptions of awe-inspiring manufacturing processes, about whose exact purpose the consumer is usually left in the dark. More and more, therefore, the consumer of today has to judge quality by indices of quality. The size of a firm, its age, even its financial success are often regarded as indices of the quality of its produce. Hence the importance producers attach to goodwill and trade marks, hence the much advertised claims of some of them to being the biggest or oldest firm in their trade.

Another important index of quality is price. Economists are wont to minimize the importance of this factor, fearing the havoc it may wreak with the whole theory of choice. But 'mass observation' of one's friends and their wives shows that more often than not people judge quality by price. The word 'cheap' usually means inferior quality nowadays; and in the United States 'expensive' is in the process of losing its original meaning and becoming a synonym for superior quality. Worse still, one of the largest American breweries uses the advertising slogan: 'Michelob, America's highest-priced beer!'

The habit of judging quality by price, however, is not necessarily irrational. It merely implies a belief that price is determined by the competitive interplay of the rational forces of supply and demand; and this belief may be either true or false. It is true and perfectly justified when the majority of buyers are experts and know what they buy. In such a case differences in price can be trusted to reflect differences in quality as appraised by experts. It is perfectly rational, therefore, for a layman to judge quality by price when he wants to buy something in an experts' market. He can assume that the prices facing him are what they are because others found them reasonable and justified; and these others, unlike him, are expert buyers.

In a layman's market, however, it is not rational to judge quality by price. I have just argued before that laymen tend increasingly to rely on indices, often meaningless indices, for appraising quality. When they do this, and to the extent that they do this, their opinion ceases to be trustworthy. But relative prices only express the average buyer's opinion of the relative worth of alternative offers. Hence, when the average buyer's opinion ceases to be trustworthy, relative prices also cease to be trustworthy indices of quality.

The situation becomes paradoxical when price is the index by which the average buyer judges quality. In a market where this happens price ceases to be governed by competition and becomes instead an instrument wherewith the seller can influence his customers' opinions of the quality of his wares. A commodity offered at a lower price than competing commodities will be both more attractive to the consumer on account of its greater cheapness and less attractive on account of its suspected inferior quality. If all consumers would judge quality by price alone, these two factors would counterbalance each other exactly and price competition would become impossible. Such extreme cases may not occur very often; nevertheless, the fact that a price reduction is so double-edged a weapon is probably the main reason why producers today are so reluctant to lower price and prefer to compete by improving the quality of their produce, by offering special bonuses, credit facilities or similar attractions, and by advertising all these things.

When it occurs, price competition usually takes the form of the seller trying to introduce into the buyer's consciousness two distinct prices in connection with each commodity. One of them is the price to be paid for the commodity, the other is the price which is to indicate its worth. The sale of 'Fifty Shilling Clothes' at thirty-five shillings before the war, or of 'dollar watches' at eighty-nine cents in America, are examples of this practice. Further examples are the granting of special discounts; and special sales at reduced prices, where both the old and the new reduced price are marked on the price tag and the consumer judges the cheapness of the bargain by the difference between the two prices.

In a certain sense we always attribute two prices to every commodity. We think of a commodity's traditional past price as its 'normal' or 'fair' price, which denotes its worth. We contrast this price with the commodity's actual price whenever the two happen to be different. Only when the two prices differ from each other are we conscious of a commodity being cheap or expensive. Price competition, therefore, operates in markets of staple commodities, whose past price is likely to be known to the buyer.

The situation is different in markets where new models or new brands are frequently introduced. A new commodity has no traditional price, no past reputation. Its quality, therefore, is likely to be appraised partly or wholly on the basis of its present price. To take an example, imagine an enterprising businessman who wants to enter, say, the fountain pen industry. Assume that he can make pens as good and as good-looking at those currently sold at and around thirty shillings. Assume further that he estimates his costs and his elasticity of demand to be such that his optimum price would be fifteen shillings. The question is, should he start selling his fountain pens at fifteen shillings? If he did, without further ado, his pens would be regarded as equivalent in quality to other pens sold at around fifteen shillings and would compete with these only. Its superiority may assert itself in the long run; but even then it is doubtful if it would ever compete with and be considered equal to thirty shilling fountain pens. Hence, if he wants to compete with these pens, he must adopt some other policy.

He might try to persuade the public by advertising that his fountain pens are as good in quality as those presently sold at twice their price. But such an advertising campaign may be forbidding in cost and may not even achieve its aim. The simplest and most economical way to convince the consuming public that a new commodity is equal in quality to its already established competitors is to sell it at the same price at which they are being sold. The best thing, therefore, that our businessman can do is to sell his pens at thirty shillings each and make them more shiny, more streamlined, or more complicated, than are competing thirty shilling pens.

Once his pen has become known and its reputation firmly established, he will be able to increase his sales by lowering price. But at that stage this may no longer be his most profitable behaviour. For by then he will have established a faithful *clientèle*, which would continue buying his pens even at their actual price. By lowering price, therefore, he would reduce his income from this section of his market. He can avoid this loss of income by continuing to sell his old pen at its old price and introducing a new additional model at a lower price. Alternatively, he may lower the price of his old model and introduce the new model at the old price. He will adopt one of these two policies whenever the cost of producing and marketing several models is less than the loss of income that would result from lowering the price of a single model. Experience shows that this must very often be the case.

The above argument holds good not only about new entrants to an industry but also about already established firms. They, too, if they think that their actual price is above the optimum, may find it more profitable to introduce an additional model at a cheaper price than to lower the price of their original model. Similarly, if their old price is below what they believe to be the optimum, they are likely to find it profitable either to introduce a new, more expensive, model or to raise the price of the old model and introduce a new model at the lower price. The different models cater to the needs of different income groups and their number depends on the distribution of incomes and the differential cost of producing and marketing more instead of fewer models. The distribution of incomes determines the range of prices, the cost of producing and marketing limits the number of models within a given price range.

The different models will seldom be completely identical in quality. They could be, if people judged quality entirely by price. But as a rule price is only one of the factors that determine the consumer's judgment; and accordingly the more expensive models will not only *look* different in order to fool the public, often they will also *be* different (and better) than their cheaper variants. Nevertheless, it seems reasonable to speak of price discrimination whenever differences in price are out of proportion to differences in quality. We shall say, therefore, that a producer practices price discrimination if he offers similar goods at different prices and with different percentage profit margins. A producer will be said to charge discriminatory prices if he adds, say, a 40 per cent mark-up to the cost of his better quality model and only 25 per cent to the cost of its cheaper variant.

The offer by the same producer of several variants of his produce need not necessarily entail price discrimination. In an expert's market product differentiation may even be a form of increasing competition. Imagine as an example two dress designers, one of which, say Hunter, designs sports dresses and costumes, and the other, say Jaguar, specializes on more feminine styles. They cater for different needs, different tastes, and do not compete very much one with another. But assume next that they want to enlarge their markets and decide to do this by encroaching each upon the other's field. The simplest way of doing this is for both of them to enlarge the range of their models. To retain their old customers both of them will continue making their old styles; but in addition they will also design additional styles calculated to encroach upon the other's preserve. The net result will be that both will cover the entire range of different styles, they will become more competitive with each other, and, if oligopolistic elements do not complicate the picture, the profit margins of both of them will be reduced.

The argument is exactly the same when the two competitors cater, not for different tastes, but for different income groups. Assume that A. & B. Modes and Jaguar decide to encroach one upon the other's field; the first by starting a new *de-luxe* department; the second, by launching low-priced popular models. If the buyers are experts, as women usually are in matters of dress, the result will be increased competition and a fall in both producers' profit margins. The percentage profit margins on models of different quality will be the same, unless there are special factors present making for price discrimination. One, and perhaps the most important cause of price discrimination we have contracted out by assumption: the inexpertness of buyers and their habit of judging quality by price. But there are also other reasons for price discrimination. One of them is Harrod's law of diminishing price elasticity. Well-to-do people can afford to be more casual and careless in their purchases than the poor; and producers can exploit this fact by charging higher percentage mark-ups on goods and services destined for the rich. Another basis for price discrimination is the premium some people put on certain goods and services merely for the sake of their expensiveness. A person may know that the more expensive model is no better than the cheaper one and yet prefer it for the mere fact that it is more expensive. He may want his friends and neighbours to know that he can afford spending all that money, or he may feel that his prestige and social position require that he should always buy the most expensive of everything. This is not quite the same thing as judging quality by price; but, as will be shown below, it is a consequence of it.

The habit of judging quality by price, therefore, leads directly and indirectly to price discrimination. This is a form of monopoly and gives rise to monopoly profits; but, unlike other forms of monopoly, it need not increase the inequality of incomes, and may even mitigate them. Hence the use of price discrimination as a social policy by publicly-owned railways, public utilities, hospitals and charitable institutions. At the same time, however, price discrimination is often assailed on the ground that it is undemocratic. To clarify these issues we shall discuss the hypothetical limiting case of perfect price discrimination.

Imagine a society in which the consumer appraises every commodity entirely by its price. This will enable producers to sell at different prices and as different in quality commodities that are essentially identical. Assume further that in this hypothetical society there is a high degree of uniformity of opinion concerning the ideal pattern of life. In other words, assume that people are more or less agreed on the list of commodities and services whose possession and enjoyment they regard as necessary ingredients of a good life. Actually, such a uniformity of tastes comes about very easily when fashionable living is widely publicized by the Press and the cinema. Given these three conditions, the consumer's habit of judging quality by price, the offer of essentially identical commodities at different prices, and the uniformity of tastes, people with different incomes will buy the same commodities at different prices under the illusion that they are buying qualitatively different goods. The Joneses, with an income double that of the Smiths, will spend twice as much as do the Smiths on what is essentially the same home, the same motor-car, the same wireless set, and the same of all the other amenities of life. Thus, above a certain lower limit, people will buy themselves essentially the same standard of living by spending varying money incomes. According to our assumptions even the producers, whose profits are increased by price discrimination, will derive no benefit from it; for they, too, in their capacity of consumers, will be subject to the common delusion that higher price means better quality.[1] This situation, of course, driven to these extremes, is frankly unrealistic. But while I have carried the argument *ad absurdum* deliberately; to a limited extent the above picture is a fairly realistic description of modern capitalistic society. Its three pre-conditions mentioned above do obtain in modern society to some extent—in the United States even to a very large extent. Similarly, it is also true today that as a result of price discrimination inequalities in real income are far smaller than are inequalities of money income or expenditure.

But to return to our example of the limiting case, could such a state of affairs be described as egalitarian? From a purely materialistic point of view it certainly could. For, one might argue, what does it matter if the distribution of money incomes is unequal, so long as people's standards of living are essentially the same? Nevertheless, one must remember that economic power is distributed in accordance with the distribution of money income and money wealth; and people value power not only for the material advantages it might yield but for its own sake as well. Furthermore, when a society has acquired the habit of judging goods and services by their price, it will naturally tend to appraise also human beings by their price. This means that as inequalities in real income diminish, people attach greater and greater importance to money incomes and tend more and more to appraise their fellow beings by 'the money they are worth'. Thus, the levelling of inequalities in real income by price discrimination does not diminish inequalities in social status but only makes the latter more dependent on money income. On balance, therefore, there is not much to be said in favour of the habit of judging quality by price. It may level out inequalities of real income; but it does so only in the upper reaches of the income range, which, from the point of view of equity, are much less important than the lower part of the scale. In exchange, the judging of quality by price tends to lead to the rather obnoxious habit of judging human beings by false standards.

It is in this connection that another basis for price discrimination mentioned above, arises. We tend to appraise

---

[1] This type of price discrimination corresponds to what Professor Pigou in his *Economics of Welfare* has termed price discrimination of the second degree.

other people's income by their conspicuous expenditure. The layman may know nothing about the technical intricacies of motor-cars; but he usually knows a great deal about the prices of different makes and models and is wont to estimate the incomes of their owners on that basis. People may, therefore, come to regard spending and the buying of expensive goods as ways of raising and maintaining their social status. When they do this, commodities and services acquire a value in their eyes by the mere fact that they are expensive—provided that their expensiveness is conspicuous. Hence, when a society begins to appraise the value of goods *by* their price, it may end by valuing them *for* their price.

The above speculations throw light on the general problem of price discrimination. They show, first of all, that price discrimination mitigates inequalities of income. From this point of view it resembles progressive income taxation—especially when the discriminating firm is in public ownership. When it is in private ownership, the gains from discrimination swell private profits and thereby tend to undo the levelling effect of price discrimination. Secondly, our discussion also shows in what sense and under what circumstances price discrimination can be said to be undemocratic. We have seen that price discrimination comes about when the law of diminishing elasticity of demand obtains, when people judge quality by price, or when they value goods because of their expensiveness. In the last-mentioned case the consumer pays for the snob value or social distinction that conspicuous expenditure entails. When this factor is the main basis of price discrimination, the latter underlines and renders more conspicuous the social differentiation on which it is based. This is especially true when the producer, to increase his profits, places special stress on the social distinction conferred by the more expensive variant of his offer. In such cases people are apt to resent price discrimination as undemocratic.

Chapter 12

IGNORANCE AS A SOURCE
OF OLIGOPOLY POWER

1950

Before starting out to discuss ignorance as a source of oligopoly power, I should like to recall to you the meaning of oligopoly power. We think of competition as a force that tends to eliminate profits; and of monopoly or oligopoly power as something that restrains competition and thereby prevents the elimination of profits. Oligopoly power, therefore, is the power to restrain competition. Professor Chamberlin has shown that we must distinguish two kinds of restraints on competition. One of these is the obstacles of entry, which keep profits from attracting newcomers to a market and so prevent the elimination of profits by the additional competition of these newcomers. The other kind of restraint on competition is that imposed on the market behaviour of established firms, which enables them to raise prices higher relatively to costs than they could in the absence of such restraints.

Both types of restraints may result from natural circumstances or be imposed by the deliberate action of a group of firms acting in collusion. When we talk about institutional or sociological causes of oligopoly, we have in mind factors that constitute natural restraints on competition or facilitate collusion to impose artificial restraints. In particular, a given factor may create natural obstacles to entry, natural restraints on competition among established firms; and it may facilitate collusion for deliberately imposing either or both types of restraints.

Technological economies of scale, for example, constitute a natural obstacle to entry; and they also facilitate collusion by keeping the number of competitors small. Buyers' ignorance and sales techniques catering to buyers' ignorance are perhaps an even more important source of oligopoly power. They, too, give rise to natural obstacles to entry; they, too, facilitate collusion by keeping the number of competitors small; and in addition they also impose natural restraints on competition among established competitors.

Marshall and his contemporaries knew that the degree of competition depended on the buyers' information; but they believed, falsely I think, that the buyers' information in turn depended on the organization of the market. They thought that buyers' information and competition were perfect in the international commodity exchanges, because these markets happened to be highly organized. This view explains their optimism about the future of competition. They expected buyers' information, and with it competition, to increase as a result of the improvement of the technical means of communication and market organization.

Today, looking back on historical developments, it would seem that this view was wrong. In fact, I should say that the very opposite of Marshall's view is correct. I should regard the buyer's information as cause and the market's organization as effect; and I believe that the market's perfection depends on the buyer's expertness. For it is only the expert buyer who insists on comparing rival products before every purchase; and it is only his insistence on making comparisons that forces the seller—or rather makes it profitable for him—to make his product easily comparable to competing products. Hence, the geographical concentration of the expert's market and the grading and standardization of products in such a market should not be considered data, as Marshall did. They are the result of a deliberate effort on the part of producers; and I believe that such an effort will only be made in the expert's market, in response to the expert buyer's demand for easy comparability.

On this view, of course, which regards market organization and the standardization or differentiation of products as variables that depend on the buyers' information, one cannot share Marshall's optimism about the future. The expert buyer has always been an exception; and the consumer is not only an inexpert buyer but the increasing complexity of consumers' goods is constantly increasing his ignorance.

But how and in what sense does the buyer's ignorance

restrain competition? We know that the expertness of buyers leads to standardization, which implies that when the buyers are inexpert, the inducement to standardize is absent. We can even go farther than this. It can be shown that in the ignorant market every producer finds it profitable to differentiate his product, not indeed in any objective sense of the word, but by playing on the buyer's ignorance and creating the impression in one way or another that his product is different from competing products. Such differentiation lowers demand elasticities and makes higher profit margins possible; but this, while it lowers competition, is probably a very minor factor, which can hardly be called a competitive restraint. For a discussion of further restraints, however, we must first ask ourselves how exactly the ignorant buyer behaves.

An ignorant buyer is a person who is unable to judge the quality of the products he buys by their intrinsic merit. Unable to appraise products by objective standards, he is forced to base his judgment on indices of quality, such as the price of products and the size, long-standing and general reputation of the producing firm. Moreover, aware of the shaky basis and insufficiency of his judgment, the ignorant buyer dare not rely on his judgment alone and falls prey to the emotional suggestion of advertising.

That this type of consumer behaviour is important in many markets needs no proof. But how does it give rise to oligopoly power? It is apparent to begin with that the ignorant buyer's inability to appraise the quality of goods on their own merits deprives the producer of the inducement to engage in quality competition. For it is pointless to offer improved quality to customers who cannot distinguish good quality from bad. Similarly, the ignorant buyer's habit of judging quality by price weakens also price competition. For the offer of a lower price will largely defeat its purpose in markets where a low price is regarded as a sign of inferior quality. In such markets a price change will lead few buyers to transfer their custom from one producer to another. Hence, the price elasticity of demand will be low in such markets. It may be almost as low as it would be if collusion among rival producers had suspended price competition among them.

Needless to say, consumers' ignorance is never absolute; and they never judge quality by price alone. Accordingly, quality and price competition are limited rather than totally absent in the ignorant market; but such limitation may be substantial and give rise to very high profit margins.

When quality and price competition are limited, other forms of competition tend to be intensified. Hence the great importance of advertising and of new models and eye-catching features in the uninformed market. These forms of competition, however, can never replace price and quality competition fully; and the lowering of price and quality competition lowers competition in general. Moreover, since advertising and other such competitive weapons are obviously wasteful and socially undesirable, their preponderance in modern society has considerably weakened people's belief in the usefulness of competition. Competition by such methods may be no easier to limit by collusion than price and quality competition; but public opinion is certain to be less opposed to collusion in restraint of such forms of competition.

The limitations on price and quality competition in the un-informed market are what may be called the natural restraints on competition among established competitors. But the main manifestations of oligopoly power are restraints on potential competition from newcomers. Such restraints are due in the uninformed market to the importance of advertising, service and goodwill.

I need not enlarge here on the fact that the importance and efficacy of advertising increases with the market's ignorance. But the importance of advertising would not, by itself, dis-criminate against newcomers if it were not for the fact that advertising seems to yield increasing returns to scale. This means that as far as the effectiveness of advertising is con-cerned, the large firm has an advantage over the small firm, and the new firm must operate on a large scale from the outset if it is to compete on equal terms with established competitors. In other words, the need for advertising in the uninformed market creates the same protection for established firms and the same obstacles to the entry of new firms as the existence of technological economies of scale.

A further and very similar obstacle to entry in the ignorant market is due to the importance that the buyer of durable goods attaches to the provision of repair and maintenance services by the producer from whom he buys. The need for such services is created, of course, by the technical complexity of durable goods. But the consumer's insistence that such services be provided and guaranteed by the producers themselves is to a large extent due to consumers' ignorance. For the ignorant buyer knows more about the nature, availability, and quality of the services his car and appliances need than he knows about the quality of these products themselves; and he often believes, and is led to believe, that each brand of product requires special service. He wants an expert's assurance that adequate repair service for the product he buys will be available; and he believes that the best assurance he can get is the producer's guarantee to provide such services himself. Hence the consumer's preference for the products of manufacturers who can offer him repair and maintenance service as well. But the provision of services, just like advertising, yields increasing returns to scale; which means that the importance the uninformed consumer attaches to them creates the same advantages for the large and obstacles for the new firm as the importance of advertising and the technological economies of scale. It is worth mentioning in this connection that the marketing difficulties encountered in this country both by Kaiser-Frazer and by the British motor-car manufacturers have stemmed mainly from this source.

But by far the most important obstacle to entering the uninformed market is the ignorant buyer's habit of judging products by the size, age and reputation of the manufacturing firm—in short, by the goodwill of the firm. Given his inability to appraise goods on their own merit, this may be the most rational thing that the buyer can do; but it gives a very important advantage to the large firm over the small and to the established producer over the unknown newcomer. The more ignorant are the buyers and the more their ignorance forces them to rely on the producer's goodwill for judging the quality of his products, the more important becomes this type of discrimination.

The established firm's advantage over newcomers is due to the mere fact that it is already established and that therefore its name is known and it has established trade connections and an established group of customers. The importance of this advantage is measured by the high price that is sometimes asked and paid for the mere use of a name or trade-mark.

In fact, the price for which established goodwill is bought and sold may be regarded as a measure of the value of oligopoly power that is due to buyers' ignorance.

A new firm, of course, need not buy an established goodwill; it can always create a new one. A new name and a new reputation can be built up from scratch; but in the uninformed market this may take a major advertising campaign. In either case, therefore, a newcomer must pay for his goodwill. This payment represents a kind of entrance fee to the ignorant buyers' market; and the existence of this entrance fee protects the oligopoly profits of established firms.

Manufacturers are often aware of the fact that the security of their oligopoly position depends on and increases with the ignorance of their customers. At least they often pursue an advertising policy that seems deliberately aimed at impressing the consumer with his own ignorance. Hence the stress in some advertisements on the technical or chemical complexity of products. Hence the emphasis on the need for costly research and elaborate testing equipment for maintaining high standards of quality. All such advertising carries the suggestion that the consumer, a mere layman, would be unwise to judge quality unaided, by mere inspection, and should rely instead on the guarantees offered by the reputation of established manufacturers. The same idea is expressed more succinctly in the advertisements that enjoin the consumer to buy only the products of reputable firms or to buy only nationally advertised goods.

To sum up the above argument, consumers' ignorance creates oligopoly power and oligopoly profits in three ways: it limits price and quality competition among established firms, it protects these firms from the potential competition of newcomers by setting a high entrance fee to their market, and it facilitates collusion by limiting the number of established firms. When one recalls that the decline of price competition and the increasing cost of goodwill are among the main trends in recent economic development, one realizes how important a source of oligopoly consumers' ignorance is. In fact, one may wonder why this factor has received so little attention in the past. One probable reason is that very little can be done about it. The consumer's ignorance is not something that he need be ashamed of. To a very large extent it is the inevitable result of our highly technical civilization. Another reason is that very often we think of the producer's profit not as the result of his exploiting the ignorance of his customers but as the well-earned remuneration of his expertness. For example, if I buy a painting in an art gallery, the price I pay is bound to be very much higher than the price received by the painter. Out of the difference come the gallery's profits; and as an economist I am trying to explain these profits. Should I regard them as the gallery's fee for having made an expert appraisal of the painting; or should I say that the gallery is exploiting my lack of artistic judgment, which prevents my going directly to the painter in Greenwich Village for fear of making a fool of myself and a financial blunder in addition?

The first explanation is undoubtedly more attractive; but there is one trouble with it. How do I know that the gallery has exercised expert judgment and has exercised it for my benefit? If I think so mainly because it has an imposing shop front and thick carpets, then the second explanation is likely to be more correct—and it certainly is the more honest one.

Chapter 13

WHAT PRICE ECONOMIC PROGRESS?[1]

1959

The optimistic philosophers of the eighteenth and nineteenth centuries expected economic progress to accomplish many wonderful things. It was going to bring about 'the greatest possible abundance of objects suitable to our enjoyment, and the greatest liberty to profit by them';[2] it was expected to free man increasingly from daily toil and thus to provide him with more time to cultivate his mind. In short, they hoped that progress would turn more and more people into philosophers in their own image, engaged in the leisurely and philosophical contemplation of the world and its wonders.

In a material sense, and measured in terms of output per man-hour or income per head, economic progress in the West has achieved or surpassed these men's wildest hopes. The consequent rise in our standard of living is a genuine and substantial gain; but the potentialities it offers we certainly employ very differently from the way they envisaged. What was wrong with their vision; or, to turn the question around, what is wrong with us that we do not measure up to their hopes? In the following pages we shall give a partial answer to this question and show that economic progress itself influences and changes man's aspirations. We shall argue that economic progress in our society has wrought cultural and social changes that divert time and energy from intellectual pursuits and 'idle' speculation, lower the prestige of learning, and diminish the availability of channels for intellectual discussion and the dissemination of new ideas. These and some related consequences

---

[1] I wish to express my gratitude to Mrs Marjorie Fisk Lowenthal for many helpful suggestions and criticisms.
[2] Mercier de la Rivière in *L'Ordre Naturel et Essentiel des Sociétés Politiques* (1767), quoted and translated by J. B. Bury, *The Idea of Progress*.

are part of the price we pay for economic progress in our society.

From a purely materialistic point of view, the price of economic progress is the cost of the resources invested in plant, equipment, scientific research, training, and whatever else contributes to expanding and improving productive capacity. These are direct and easily quantifiable costs. The undesirable social and cultural effects of progress are costs additional to these, indirect, intangible, less easily quantifiable, but no less real.

Many of these social and cultural effects are identical with those features of modern American life and society that have for some time occupied the attention of sociologists and social psychologists in this country. In discussing these effects therefore, we shall be dealing with well-known and much discussed phenomena; but we hope to offer something new by tracing them back to economic progress as one of their causes.

The people most aware of the existence of a causal relation between economic progress and certain cultural features of modern society are perhaps those European intellectuals to whom economic progress means Americanization and who fear that Americanization in the economic sphere would bring with it some of those elements of American culture and civilization that they dislike. America to them means not only a high standard of living but also excessive conformity, a hectic life, an atmosphere unfavourable to intellectual and cultural pursuits; and they feel in a vague way that one cannot have one side of the American coin without also having the other. We propose to show that these fears are indeed justified to some extent and, to the extent that they are justified, they imply that these undesirable cultural elements are characteristic, not so much of America, as of the advanced economy. They are the price of economic progress.

It is true, of course, that special circumstances—national characteristics—have been at work in America favouring economic progress; and that these, being truly national characteristics, would not follow in the wake of economic development elsewhere. The best known of these national characteristics is puritanism, whose origins and significance for capitalist development are too well known to be repeated here. Another one worth mentioning is the American habit of expressing all values in terms of money, which may first have developed in those early immigrants who came here solely for economic gain. Many of these, finding the work hard and the life devoid of many of their accustomed social and cultural amenities, settled or planned to settle down, not to creating a satisfactory mode of life but merely to a temporary period of hard work and frugal living. During this period they hoped to amass a fortune to be enjoyed later, after their return to the home country and in its accustomed social and cultural environment. Such separation or planned separation of the years of earning (work) from the years of spending (leisure) was highly conducive to making all valuations in terms of money; and once this habit was acquired, it rendered the individual's economic striving more single-minded, different people's sets of values more alike, and the community's total economic activity more uniform—all of which is conducive to fast economic progress. These, however, are conditions of economic progress peculiar to the United States and mentioned here only in passing. Our main concern, to which we now turn, will be the consequences likely to result from economic progress wherever it occurs.

Two features of the advanced economy have important cultural and social implications. One is the high cost of labour, the other large-scale organization and extreme specialization.

THE IMPLICATIONS OF
THE HIGH COST OF LABOUR

Economic progress consists mainly in the rising productivity of labour and consequent growth of national income. Market forces in our economy cause the earnings of labour to rise more or less in proportion with its productivity; and the consequent rise in labour's standard of living is among the main achievements of economic progress. But a rise in labour's earnings is, from another point of view, a rise in its cost. Parallel rises in labour cost and labour productivity have mutually offsetting effects on costs of production; and this is what we observe when we look at the economy taken as a whole. When one looks closer, however, one becomes aware of differences in the rate at which productivity rises in different industries and fields of activity, and also of differences in the rate at which earnings rise in different occupations. The two sets of differences do not always run parallel: now the rise in productivity, now the rise in earnings prevails, causing costs of production to fall in some fields and to rise in others. The resulting distortion in the structure of costs, prices, earnings and profitabilities is a normal manifestation of economic life; but it has some undesirable cultural consequences often overlooked. These appear most often in industries and fields of activity whose productivity lags behind, which are generally the ones that suffer the growing pains of the economy.

For the laggard sectors of the economy are usually in competition with the more progressive ones; and it is the pressure of this competition that causes the trouble. If they compete with the more progressive industries mainly in the labour market, they face rising costs and are forced to raise prices; if they compete mainly in the product market, they experience lower earnings and are forced to pay lower wages; if they compete in both labour and product markets, their profits diminish, which puts them under pressure to raise their productivity. Each of these three cases has important cultural implications.

THE SHIFT IN RELATIVE PRICES

Every tourist is aware of differences in relative prices that economic development brings about, and each has his pet grievance concerning the high American price of some commodity that is more accessible in less developed countries. But the commodities whose prices have been raised the most by the rising cost of labour are leisure and personal services. For the price of leisure, being the income sacrificed in taking one's leisure, *is* the cost of labour looked at from the seller's (worker's) point of view,[1] so it necessarily rises with the cost of labour. As to personal services, such as domestic service, household repairs, hairdressers' services, etc., their prices have

[1] Strictly speaking, this is not entirely true, because the price of leisure is the income forgone in taking one's leisure *less* the income tax that would have been levied on that income; and the income tax is a secularly increasing proportion of income. The price of leisure therefore has been rising somewhat more slowly than the price of labour and probably a little more slowly also than the price of personal services.

risen in (or almost in) proportion with the cost of labour, because productivity in rendering these services has risen hardly or not at all. One would expect the rise in these prices (relative to the prices of material goods) to have induced the consuming public to buy less leisure and fewer personal services, except to the extent that the rise in real incomes enables people to buy more of everything, including leisure and personal services.[1]

What is the evidence? When one contrasts the regular, routinized, and contractually regulated employment of labour in the developed economies against the seasonal, intermittent and patriarchically controlled farm labour with its many forms of disguised unemployment in the under-developed countries, then it seems obvious that the former have more work and less leisure than the latter. The major increase in work and diminution in leisure, however, seems to have occurred during the early stages of industrialization. More recently, the dominant force would seem to be the shortening of the working week. In the United States, for example, in manufacturing—the only sector with a long and comparable statistical record—the working week has become 20 per cent shorter over half a century, having declined from 51 hours in 1909 to 40½ hours in 1956.[2] If we assume the same shortening of the working week in all sectors of the economy, this means a reduction of sixteen million man-years in the amount of work performed by the 1956 labour force of sixty-four million.

This trend, let it be noted, need not indicate an increased *desire* for leisure. For one thing, fifty years ago, when unions were in their infancy, the length of the working week may

[1] At first sight, the crucial question seems to be whether incomes have risen more or less than the price of leisure and personal services; but on second thought this turns out to be unimportant. For even if incomes had risen in proportion with the prices of these commodities, people might still buy less of them than before, depending on the prices of other commodities. Hence, information on price and income changes alone tells us little or nothing concerning the change in people's expenditure pattern. This has to be examined directly.

[2] The statistical series used is the BLS monthly data on average weekly hours of work, published in the *Monthly Labour Review* and carried back to 1909 in the *Historical Statistics of the United States* (series D 118). Using this series as representative of all employment may underestimate the shortening of the working week, since labour in commerce and the service industries was organized much later than manufacturing, and union organization has probably given the main impetus to the reduction in hours of work.

have been the result more of employers' demands than of workers' wishes. For another, there is some evidence that the present short working week is not entirely to the workers' liking. It is a matter of union strategy to demand, not higher wages, but shorter hours with the same take-home pay, thus asking for higher wages only by implication; and there are signs of increasing dissatisfaction with this policy on the part of workers, many of whom would prefer to work longer hours for higher pay.[1]

But whether or not it is wanted, the shorter working week is here. The question is whether it implies correspondingly more leisure; and there are reasons for thinking that it does not. To begin with, the percentage of married women working has risen, from 5 ½ per cent in 1900 to 30.2 per cent in 1956— their total number amounting in 1956 to 12,278,000. This means that today's labour force contains over ten million (18 per cent) more people that it would if the proportion of married women working had remained what it was in 1900.[2] On this count therefore the amount of work performed has increased by ten million man-years.

Secondly, the number of workers who hold more than one job is also increasing. In 1956, 6.9 per cent of employed men and 5.5 per cent of the entire labour force had more than one job; this is double the percentage of multiple job holders in 1943, the earliest date for which these data are available. The number of multiple job holders in 1956 was over three and a half million; and although on their second jobs they worked only a twelve-hour week on the average, even so they added about one million (full-time) man-years to the amount of work performed.[3]

These two factors already offset two-thirds of the gain in

---

[1] Witness the increase in multiple job holdings cited below, and the fact that multiple job holding is especially prevalent in industries with a very short working week. On this latter, see Harvey Swados, 'Less Work—Less Leisure, Akron tests the Six-Hour Day', *The Nation*, February 22, 1958.

[2] A part of this increase, however, may reflect merely the lower age at which women get married nowadays. The data are from Bureau of the Census, *Current Population Reports*, Series P-50 No. 73, and the *Statistical Abstract of the United States*. It would have been more appropriate to use the proportion in the labour force of 'married women with husband present'; but this category does not go back to the beginning of the century.

[3] Cf. US Bureau of the Census: *Current Population Reports, Labor Force*, Series P-50 No. 30 and 80.

leisure due to the shorter working week; and they are not the only ones. Until recently, the continuing shift of labour from farming into the service industries was probably another factor, although by today, the diversification of agriculture has greatly reduced the seasonal fluctuations and increased the total amount of the work performed by farmers and farm-workers.[1] The total amount of work performed may still have diminished and the amount of leisure available increased in the American economy over the last half a century but not by much, certainly by much less than the shortening of the working week would suggest.

More important perhaps has been the change in the distribution of leisure among social classes and income groups, and the change in people's *use* of leisure. Statistics of the length of the working week by occupation suggest that the main beneficiaries of the shorter working week are the manual and lesser clerical workers; it is doubtful if businessmen, managers, officials and professional people have benefited at all.[2] And these latter groups are virtually certain to have lost in terms of leisure time if the effect of the rising cost of personal services is also taken into account.

We have mentioned already that the higher relative price of personal services could be expected to discourage demand; and this expectation is fully borne out by the evidence. The number of (full- and part-time) domestic servants in the United States, while stable in absolute terms, has declined relatively, from 94.3 servants per 1,000 families in 1900 to 35.3 servants per 1,000 families in 1950. This means that in 1950, the number of domestic servants was more than three million smaller than it would have been had it retained the 1900 ratio to the number of families; and these figures understate the decline by about 10-20 per cent, because the definition of domestic servant used in 1950 is more inclusive than that used

[1] The proportion of the active population engaged in farming is declining in most developed countries. In the United States it has declined from 71.8 per cent in 1820 to 63.7 per cent in 1850, 37.5 per cent in 1900 and 11.6 per cent in 1950. Information on seasonal changes in the working week and on its length in different occupations is available for the United States in us Bureau of the Census, *Current Population Reports, Labor Force*, Series P-50 No. 72, 'Annual Report on the Labor Force 1956'; but unfortunately 1955 is the earliest year for which these data are available.
[2] Cf. the 'Annual Report on the Labor Force 1956' cited in the previous footnote.

in 1900.[1] Also, the amount of domestic service performed by domestic servants has further diminished because their working week has become shorter and because today (in all probability) a larger proportion of them work on a part-time basis.[2]

The significance of this decline is that it implies an increase in the amount of services people perform for themselves, since they achieve the saving on personal services largely at the cost of their own leisure. It is true that labour-saving innovations have greatly eased the burden of householding; and that families that in 1900 would have had servants, today have smaller houses. On the other hand, the introduction of automatic household appliances seems to have raised both standards of householding and the number of tasks performed within the household.[3] If we assume that the first two factors offset the shortening of the working week, the increase in the proportion of part-time household workers, and the higher standards and greater quantity of householding, then the three million reduction in the relative number of domestic servants quoted above becomes a rough measure of the additional householding people do for themselves. This would mean a three million man-years reduction in the amount of leisure,[4]

[1] Cf. George J. Stigler, *Domestic Servants in the United States 1900-1940* (NBER Occasional Paper No. 24); Census of Population 1940, Abba M. Edwards, *Comparative Occupation and Industry Statistics, 1940 and 1930*; and Census of Population 1950, vol. 2, Part II.

[2] The prevalence of part-time work among domestic servants is shown by the shortness of the average working week of full- *and* part-time domestic servants. This was 29.2 hours in 1956 (cf. 'Annual Report on the Labor Force 1956'); whereas full-time domestic servants are generally believed to work longer hours (by about one fifth. Cf. Stigler, *op. cit.*, p. 19) than production workers, whose average in 1956 was over 40 hours.

[3] E.g. the introduction of home freezers has encouraged the home preserving of food; the introduction of washing machines and ironers has encouraged home laundering and pressing. The latter's importance may be judged by the very slow rise of consumers' expenditure on commercial laundry services. In 1929, this equalled consumers' expenditure on dry cleaning and dyeing; by 1956, it was only half as great. (See the National Income numbers of the *Survey of Current Business*, Table 30.) Had it risen in proportion with expenditure on dry cleaning and dyeing—which it probably would have in the absence of home laundries and ironers—commercial laundries would now employ an additional 330,000 workers. Hence, on this count alone housewives perform an additional 330,000 man-years of housework—for home laundries and ironers can hardly be more labour-saving than the equipment used in commercial laundries.

[4] Needless to say, the three million people who did *not* go into domestic service do not have that much more leisure on this account, since they can be presumed to have gone into other occupations instead.

which one is tempted at first, either to add on to the eleven million man-years reduction due to the increased proportion of women working and greater prevalence of multiple job holding, or to distribute evenly over all households and express as a 2.1 hour per week reduction of leisure per household.[1] It would be misleading, however, either to add to a national total or to distribute evenly over all households this loss of leisure, which is suffered not by all families but only by those who formerly, with the relative price of domestic service lower, would have employed domestic servants. Distributed over this smaller group, which comprises the professional classes and others in the middle-income range, the loss of leisure per family becomes very much greater. At the same time, it also becomes apparent that people in the lower income groups, who would not have employed domestic help even at a lower relative price, have gained on balance, since they too have benefited by the increased productivity of modern household appliances.

Domestic service is not the only personal service whose price has been raised by the rising cost of labour. The same is also true of household repair services of all kinds; and the effect of the rise in their prices on the distribution of leisure is very similar. The great expansion of the industry that provides the tools for the do-it-yourself man and the greatly increased percentage of household paints sold to the non-professional painter amply demonstrate the increasing tendency for household repairs to be done by the householder himself.[2] Equally suggestive is the questionnaire survey referred to above, according to which the average American husband spends three hours per week as a home handyman, two hours as a garage mechanic, and three hours as a gardener. We have no corresponding estimates for earlier years with which to compare the above and establish the nature of the trend over time; but the main conclusions seem obvious enough. The higher price of house repair and maintenance has caused the professional

[1] This last figure is very close to the two hours a week that the average American husband spends in washing dishes and helping in the kitchen, according to a recent questionnaire survey by the Institute for Motivational Research (quoted in *This Week* magazine, March 30, 1958, pp. 12-13).
[2] Cf. the 'Summary of Information on the Do-It-Yourself Market' prepared by the US Department of Commerce and reprinted in E. Larrabee & R. Meyersohn, *Mass Leisure* (The Free Press, 1958, Glencoe, Ill.).

classes and middle-income groups to do by themselves work that in an earlier age they would have had done by others; and this means an equivalent reduction in their leisure time. People in the lower income groups on the other hand have probably always done their own household repair; and they are likely therefore to have gained in terms of leisure, since they benefit by the technical improvements that render this type of work easier and quicker.

Needless to add, some of the activities referred to here as encroachments on leisure are far from unpleasant and are regarded by many people as forms of leisure. Indeed, when increasing specialization renders most factory and office jobs increasingly monotonous, exchanging part of such a job for the greater challenge and variety of improving or embellishing one's home is bound to be attractive. But our concern here is with leisure time available for intellectual and cultural activities. However enjoyable do-it-yourself activities may be, they do divert time and energy from intellectual pursuits.

We conclude therefore that the rise in the relative cost of personal services has greatly contributed to the redistribution of leisure (or rather of the part of it available for intellectual pursuits) from professional and middle-income groups to the working classes.[1] Yet another factor that pulls in the same direction is the move of the middle-income groups to suburbia, since the time they spend in commuting also encroaches upon their leisure.

This trend towards 'leisure for the masses, toil for the classes' is welcome from the point of view of social justice; but it is not conducive to the further progress of society. Leisurely contemplation and 'idle' speculation seem to be necessary conditions of creative intellectual activity. The professional classes, being the best educated, are the best able to make intellectual use of their leisure; and this is attested by the fact

[1] Another group that has suffered from the higher cost and lesser availability of personal services is that of people who for one reason or another live alone. The most important among these are old people. Their spendable income out of pensions and savings is usually less than what they were used to in their younger days, they need more personal service than others on account of their age, and they—when widowed and living alone—have to pay for services that members of a family household perform free for each other. This is an important part of the 'problem of the aged'; and it is becoming more serious and intractable as the cost of labour—and with it the cost of personal services—rises.

that most of the political, cultural and technical progress of the past has been their achievement. A diminution in the amount of leisure available to them must therefore be regarded as undesirable from society's point of view. This judgment, however, does not necessarily imply that professional people are the step-children of economic progress in our society. For that is a matter which has to do with the distribution not of leisure but of income—a subject we shall take up in the next section. Here we are concerned solely with the availability and distribution of leisure; and if professional people obtain less leisure today than they used to, and devote less of it to intellectual pursuits, the reason need not be that they can afford less leisure than before, it may simply be that, facing a different structure of relative prices, this is the way they have chosen to allocate their expenditures and organize their lives.

We turn now to the changing *use* of leisure time. The high productivity and consequent high cost of labour have made people increasingly conscious of the fact that time is money; and this seems to have engendered the belief that time should be fully and efficiently utilized both in work and in leisure—although the efficient utilization of leisure is, of course, a contradiction in terms.

It is only natural that the pace of work should be speeded up and working time better utilized as the cost of labour rises; and there is every indication that this is what has happened in the United States, the country with the highest cost of labour. As to the pace of leisure and leisure activities, it is speeded up both directly, by the high cost of labour, and indirectly, through transference of the pace and habits of work. The high cost of labour renders the European coffeehouse, with its leisurely and often intellectual atmosphere, an unprofitable business proposition in the United States; and it puts pressure upon restaurants to speed up their turnover through quick service, large-scale operation, overcrowding, and other means of hurrying the customer. Indirectly, the habits and pace of work are carried over into leisure activities owing simply to man's inability to change at short notice his ingrained habits and accustomed pace. Hence the tendency to attend machines, such as TV, radio or movies, and let them set the pace; hence the preference for organized leisure, for doing things; and the attitude of regarding idle conversation and leisurely contemplation as a waste of time—even of leisure time.

Leisure, however, and personal services are merely extreme examples of goods whose relative prices have risen. Other services that have become relatively more expensive owing to the lagging productivity of the labour rendering them are urban public transportation, postal and telegraphic communication, and most of the administrative services rendered by Government. Whether the scope for raising labour productivity in these fields is genuinely limited, or whether the inducement to raise productivity is lacking in the public domain, is irrelevant from our point of view. Whatever the reason, these services have become dearer compared to other goods; and this fact, combined with the public's reluctance to spend more on them, has occasionally led to the reduction in their supply or worsening of their quality. Hence the paradox that sometimes the richest countries seem the least able to afford these services.[1]

The Shift in Relative Earnings

The second category of effects of the high and rising cost of labour is the change in relative earnings brought about by the uneven rate of progress in different industries and fields of activity. The main fields in which lagging productivity has caused relative earnings to fall are the learned professions. Their productivity can be increased relatively little; and their life is sufficiently different from that of other people for a fall in their relative earnings to have no short-run effect on the numbers entering the professions. Indeed, hand-in-hand with the fall in the relative earnings of teachers, academic people, civil servants, lawyers, etc., their relative numbers have increased—presumably owing to the lesser cost of acquiring the education needed to enter these professions.

Two sets of statistics show that economic progress lowers the earnings of professional people in relation to those of others. First of all, an international comparison of thirty-eight countries has shown a much greater disparity between the earnings of professional people and of manual workers in

---

[1] Cf. J. K. Galbraith, *The Affluent Society* (Houghton Mifflin, Boston, 1958), *passim* for additional reasons why demand for public services is relatively small in the United States.

underdeveloped than in developed countries.[1] For example, a senior natural scientist, the head of the national meteorological service, earns thirty times as much as an office messenger in India but only five and a half times as much in the United States. In the Western European countries, and in Canada, Australia and New Zealand, the ratio is close to the US ratio; in South America and Asia it is closer to though not quite as high as that for India.

Essentially the same picture is shown also by the statistics of the trend of earnings over time. The decline of the economic position of professional people and intellectuals in the United States is too well known to need comment here; but it is worth mentioning that this trend seems to extend to all the economically developed countries. For example in Canada, the income of professional people rose only one quarter as fast as the income of industrial workers over the period 1911-51.[2] The situation is very similar in Germany, where over the shorter period of 1936-55, the average income of the free professions rose by only half as much as the incomes of the rest of the economy.[3]

This is a sad state of affairs for the professional people themselves; but what is the significance of their declining economic position from society's point of view? Let us note first of all that professional people are among the few groups whose working week has not been reduced over time. On the contrary, under pressure of the fall in their incomes, many professional people have tried to increase or supplement their incomes by additional work. Also, they are among those hardest hit by the rising cost of personal services. Hence the redistribution of leisure already mentioned, with professional people suffering the most drastic curtailment of their free time—and they are the group the best able to use leisure time for intellectual and cultural activities. For many professional people have functions going beyond those that, in a narrow sense, they are paid for. These additional functions are often

[1] Cf. 'Salaries and Hours of Work in Government Service: An International Comparison', *International Labour Review*, vol. LXVIII (1953), No. 4-5.
[2] Cf. J. F. Haberer & F. L. W. McKim, 'The Economic Position of Canadian Scientists and Engineers', *The Canadian Mining and Metallurgical Bulletin*, October 1956, pp. 721-5.
[3] Cf. Gerhard Wolff, 'Der Anteil der freien Berufe am Sozialprodukt', *Das Geistige Kapital*, März 1956, pp. 34-6.

the most important and the most creative; and they can be so erratic, their nature and usefulness so unpredictable, that they cannot be contracted for but must be performed in what, by other people's standards, is considered leisure time.[1]

Secondly, the smaller share of professional people in the national income has diminished their share in consumers' demand and hence diminished the weight allotted to their tastes and preferences in the allocation of resources and the planning of production.[2] If we regard professional people as cultural leaders of our society, then their loss of influence over production decisions must be considered a loss to society. This loss of influence may have something to do with the decline, for example, of book publishing—a subject to which we shall return in the next section.

A third effect of the declining economic status of the professions is a corresponding decline in their prestige—and in the prestige of learning itself. This is especially so in the United States, with its tendency of expressing all values in terms of money and hence of valuing everything according to its price. The low price, then, that society puts on learning and the learned may have much to do with anti-intellectualism, with the neglect of basic research and basic science as against problem-oriented research; and perhaps also with the neglect of general education in favour of vocational training.

Furthermore, the decline in earnings and prestige may in the long run lower the quality and restrict the number of young people entering the professions. This again is a subject so much in the public eye at present as to need no further discussion here.

The Pressure to Mass Produce

Having dealt with some of the implications of the changes in relative prices and relative earnings, we proceed to discuss some consequences of the change in relative profitabilities.

Economic progress in our age is closely linked with mass production, because the lowering of costs usually depends on

[1] For a discussion of the inherent difficulties of paying scientists, in the form of grants or research contracts, for their most creative and original work, see Warren Weaver, 'The Encouragement of Science', *Scientific American*, September 1958, pp. 170-8.
[2] This was pointed out to us by Professor Lorie Tarshis of Stanford University.

economies of scale. At first sight there seems nothing wrong with this. Indeed, to bring within reach of the many what before was accessible only to the few is among the noblest achievements of economic progress. Very often, however, the advantages of mass production are obtained at the sacrifice of quality and variety.

In fact, the low cost of mass production often hinges on a restriction of variety and lowering of quality. In addition, the sale of many products cannot be raised significantly by price reduction alone, changes in quality may also be needed to make them appeal to a wider public and its less educated taste. Finally, and this is the main point, mass production does not remain confined to the fields that provide the greatest scope for it, competition imposes it in other fields too. When some firms in some fields engage in mass production at lower costs, they divert demand from and raise costs against competing firms in related fields; and the combination of falling demand and rising costs puts pressure on these other firms to adopt mass-production methods too. When such pressure stimulates technical advance, well and good; but in fields where the scope for technical improvements is limited, the pressure of dwindling profits merely lowers standards, restricts variety, and worsens quality. There are many examples of this; paramount among those involving cultural standards are the theatre and book publishing.

The first means of mass producing theatrical entertainment was the cinema; and it will serve to exemplify the effects also of the radio and television. The economics of the mass market are such that it is almost always more profitable to cater to the tastes of the unsophisticated majority than to those of the sophisticated minority, however saturated the former and unsatisfied the latter segment of the market may be.[1] Thus, the

[1] This is so, because the same artistic and literary ability needed to make sophisticated films is (or seems to the entrepreneur) appropriate also to the making of better-than-average unsophisticated films. A better-than-average film, however, is always expected to capture the entire market it is designed to cater to, however saturated this may be with average films. It follows that in a country like the United States, where the unsophisticated segment of the market is much larger than the sophisticated segment, any producer set to make a sophisticated film will be under pressure to compromise and produce instead a 'superior' unsophisticated film; and only a strong artistic conscience or a serious lack of capital will enable him to withstand such pressure. This explains why most serious films stem from small countries,

cinema, catering to a mass audience, provides entertainment designed to appeal to a large and hence unsophisticated public.

There remains, of course, the legitimate theatre to perform serious drama; but it, too, has suffered from the competition of the movies, the radio and television; and it has become less willing to perform its traditional function as a result. The decline of the theatre due to increased competition has been serious enough. From 1927-28 to 1952-53, the number of New York theatres open declined by 69 per cent, from 71 to 22, the number of road companies operating fell 55½ per cent, from 72 to 32 (there used to be 308 in 1900-04), that of stock companies fell 46 per cent, from 257 to 139. More serious, however, than the decline in the number of theatres open and companies operating was the 77 per cent decline in the number of plays produced, from 280 to 65 over the same period.[1] This implies an increase in the average run of a play; and indeed, there is independent evidence of a very great increase in the number and proportion of so-called long runs —plays that pass 500 performances.[2] Actors' Equity regards this as the one bright spot in their otherwise gloomy sky; but from the cultural point of view it is undesirable, because it implies that producers, facing a decline in demand and rise in costs, are maintaining profits by shunning the more controversial plays and concentrating on the production of the safer and more popular ones. Needless to say, our concern is not with the displacement of sophisticated comedy by musicals but with the decline of serious drama. After all, the theatre has for a long time been an important forum in which to present serious social, psychological and political problems for discussion and analysis by the intelligent public; and the narrowing of this forum must be considered a loss to society.

Book publishing presents very much the same picture. Here, increased competition comes from the fact that the growing importance of advertising—itself the result of the growing importance of mass production—has rendered radio and television highly profitable and magazines and periodicals less

where the smallness of the language area limits the market for unsophisticated films; whereas serious films, for which language is a lesser barrier, have, thanks to exports, a relatively large market.

[1] Cf. A. Hewitt, 'Five Short Years', *Equity*, Jan. 1954, pp. 5-13 and 21; and A. L. Bernheim, *The Business of the Theatre*, New York, 1932.

[2] Cf. *Equity, loc. cit.*

dependent on the consumers' dollar. The resulting expansion of radio and television programmes and the fall in magazine prices relative to book prices have lowered the demand and raised the costs faced by book publishers. Hence the complaint, frequently voiced in *Publishers' Weekly*, that publishing costs are rising faster than the price of books.[1] The result is that to yield a profit, a book has to sell many more copies today than it used to. According to Mr Leon E. Seltzer, director of the Stanford University Press, the break-even point (i.e. the number of copies that must be sold to repay expenses) has doubled over the last ten years. Similar statements have been made by Mr Leonard Woolf of the Hogarth Press in England, and by many others.[2]

The result is increased selectivity of an undesirable nature in the works chosen for publication. Under the pressure of declining profits, textbooks and potential best-sellers crowd out scientific and scholarly works, monographs, and anything that is new and unusual and therefore unlikely to appeal to the mass public. In short, the attempt to offset declining profits through larger sales introduces a conservative and anti-intellectual bias in book publishing just as the striving for longer runs downgrades the theatre.

This trend may be great enough to affect even the absolute number of books published. Statistics of the number of new titles and new editions published certainly suggest this; and while these statistics are generally viewed with suspicion, they show the same trend in so many of the advanced countries that they can hardly be ignored. The number of titles published has declined in practically all the advanced countries, except England, the Netherlands, and Russia. France reached the peak in the late 1880s, the United States, Germany, Japan, Denmark, etc., reached it just before World War I, although Germany and France topped their peak for a short moment in 1925 and the United States had reattained its 1910 peak by 1958. Before World War I, US books published exceeded the

---

[1] E.g. *Publisher's Weekly*, July 1, 1958, p. 70, summarizing a finding according to which average publishing costs rose 100 per cent over the period 1940-1957; whereas average book prices rose by only 60-70 per cent over the same period.
[2] Cf. Leonard Woolf, 'The Future of the Serious Writer', in *Books in a Changing World*, special number of *The Times Literary Supplement*, August 15, 1958, p. xviii.

P

number of British book titles, today the US figure is barely 60 per cent of the British; and it trails, as it always has, the Russian, Japanese, and German figures as well.[1]

Yet another example of this same anti-intellectual trend that is at least worth mentioning is the newspaper. It, too, is suffering from the increased competition of magazines, radio and television; it, too, is trying to maintain profits through increased circulation, and to increase circulation by appealing to a wider public. Here again, however, to appeal to a wider public means lowering intellectual standards, which in the case of the newspapers implies promoting to the front page crime, divorce cases and gossip, and leaving out an increasing proportion of serious political and foreign news.

THE IMPLICATIONS OF EXTREME SPECIALIZATION AND HIGH COMPLEXITY

So far we were concerned with some implications of the rising cost of labour; and we now propose to deal with a few of the consequences of the high degree of specialization and technical complexity that characterize the advanced economy.

The Political Implications

The political implications of extreme specialization are perhaps the best known and most obvious. Let us recall that democracy is rule by dilettantes—a dilettante government controlled by a dilettante Congress, itself controlled by a dilettante electorate; dilettantes not in a pejorative sense but in the sense of not being experts in the various fields in which they have to pass judgment. With increasing specialization, however, and with the increasing technical complexity of each field of specialization, dilettante rule becomes both more difficult and more dangerous—a trend that seems so obvious at the present time that we will not elaborate on it any further.

One aspect, though, may be worth mentioning. Increased specialization of knowledge tends to turn professional people

[1] Cf. *Publishers' Weekly* annual surveys, usually contained in the January 3rd issue; and the United Nations, *Statistical Yearbook for 1957*. The data refer to new titles and new editions of old titles. The scepticism with which publishers view these data is engendered partly by the difficulty and arbitrariness of defining a book and distinguishing it from a pamphlet, and partly by the difficulty of drawing the line that excludes official government papers and memoranda.

from intellectuals into technicians. This means that as each of them gets to know more and more about less and less, he becomes not only more of an authority in his own field but also more willing to accept the authority of others on matters outside his own field. In other words, specialization renders the professional classes not only a better tool of authority but also a more pliable one, and makes them abdicate to an increasing extent their traditional rôle of upholders of political liberties.

A Psychological Effect

Further well-known implications of mass production and extreme specialization are psychological; they often have been described by more competent observers, but we shall mention them here nevertheless, for completeness' sake. They have to do with man's increasing isolation, partly from his environment, and partly from his fellow human beings.

A rudimentary understanding of man's use and control of nature, of the nature and origin of the objects around him, and of the way in which different tasks are performed and divided among different people, seems a good in itself, perhaps even a psychological necessity. Not so long ago, most people acquired understanding by just looking around and exercising their natural curiosity. They knew the provenance of the foods, materials and tools they used daily; and the division of labour was simple enough to be explained in terms of the butcher, the baker, the candlestickmaker.

Today, in the age of push-button appliances, ready-mix foods, plastics, and synthetic fabrics, this is becoming increasingly difficult. We use many materials of whose provenance we know next to nothing; we are surrounded by household implements we know how to operate but whose working principles we ignore; and we are more and more at a loss when trying to answer the simplest questions of our children concerning the nature of the everyday objects around them. This applies not only to the atom but even to the shirts on our backs. Hence man's feeling today of the utter dependence of his everyday life on a complex technical and social organization about whose working, outside his own narrow sphere, he is largely in the dark; and this, too, contributes to his feeling of impotence in relation to organized society.

We are not competent to judge the psychological effects of this state of affairs; nor do we know the extent, if any, to which it is resulting in neuroses and other disorders. That it is felt to be an unsatisfactory state of affairs, however, is attested by some indirect evidence, especially the renewed interest in handicrafts. It is a striking fact that the United States, the very country where handicrafts have become the most obsolete and unprofitable, should also be the country that puts the greatest stress on the teaching of handicrafts in schools and where handicrafts as a hobby are the most popular. This is partly explained by the high cost of household repair already mentioned, which in some respects forces the household to become an increasingly self-sufficient Robinson Crusoe type economy; but another and possibly more important part of the explanation is man's need to compensate for his increasing remoteness from the material world around him. Let us hope that making one's own ashtrays, finishing one's own furniture, and doing one's own plumbing, painting and papering accomplish this. But even if they do, they do it at the cost of time—and a lot of time—being diverted from more intellectual pursuits. This is especially true of school, where pottery, weaving, glove-making, etc., divert time and energy not only from the humanities but probably also from the three Rs.

Another Psychological Effect

Let us now deal with another psychological effect of an advanced economy: man's increasing alienation from his fellow men. With the growing size of the economic unit, the average person no longer deals with his employer, his grocer, his banker; instead, he has dealings with firms that are forever growing larger and more impersonal, more bureaucratic and more rigid, and hence more inhuman and frightening. They are represented by employees whose very blandness and politeness render the organization they represent all the more remote and inaccessible. This situation, the frightening aspect of man's being surrounded by giant organizations, the frustration of there being no particular human being to be angry at or hold responsible for the occasional cruelty, rigidity and administrative inefficiency of these giant organizations—all this has been amply described and analysed by Erich Fromm and other members of the American neo-Freudian school of psychologists. Added to this is the fact that even the few human contacts remaining have been rendered less human and personal by the rising cost of labour and the increasing economy of its use. Our relations with the corner grocer, the elevator man, the waiters in our favourite restaurant and the family doctor used to be fairly close and friendly. Today, in the age of medical groups, of cafeterias and supermarkets, of vending machines and automatic elevators, and of various other forms of self-service, such human contacts have become fewer, shorter, and very much less personal. Even in factories, automation is thinning out the number of workers to such an extent as to create isolation.[1] If one adds to this the move to the suburbs and the decline of metropolitan public transportation, both of which force people to spend a large part of their time sitting alone in the gilded cage of their automobile, then one has a fairly complete picture of how, thanks to his rising standard of living, modern man is increasingly left alone— not, indeed, with his thoughts, but with his gadgets.

Now what does man do when he finds himself increasingly cut off from personal contact with his fellow man? He tries to establish closer contacts with woman. Here again, one finds the instinctive desire to compensate for the loss of human contacts outside the family by seeking earlier and stronger contacts within the family. As is well known, the median age of marriage is steadily declining in all the advanced countries. In this country, the median age of first marriage for men has declined from 26.1 years in 1890 to 22.7 years in 1955; for women it has declined from 22 to 20.2 years over the same period. Also, the median age of marriage is lower in the United States than in any of the Western European countries; although there, too, it is declining over time.

There are, of course, several reasons for early marriage in the United States. One is, probably, that being better off, Americans can afford to marry early. Another one may be the stricter sexual morality of the United States. It is very likely, however, that a further and important reason is the scarcity of human contacts and people's greater loneliness out-

[1] Cf. the short account in the December 2, 1958, *New York Times* of a seven-month investigation of conditions at the Renault plant at Billancourt by a group of psychiatrists. According to their report, 'Workers in factories where automation is well advanced are in danger of succumbing to mental disturbances stemming from a sense of isolation and loneliness.'

side marriage and the family circle. The high cost of personal
services may also be a factor.

The trend towards earlier marriage is being welcomed by
many people and from many different points of view. From
the cultural and intellectual point of view, however, it is
probably a bad thing. For the time between a person's emanci-
pation from his parents and the establishment of his own
family is among the intellectually most fertile periods of his
life. It is then that people are the most anxious and the most
able to explore new fields and avenues of knowledge and to
think and argue about intellectual problems. Early marriage,
with its family obligations, tends to cut short this period of
life. Indeed, the ever-increasing percentage of married couples
among university students may well dampen the spirit of
intellectual inquisitiveness and adventure that is so essential a
part of university life.[1]

We have discussed above a few of the consequences of economic progress that seem to have contributed to changing its
direction and diverting its path from the course envisaged by
the eighteenth-century believers in progress. We want to stress
once again that the great rise in the standard of living and the
decline in its inequalities brought about by economic progress
are real benefits, well worth paying a price for. The purpose
of this discussion was to point out that there is a price and to
analyse its nature. The question we wish to raise in closing
is not whether the price is too high but whether it has to be
paid, and be paid in full.

Some of the undesirable features of the advanced economy
are probably here to stay. The technical complexity of our
civilization and the organization of society and the economy
into very large administrative units seem to be unavoidable;
and so are, in all probability, many of their political and
psychological effects. Those consequences, however, of economic progress that have to do with the changing structure of

[1] The fact that married students usually have better grades than unmarried
ones does not contradict the above thesis. It only shows that married students
are, indeed, more diligent and more anxious to finish their studies and settle
down to a secure job. Today, about 20 per cent of undergraduates are
married in this country, and many universities and colleges provide special
housing for them; whereas not so long ago many colleges barred the married
student or admitted him only as a special exception.

relative prices, earnings and profitabilities are peculiar to economies where market forces are given free rein; and they can be mitigated or avoided by subsidizing certain activities and services or by taking them out of the realm of the market altogether. To some extent, this is being done and always has been done. In the United States, for example, the university presses, subsidized from various sources, publish works whose publication is desirable from a cultural, scholarly or scientific point of view but would not be profitable by commercial standards. Similar purposes are served by the foundations and grants they are giving to basic research, to education, to hospitals, to certain educational and cultural radio and television stations, to some semi-professional theatre groups, etc. In the continental countries of Europe, the same functions are performed by the State; one need only recall their State-owned radio and television networks, and their National theatres and State operas.

Indeed, the need for the State or for non-profit organizations to modify, supplement or supplant the market mechanism in certain areas has always been recognized in our society. We have tried to show that economic progress renders this need ever greater and widens the areas where it arises.

Chapter 14

A CRITIQUE OF PRESENT AND PROPOSED STANDARDS

1960

There are several aims and standards that may be set for an economy; and I propose to consider three of these: to maximize consumer satisfaction, to promote growth, and to provide economic security. I shall deal mainly with the first of these, because most economists in this country consider it the primary aim of economic activity; and I shall deal briefly with the other two, treating them as proposed aims, although they are, of course, the primary aims of economic policy in many other countries.

To regard the satisfaction of the consumer as the aim of economic organization and conformity to consumers' preferences as the standard by which to judge the performance of an economy—these are the precepts of neoclassical economics, which still dominate most of our thinking. Not the least reason for this is the attractiveness of the neoclassical precepts. Their use has encouraged economists to look upon their subject as an objective science and, in some sense, a democratic one. Economics is objective, inasmuch as the criterion of consumers' preferences is given from the outside, treated by the economist as a datum, and revealed to him by consumers' actual behaviour in the market. The democratic nature of economics derives from the economist's habit of identifying the consumer with the people and consumers' sovereignty with the sovereignty of the people.

This, admittedly, is a vastly oversimplified picture. To begin with, society's preferences as revealed by the market are aggregated from the preferences of individuals in such a way that each person's preferences are weighted by his expenditures. And since the distribution of expenditures depends on the distribution of income and wealth, so does also the weighted aggregate of consumers' preferences. The economist, therefore, who accepts the standard of consumers' preferences as revealed by the market has accepted as given not only each individual's tastes but also the distribution of income and wealth, which determines the aggregation of these tastes. Needless to say, while a good case can be made for considering sacrosanct individuals' tastes, it is an altogether different proposition so to consider the actual distribution of income and wealth. Economists generally slur over this awkward fact, possibly because it might be argued that consumers' tastes are similar enough for a change in weighting to make no significant difference to their aggregated preference system.

Yet another difficulty—though one that relates only to collective and not to market goods—is that of aggregating individual preference functions in a democratic way into a meaningful (transitive) social welfare function. This is well known through Arrow's work and I shall not go into it here.

Many, perhaps most, economists choose to ignore these difficulties, regarding them as esoteric and leaving them to the welfare economist to handle as best he can. But no sooner have welfare economics and welfare economists been swept under the table than a new and even more formidable set of difficulties arises; and today the principle of consumer sovereignty itself is being called into question. Some people question the consumer's competence to decide what is best for him; others argue that certain issues he cannot decide because the market provides him with misleading or inadequate information; still others feel that the market makes available too narrow a range of alternatives for the consumer to choose from. I shall deal with each of these cases in turn.

The consumer's competence is denied by Professors Baran and Galbraith. Baran argues that the consumer's values and aspirations are variable and moulded by the structure of the society and economy in which he lives. Even producers regard as variable—and spend 4 per cent of the national income on influencing—the very consumers' preferences that economists regard as data. It is absurd, therefore, in Baran's view, to judge the productive performance of an economy by a standard that is itself changing and influenced by the nature of that economy, especially since much of this influence is exerted by the self-same producers whose performance is being judged. He argues that just as society refuses to accept, and let the economy cater to, the tastes of drug addicts, so it should scrutinize and overrule if necessary the more foolish, frivolous, and irrational aspects of any consumer's preferences. He gives a catalogue of the resources wasted as a result of consumers' irrationality, including among others the resources devoted to advertising and salesmanship, to the production of automobile fins, to the annual retooling of the automobile industry, and to other industries' activities aimed at creating planned obsolescence.

Baran's criticism is well taken; but he becomes less convincing when he advocates the use of 'objective reason' and 'rational judgment' as guides to economic activity. He realizes that these criteria are easier to apply for ascertaining man's biological needs than his cultural requirements; but he feels nevertheless that research could establish objective judgments on the latter as well.

He fails to see that when it comes to allocating resources between the production, say, of books on the one hand and of television programmes on the other, objective reason ceases to be a guide. One man's judgment on these matters may be wiser and more sensible than another's; it may take more, better and more reasonable considerations into account; but it still remains one man's subjective preference pitted against another's. It is important to realize this, because in accepting the impossibility of applying objective criteria to choices of this kind one is forced to face the practical problem of how to guard both against the waste and misallocation Baran rightly castigates and against too arbitrary and authoritarian methods in the making of economic decisions. By putting his faith in objective reason, Baran never seems to face up to this problem, although if nothing else, then the Communist countries' increasing reliance on consumers' preference should have warned him about the difficulty of using any other criterion as a guide to resource allocation.[1]

J. K. Galbraith in the *Affluent Society* reaches very similar conclusions. He too mistrusts the consumer's judgment as a

[1] Cf. UN/ECE *Economic Survey of Europe in 1958*, pp. iv, 25 ff, for a discussion of how the Eastern European countries are using family expenditure data for planning production.

guide and arbiter of resource allocation, although he considers the consumer's unreliability the result of his high standard of living. He revives the law of diminishing marginal utility to argue that the rise in the consumer's real income renders him increasingly unsure, diffident, and suggestible in his consumption decisions; and he quotes the great rise in advertising expenditures to support his explanation. He is unconcerned about the resulting misallocation of resources as between different consumers' goods, and rightly so; for if the consumer himself cares so little about how he spends his marginal dollar, why should the economist care more?

He is concerned, however, with what he considers a serious misallocation between consumers' goods on the one hand and collective goods on the other. He feels that the American public spends too much on consumers' goods and too little on collective goods, under the impact partly of advertising, which promotes only the former, and partly of a conventional wisdom, which views with suspicion most services provided by government. He thinks that if the judgment of consumers were not warped by salesmanship and distrust of government, they would see as clearly as he does the anomaly of luxurious housing in noisy and overcrowded cities, of well-fed and well-clothed children in bad schools, and of high living under the shadow of economic insecurity.

The second group of objections to consumer sovereignty has to do with the inadequacy of the market information on whose basis the consumer makes his decisions. Part of this inadequacy stems from the increasing technical and chemical complexity of consumers' goods; and on this little can be said, except that the main and obvious remedy lies in the establishment and rigid enforcement of strict standards to protect the consumer from fraud and health hazards.

Inadequate also is the information on which the individual's decision between consumption and saving is based. This determines the propensity to save, which in turn is one of the determinants of the growth rate of the economy; and many economists, especially the theorists of economic growth, deny the consumer's competence for making this decision. Their doubts are probably aroused by the great dependence of saving on income distribution; and they argue either with Pigou that the duly appointed government is more competent than the consumer to make a decision that will affect the welfare of unborn generations, or with Higgins that there usually is a conflict between the public's preferences as expressed at the polls and as revealed in the market place, and that in such cases the public's politically expressed preferences should be determining, since they are formulated with greater care and a higher degree of rationality.

Both these arguments are forceful. Yet another argument, however, against relying on the market in this matter is that even if consumers' savings decisions were fully rational and based on their desires to add to their future incomes, total private savings would still not buy the amount of growth consumers want, in the same way in which consumers' total spending on bread buys the total amount of bread they want. A parallelism between savings decisions and spending decisions would exist only if each person received and expected to receive no less and no more of an addition to his (and his descendants') income than the contribution his savings make to the growth of the economy. This condition, although fulfilled in the world of Ricardo's *Principles*, is not fulfilled in our world today. To begin with, wage and salary earners have too little inducement to save for the sake of higher incomes, because they expect their and their descendants' incomes to rise with the growth of the economy quite independently of their own savings. The independent businessman and the rentier are the only members of our economy who must save to raise their incomes; but death duties and the double taxation of savings prevent their obtaining for themselves and their families the full contribution of their savings to the growth of the economy; and this is presumed to weaken also their incentive to save. Corporations come closest to obtaining the full contribution their savings make to growth; but it would be far fetched to regard corporate savings as determined by the savings decisions of individuals. All in all, the total growth created by individual savings-decisions in our economy is very tenuously related to and probably much lower than the amount of growth the community would wish to have and be willing to pay for if the market would reflect correctly the choice between present consumption and additional future income.

The third group of objections to consumer sovereignty is

aimed at the inadequacy of the alternatives provided by the market. Whatever the consumer's competence to make decisions and whatever the information on which he bases his decisions, he can only choose from among the alternatives the market provides; and these may be unduly limited. In the past, the market seems to have provided a large enough variety of products fairly evenly distributed over the entire range of consumers' tastes so as to give a kind of best fit, with not too large a gap between market availabilities and consumers' wants for any one consumer. Today, however, economies of scale are changing this situation. Technical progress usually cheapens production only when large numbers are produced; and the resulting differences between the costs of small- and large-scale production restrict the variety of products in at least two ways. First, the minimum volume that demand for a product must exceed in order to render its production profitable is forever increasing; and this reduces the availability of many products and variants of products. For example, public carriers are increasingly making losses on their less frequented routes; and live music, the legitimate theatre, and the publication of scientific and scholarly works are increasingly in need of subsidies for survival.

Second, the range of products tends to conform less and less to the range of consumers' wants even in the realm of profitable production. When economies of scale were small, a newcomer would enter or an established producer expand his market by offering a product slightly different from those already marketed and designed to cater to the special requirements of a hitherto untapped segment of the market. Today, in the age of mass production, it usually seems more profitable to design every product for the majority, however saturated majority demand may be already, and to expand the market by moulding minority preferences through advertising or the offer of fringe benefits and added features. Hence the secular increase in the uniformity and decline in the range of products in almost every field. This need not always lead to a loss of welfare but it does render the market less liberal. The individual consumer is still free to fill his shopping bag with whatever collection of goods he wishes; but the nature of the goods from which he chooses is imposed upon him by the tastes and wants of the majority. This is why the rationale of the majority's preferences, the influences that mould its wants, and the motives of those that influence it, seem to have become the concern of every consumer.

In addition to this reduction in the number and variety of products, consumers' choice is further limited by the progressive substitution of non-price for price competition, which tends increasingly to offer consumers a choice from among competing packages of goods, with no possibility to buy only part of the package and reject the rest. Each package contains beside the product itself a number of fringe benefits, which range from the good and the indifferent to the objectionable, and most of which the consumer would not buy, at least not in the form and quantities provided, if he had the choice. The most important of these fringe benefits is, of course, advertising and all the free services paid out of advertising.

I have dealt in such detail with the objections and qualifications to consumer sovereignty, because our accepted notions favour it. As to the other alternative aims of economic activity, I shall analyse the arguments in favour, because our accepted notions are against them.

It has been said by Peter Wiles, of New College, Oxford, that we must choose between choice and growth, and that growth is the better choice. It certainly is true that if we can make the cake grow bigger faster, then the way in which it is divided and utilized becomes that much the less important; it is also true that the economist's preoccupation with consumer's choice has led him to neglect problems of growth, which is all the more inexcusable if my earlier argument is correct that the growth rate of the laissez faire economy does not reflect consumers' preferences. I also suspect that the economist may well be more effective in promoting growth than he has been in improving resource allocation; but so far this is only a hope. In any case, the state has assumed responsibility for promoting growth in a number of countries, with budgetary surpluses supplementing private savings, and with growth becoming the primary aim of fiscal and monetary policy, superseding or absorbing such other aims as price stability or full employment. In the light of the foregoing arguments, all this seems economically sound and rational; the only arbitrary element is the particular rate of growth aimed at. The faster the growth, the higher its cost; and no one has yet defined the optimum rate of growth at which gains and costs balance. All, so far, use the political criterion for growth: keeping up with the neighbours is good and desirable and surpassing the neighbours is bad and proof of aggressive intentions.

Coming at last to the aim of economic security, I shall only deal with the part of it that first comes to mind when the welfare state is mentioned: the provision by government of social services. Many of these could also be provided individually, through the market; and the fact that the electorates of so many countries have opted for their collective provision by government has led many American economists to suspect a preference for paternalism. There are, however, some perfectly good economic reasons why some—perhaps most—societies should prefer to provide these services collectively.

One reason is the expectation that the government will often provide better services cheaper. In the market, consumers can choose only among the alternatives available; and available private health insurance schemes, for example, are notoriously inadequate and limited in coverage. Similarly, no private insurance company will underwrite a pension scheme that insures against a rise in the cost of living, while the government, operating on a pay-as-you-go instead of on an actuarial basis, can do so and at reasonable cost. In an age of secular inflation this is an important argument.

Second, the collective provision of free services paid out of general taxation inevitably redistributes income in favour of the poor; and by voting for it the public expresses its preference for lesser inequalities. This is not an efficient way of redistributing income; but neither is progressive taxation beyond the point where it affects incentive. A further objection to collective services is that they always contain an element of compulsion, since the majority compels a minority to pay through taxation for services they would prefer to be free individually to buy or not to buy in the market. Hence the feeling that collective services violate the principle of consumer sovereignty. On the other hand, any kind of redistribution is virtually certain to involve compulsion; and if by voting for collective services the public expresses its desire to mitigate inequalities of income, it can hardly put such preferences into effect without an element of compulsion.

A third argument in favour of collective services is that the compulsion involved may be something the public wants to impose upon itself. To begin with, the theory of rational consumer behaviour paints too simple a picture of human nature when it implies that a rational person is equally rational in all his actions. People may, in different situations, have very different ideas on how to apportion their income between present consumption and provision for old age, sickness and accident; and they may wish, in their serious moments, to put compulsion upon themselves in the form of higher taxes to guard against the temptations of the market place. Second, part of consumption in modern society aims at keeping up with or surpassing the Joneses; and it is easier to sacrifice part of one's present consumption to pay for social insurance if the Joneses have to do likewise.

To condemn these features of the welfare state as paternalistic would amount to condemning the preferences of the people who voted for the welfare state. This might well be justified; but it is inconsistent with an attitude that considers sacrosanct people's preferences when expressed in the market. Indeed, the main lesson to be learned from all this, from my account of the criticisms and shortcomings of consumers' sovereignty and of the benefits and advantages of alternative aims, is that the economist can no longer regard his standards as given to him from outside, but must make a judgment of his own what standards to accept within what limitations and with what qualifications.

Chapter 15

ON THE PRINCIPLE OF CONSUMERS'
SOVEREIGNTY

1962

Many attacks from many quarters have been launched in recent years on the principle of consumers' sovereignty. They have questioned the economist's wisdom in putting too great and exclusive a trust in the consumer's wisdom; and it is regrettable that these attacks have shaken the public's faith in the economist but have not shaken the economist out of his established modes of thought. Indeed, American economists have largely ignored these attacks, following an old American tradition of keeping hands off welfare economics—applying its results but refusing to cast a critical look at the derivation of these results. I have been fighting this tradition for some time, because I believe that much of the criticism is valid and economists should take it to heart. I have much more to say on the subject than time to say it in, and have said much of it already, so I shall confine myself here to two issues: the choice between market and collective goods, and the problem of whether the market can cater to consumers' tastes truly and well.

The first issue stems from the realization that the sovereignty of the consumer is not at all the same thing as the sovereignty of the individual or citizen. The consumer is just one facet of the individual—the one that has to do with the consumption of goods sold through the market. The consumer's welfare therefore is only a part of man's welfare and only a part even of his economic welfare. Choosing between market and collective goods, deciding whether a given service is better provided through the market or by public spending, determining the best allocation of public funds among their various uses—all these are economic choices no different and no less important than the consumer's choice between two market goods; and

Q

yet, our society has failed to develop adequate machinery through which the public could express its preferences on these issues. For, as Galbraith pointed out, advertising, the American tradition of self-reliance, belief in the advantages of private enterprise, and the economist's excessive preoccupation with consumer's choice in the market, not only have biased the American public against collective goods but even prevent its forming and expressing rational preferences on the economic aspects of any choice involving them, so much are these issues befogged by ideological considerations. The more's the pity, because a variety of recent changes and developments are rendering these choices ever more important.

Historically, there is plenty of excuse for such bias. For many centuries, food, clothing and shelter symbolized market goods, while cathedrals, palaces and armies were the symbols of collective spending; and most of us would favour absolute priority of the first over the second group. The tendency to think in these terms persists today, although in most developed countries the choice has long ceased to be so simple. On the margin, which is where choices are made, most expenditures in a developed economy have to do with leisure; and today, society's marginal choice between market and collective expenditures is no longer a choice between more bread and more palaces but more nearly that between TV sets and other gadgets and appliances on the market side and public services and recreational and educational facilities on the collective side. This is the kind of choice that the Planning Commission of France must have had in mind when they recommended a faster expansion of collective services than of the consumption sector and warned against the social malaise that might result from catering to the consumer's every whim.[1]

Another explanation of our undue emphasis on the consumption of market goods may be the fact that our economic thinking was formulated at a time when many collective goods were free but which today are no longer free. The increase in population density and man's tendency to fill the countryside with factories, automobiles and empty beer cans have created a world in which fresh air, clean water and the enjoyment of nature are no longer free goods. Smog control and the decontamination of polluted rivers are expensive operations, and so

[1] Cf. *Le Monde*, October 17, 1961.

is the creation and maintenance of 'nature areas' in a world whose wide open spaces are rapidly being subdivided into quarter-acre lots. The external diseconomies of the production and consumption of market goods render such collective goods increasingly scarce and expensive; but economic theory, social accounting and most public policy still proceed on the fiction that external diseconomies are small enough to be neglected.

Besides the rise in living standards and the crowding of space, increased life expectancy, secular inflation, and uneven progress and the resulting change in relative prices are all among the factors that call either for more provision of collective goods and services or at least for a reconsideration of the question which goods and services should be provided collectively and which through the market. Increased life expectancy demands of the individual more and more careful long-run budgeting at the very time when secular inflation and the uncertainty it creates are diminishing the market's ability to handle long-run budgeting. This, together with the changing nature of the family, which no longer provides a place for the aged, explains the rising demand and rising recognition of demand for the collective provision of social security. Increased life expectancy is also bringing about a situation in which the leisure classes are no longer the rich but the aged, who however are at the same time also the poor of modern society. This, too, is causing many people to wish to do some reallocation of spending from market goods to collective services.[1]

Changing relative prices are another factor relevant here, because they can change people's ideas on which services should be distributed free and paid out of public funds, which should be subsidized and which sold at full cost through the market. This is so because, given the distribution of income and wealth, the inequality with which a particular good is distributed depends on its price in relation to other prices. The higher its relative price, the more unequally the market distributes it. It can happen, therefore, that the rise in the price of a good should increase the inequality of its distribution beyond the point tolerated by public opinion, which will then

---

[1] Cf. Bertrand de Jouvenel, 'Efficiency and Amenity, 40th Earl Grey Memorial Lecture', King's College, Newcastle upon Tyne; and his 'The Political Economy of Gratuity', *Virginia Quarterly Review*, Autumn, 1959.

demand either its subsidization and sale below cost or its free provision out of public funds. In this age of fast and uneven technical progress there are many instances of this happening. An illustration is the increasing public demand in developed countries for national health insurance or free medical care.

In discussing some of the factors that in today's more complex world call for greater reliance on collective goods and services, I am not forgetting the arguments against the element of compulsion and the lesser safeguards against inefficiency and waste in the public sector. In the past, we have fought these troubles the easy way by trying to minimize the public sector itself. Its growth and the increasing need for it may compel us to fight the hard way for its more satisfactory performance.

We can now proceed to our other subject: the criticism of consumers' sovereignty in the narrow sense. The two main objections here are, first, that in this age, when man's control over his fellow men's beliefs is almost as great as his control over nature, the economist should still continue to regard consumers' preferences as a datum and the standard by which to judge the performance of the economy; and, second, that even by the questionable standard of consumers' preferences, the market economy performs badly, and for reasons not even considered in traditional economic analysis.

In the days of the handicraft economy, every piece of clothing, every piece of furniture, was made to the specifications of the person who bought it; but from this position of 100 per cent consumer sovereignty we have retreated long ago. Consumers yielded their dominance first to merchants, who had the initiative in placing orders and specifying the nature and design of products for a long period, and later to manufacturers, who now decide themselves what to produce. The consumer's loss of initiative involves no great loss of sovereignty as long as he is given an adequate range of alternatives to choose from and is able to distinguish the good from the bad and to recognize solid construction, good design, and practical and imaginative ideas. These conditions, however, are the less fulfilled, the more the economy and technology progress.

Economies of scale not only cheapen large-scale production but by raising wages they also raise the cost and diminish the profitability of small-scale production. This in turn raises the minimum volume of sales necessary to render production profitable and thus leads to an ever increasing narrowing of the range of variants of products offered and neglect of minority needs and tastes in the nature and design of goods produced and marketed.

The increasing neglect of minority preferences is a bad thing, because it is illiberal, makes for uniformity, and destroys to some degree the principal merit of the market economy: its ability to cater separately and simultaneously to different people's differing needs and tastes. Also, the more the market loses this ability, the greater the extent to which majority preferences are imposed upon minorities and the more do the nature and formation of these majority preferences become matters of public concern.

Now the very failure of the market to cater to minority preferences may have undesirable effects upon the development of majority preferences as well. Even the most ardent believers in consumer sovereignty must realize that most tastes are acquired, that bad tastes are as easy to acquire as good ones, and that the best one can hope for is that by example and imitation the good will prevail over the bad if given an even chance. An additional advantage, therefore, of a market that caters to different people's differing tastes is that it gives those with informed tastes a chance to set an example to the rest of the community. Informed people, however, are always a minority; and when they are too small a minority—or economies of scale are too great—for producers to cater to their demand, then they are unable to set an example and fulfil their educative function.

Informed people are partly the experts who either as professionals or as amateurs have an intimate knowledge of a particular type of consumers' good—and it goes without saying that the expert public for music is generally a different group of people from the expert buyers of automobiles. A second part of the informed public is composed of generally educated people, who either are informed or, if not, know how to inform themselves.

I should like to see the tastes of experts catered to, because they know something about technical excellence. I should like to have the preferences of the generally educated public respected, because they have a wider perspective, apply a variety of criteria, and pay attention to the relation and connection between different criteria.

I admit, of course, that the preference for an educated taste is simply the subjective preference of educated people; but they, or most of them, have the tremendous advantage of having, at an earlier stage, been uneducated and uninformed themselves. In the early work on the theory of consumer satisfaction, the Greeks could never resolve the problem whether men or women enjoyed more the pleasures of love, because they could not draw on the experience of people who had tasted these pleasures in both capacities. In approaching our problem we have no such handicap. I cannot claim that an informed person's tastes are better by any test than an uninformed person's, or that they are more conducive to happiness or more appropriate to the atomic age; but I can claim that they are based on knowledge of a wider range of alternatives, which includes the alternatives available to the uninformed person.

Let me also recall that the issue is not whether uninformed tastes should or should not be suppressed and displaced by informed ones. I am merely deploring and criticizing the tendency of scale economies to keep the market more and more from catering to informed or, if you wish, highbrow, tastes and thus to keep these tastes from competing on an equal basis with uninformed and lowbrow tastes in moulding the preferences of the public at large.

Who, then, influences the majority's preferences and how? I can think of several channels through which is imposed what David Riesman called 'other directedness', not so much the taste of the representative consumer as what public opinion experts believe to be his taste. As already mentioned, the increasing importance of scale economies has greatly raised the penalty producers have to pay for making the wrong guesses about consumers' tastes and putting unpopular products on the market. Hence the tendency of producers in an increasing number of fields to play safe and not to risk imaginative innovations in the new products, services and publications they put on the market but to rely instead on market research into the consumer's unfulfilled desires. At its best, this can slow down genuine progress and innovation in the design of products; at its worst, it can lead to a serious misreading of the public taste and the imposition of a mythical majority taste that in fact few people share. The automobile industry, with its hand on the consumer's pulse, has for many years diagnosed a chronic yearning for longer and wider and more powerful cars; and had it not been for foreign competition, we—and they—might never have found out how wrong they were. Similarly, Hollywood used to proclaim twelve as the median age of the American movie audiences; and if it had not been for the success of foreign films, we would still live under the shadow of this depressing thought.

One trouble with such misreadings of the majority's mind is the difficulty of finding out how wrong they are. Competition seems no adequate safeguard. The consumer is all too often in the position of the voter who has but one candidate to vote for or several candidates who all stand for the same thing. And to complete the simile, the consumer too is subjected to a barrage of advertising to persuade him that he really wants the product which is the designer's realization of what the market researcher believes to be the average consumer's wishdream.

Another factor responsible for the other-directedness of the consumer's taste has to do with the increasing importance of durable goods in the consumer's market. The most important of these, cars and houses, are bought not only for consumption but also as an investment for their resale value; and buying for high resale value means buying not what one wants but what one believes other people want. The consumer buys extra trim on his car, not necessarily because he wants it, but because the salesman assures him that it will raise the blue-book value of his car in the second-hand market. He is forced to avoid all but the most conventional design and construction in his house, because to get a good mortgage the house must conform to what the appraiser believes, perhaps wrongly, the majority taste to be. Accordingly, house construction is governed to quite an extent not by what the consumer wants but what an unimaginative and not very expert middleman expects other consumers to want.

Luckily for the consumer, his writ still runs in many areas; but it is none too soon to start thinking about how to remedy the situation. Also, the above points were merely a sample of the things that are wrong with consumer's sovereignty but a sufficiently representative sample to raise the question of remedies and policies. Most economists seem reluctant to face up to these questions, presumably because they visualize the dictatorship of an economic planner as the only alternative to the present situation. Such an attitude, however, shows a misunderstanding of the issues involved. Most critics object not to the consumer's sovereignty but to the ignorance and restrictions to which his reign is subject and to the influence businessmen have over it. We cannot and do not want to turn the clock back and return to a handicraft economy; and some shortcomings we may choose to put up with. However, some of those discussed in this paper can be remedied; and we may be able to establish safeguards to assure the satisfaction of a wider range of consumers and to guard against the undue and undesirable influencing of consumer's tastes. The choice is not whether consumers or a central planner should exercise sovereignty but whether and how the producer's power to ignore some consumers and influence the preferences of others should be curbed and modified.

This is not the place to discuss in detail the nature of a constructive answer to any of these questions; but a few precedents may be mentioned. Public carriers are required to offer service in off-peak hours and on little-travelled routes; the Pure Food and Drug Administration does impose curbs on a highly competitive industry; and Britain's Independent Television Authority is an excellent and successful example of how the influencing of consumers' tastes by market research and public opinion experts can be curbed, modified and supplemented by the influence of distinguished citizens. In a slightly different area, the survival of opera and serious drama and the publication of scholarly books are assured by subsidies—from the state in Western Europe, from other sources here.

All these, of course, are examples of exceptional cases justified by special circumstances. To extend them into a general rule would be much harder and more momentous than their admission as exceptions. Also, the further such policies are extended and the more the unfettered operation of the market is encroached upon, the more value judgments are involved. And here I should like to end on a note I started out with: the economist could wash his hands of value judgments only if the public's preferences were really given and he could accept them as such. As soon as this ceases to be true and the public's preferences are influenced by economic agents and the economic environment, value judgments on whether this influence is good or bad, in need of restraint or reform, cannot be avoided. If the economist feels incompetent to make such judgments himself, he should at least admit their legitimacy and provide the analytical framework to help others to make these judgments.

Chapter 16

EQUITY

1963

Equity is a big word and a vague concept, and you may wonder what business have I, as an economist, to speak on such a topic. Economists usually pride themselves on being more down-to-earth, more rigorous, more scientific than most other social scientists; why, then, should an economist choose so nebulous a topic to discuss with his fellow economists?

My reasons are the following. An important part of the economist's task is to find out how well the production and distribution of goods and services conform to the public's wishes. The first thing to ascertain in this connection is what the public's wishes are. In the realm of private goods, economists have succeeded fairly well in doing this. The main function of the theory of consumers' demand is to deduce from consumers' market behaviour what their preferences are; we have even renamed it the theory of revealed preference to remind ourselves and our students of this fact. But while a lot of theoretical speculation and empirical work has been devoted to the private sector of the economy, the public sector is very much neglected. Some economists are ideologically opposed even to the very existence of a public sector; and they, of course, have a fine excuse for not dealing with the subject. The rest of us have no such excuse. Collective goods, provided and paid for through the public sector, are increasing in importance; but economists have done very little work on the subject, although there are plenty of problems, plenty of work to be done. It would be desirable to develop some machinery for ascertaining what the public's preferences are concerning collective goods, machinery for making these preferences known to those who decide on public expenditures, machinery to assure efficiency, adequate resource allocation, and the minimization of costs in the public sector. I believe that some of the most urgent and most important work of the economist lies in this field.

It would be desirable to know something about the public's preferences concerning the distribution of income and wealth —a collective good similar in essentials to such other collective goods as public transportation, state parks and national defence. All collective goods have a common feature that distinguishes them from private goods and consists in their inability to accommodate personal differences in tastes. In the realm of private goods, the market enables one man to drink whisky while another drinks tea, but collective goods do not and cannot cater to personal idiosyncrasies. Your national defence is my national defence; your public transportation is also my public transportation. Existing bus routes and schedules may favour your special needs more than they favour mine; but we share the same transportation system and there is no way of catering simultaneously to my preference and your distaste for buses.

The same way with distribution. Some people are in more fortunate financial circumstances than others; but we share the same degree of inequality of distribution and the same principles on which income and wealth are distributed. If the system of distribution is to conform to the public's preferences, it must conform to a consensus or to a compromise between different preferences. I propose to examine the nature of this consensus, or compromise, or mixture of consensus and compromise, and chose the title equity because it seems to stand for some minimum degree of equality people would like to see realized and on the nature of which they might be able to agree.

It is no accident that the English word equity comes from *equus*, Latin for equal. By equity people mean, if not equality, at least something that approximates it closely enough to satisfy them. The public is satisfied with something short of equality, partly, perhaps, because it is resigned to this being an imperfect world, and partly also because it recognizes the impracticability of perfect equality. The latter is unattainable as long as we need to provide economic incentive to produce the national product. Most of us believe that economic incentives are superior to most other incentives, such as coercion, or social pressure, or the threat of physical punishment; and society needs some incentive as long as the national product it wants is greater than what can be produced with the amount and kind of work the public regards and performs as play. While this has always been so, it need not remain so if automation goes very much further. Karl Marx's motto for Communism: 'From each according to his abilities, to each according to his needs', could describe a future economy of plenty, in which a puritanical limitation and satiability of wants coincides with so great an increase in the productive efficiency of work that the setting-up exercises of society, the tinkering of hobbyists with science, and the social services supplied by the young matrons of the junior league would be the only human inputs needed in an otherwise fully automated economy.

For the time being, we are far removed from such an economy; and with all the effort devoted to the creation of new wants, we may never reach it. We still need incentive to get the national product produced, most of us prefer economic to other incentives, and economic inequality is the price of having an economic incentive.

When the economist realizes that inequality is the price of obtaining the national product, he instinctively asks: how much national product for how much inequality? Is there an optimum point at which the marginal increment of national product just equals the marginal increment of inequality? The answer, for the time being, is no. We do not even know as yet whether, and if so by how much, progressive taxation lowers incentive; even less do we know the price of a dollar's worth of national product in terms of inequality; and, as I have argued, we have yet to devise machinery whereby consumers or citizens could express their preferences between a small addition to income and a slight easing of conscience over the inequality of man.

For the time being, all one can do is to guess at the public's feelings concerning equity. Differences of degree are obviously important here. The public will resent inequalities of income and wealth that are too great; and while it is hard to find the dividing line between what is and what is not too great, one can say something about the factors that determine the location of this dividing line. For one thing, society is more likely to tolerate inequalities if these are correlated with merit or people's contribution to society and its values. For another, inequalities are more acceptable to a person who feels that he has equal chances with others of reaching the top. Hence people's strong feeling against discrimination, the provision of free education in our society, and John Stuart Mill's advocacy of confiscatory (100 per cent) inheritance taxes. A third factor is the well-being of those at the bottom of the ladder. The public will the more easily tolerate inequalities, the better-off are those least favoured, the more nearly they are assured of subsistence and provided with the necessities of life. In the following, I shall concentrate on this last factor and neglect the first two, discussing only the relation between equity and the distribution of the necessities of life. Indeed, to simplify the argument, I shall not only hold constant the first two factors but pretend they are not there. In other words, I shall pretend that equity (that is, the acceptance as equitable of a given distribution of income and wealth) depends solely on the availability and distribution of the necessities of life—admittedly an over-simplification but a useful one.[1]

In this connection it is helpful first of all to ascertain how goods and services are actually distributed under the market mechanism. The distribution of income and wealth determines the consumer's share in the consumable national product; his freedom of choice enables him to obtain his share in that combination of goods and services which gives him the greatest satisfaction. In other words, the market distributes goods and services in accordance partly with people's tastes and needs, partly with the distribution of purchasing power among them. It follows that if everybody's purchasing power were equal, the distribution of each commodity would be egalitarian (by which I mean equal except for differences in tastes and needs); but it does not follow that if people's tastes and needs were identical, each commodity would be distributed uniformly with the distribution of purchasing power. For man's need of necessities is biologically limited and therefore much sooner and more abruptly saturated than his demand for luxuries. An unequal distribution of purchasing power therefore causes different commodities to be distributed very differently, rang-

[1] The argument of this paragraph owes much to comments of my friends, Professors R. Radner and H. Leibenstein.

ing from the egalitarian or near-egalitarian distribution of the cheaper necessities to a distribution of the more expensive luxuries that is likely to be much more unequal than the distribution of income and wealth. The distribution of the cheaper forms of food is virtually egalitarian in a rich country like the United States; and the distribution of most necessities is much less unequal than the distribution of income and wealth. Similarly, the amounts spent on necessities by the rich and by the poor also differ less than the income and wealth available to them; and this implies that what they have left over to save, and to spend on luxuries, must differ by more.

We are now ready to attempt a tentative definition of equity. Public opinion seems to be very much concerned with the distribution of necessities; and the first dictate of people's consciences is that the prime necessities of life should be generally available and distributed in an egalitarian way. Even great inequalities of income and wealth will not be considered oppressive as long as necessities are cheap and plentiful enough to be generally available; whereas slight inequalities of income may be considered unjust if one or more necessities are short —that is, scarce and expensive enough to become the privilege of the well-to-do. Different people's lists of necessities differ, of course, in both length and composition; but bearing these differences in mind, one can say that most people consider equitable an economic system or economic organization that leads to an egalitarian or near-egalitarian distribution of the necessities of life.[1] Once this definition is accepted, one can distinguish degrees of equity according to the number of necessities distributed in an egalitarian way; and one can define social progress or progress in equity as an increase in the number of necessities available to all on an egalitarian basis.

These definitions of equity and social progress have a number of interesting implications. To begin with, one must note the absence of any simple one-to-one correspondence between the degree of equity and the inequality of distribution of income and wealth. Given the total income of an economy and given the relative scarcities of different resources and commodities, equity will increase with a lessening of the

[1] This is admittedly a partial and incomplete definition, as pointed out in the last but one paragraph.

inequalities of income or wealth; but there are other ways of increasing equity too. For example, given an unchanging distribution of income and wealth, equity will usually increase with a rise in *per capita* income. Indeed, this latter is probably the main source of social progress in our society. Inequalities of income and wealth are probably no greater in the countries of Southern Europe than they are in the United States; and if in those countries inequities between the well-fed rich and the starving poor seem greater than in the United States, this is mainly due to the fact that the same inequality of income distribution creates greater inequities when incomes are low than when they are high.

Another peculiarity of our definition of equity is that not only does it depend on the absolute level of income as well as on its distribution, it also depends on yet a third factor, the relative scarcity or cost of production of different goods. Other things being equal, more equity results if necessities are cheap than if it is luxuries whose cost of production is low in relation to that of necessities.

To appreciate the importance of this last factor, it is useful to examine first of all a situation which public opinion regards as inequitable. Such a situation exists when some goods the public would like to see generally accessible are too expensive to become generally accessible, given the inequality of wealth and income. Such a situation can be remedied in either of two ways. One is to reduce the inequality of wealth and income distribution through progressive taxation and death duties. The other is to take the necessities whose unequal distribution through the market mechanism public opinion resents and to distribute them in an egalitarian way outside of the market mechanism.

The first is the obvious, natural and most efficient way; but it is also likely to be the less feasible politically. For a very far-reaching reduction of monetary inequalities may be necessary to assure the egalitarian distribution even of a single necessity if this is expensive and scarce in relation to demand. The second way is by far the less drastic, by far the less revolutionary whenever the number of such necessities is small. Hence the many examples in free enterprise economies of the egalitarian distribution of necessities more or less outside of the market system. Wartime rationing of food, clothing,

petrol, etc, is one example.[1] Public education, provided free
and paid for out of taxation, is another. Such distribution,
however, is often inefficient or administratively cumbersome
—problems I shall return to presently.

For the time being, let us look at the subject in the context
of secular change and economic development. Development
means a rise in incomes; and as incomes rise, the public feels
that it can afford more equity and usually wants to spend part
of its additional income on increased equity. In other words,
development increases the *demand* for equity.

At the same time, development may but need not increase
also the *supply* of equity. The rise in incomes stems from
technological progress, which may lower the cost, improve the
quality, or extend the range of the goods and services available.
But only when it lowers costs, and lowers the costs of necessities, actual or potential, only then does technical progress
automatically involve social progress as well.

It so happens that most of America's early contribution to
technical progress was precisely of this nature. We made
modest contributions to the advance of knowledge—most
scientific breakthroughs were of European origin—but we
made a large contribution to the simplification of products
and improvement of manufacturing methods calculated to
make possible mass production at low cost. This, more than
anything else, explains why, in the half-century before World
War II, America was regarded as the land of the common
man and American civilization as the civilization favouring the
common man. Our standard of living rose, because more and
more necessities, and goods coming to be considered necessities, became cheap and generally available; and this meant
social progress hand-in-hand with the rise in incomes.

Such development satisfies more or less the public's wish to
obtain part of its additional income in the form of increased
equity; but it is not the only form that economic development
can take. Indeed, it is likely that since World War II, economic
development in most Western countries has taken a different
form, involving a rise in incomes with little or no increase in
equity.

This latter kind of development results from the cheapening

[1] Cf. my 'The Political Economy of Consumers' Rationing', *Review of
Economic Statistics*, Vol. 24, pp. 114-24, for a detailed discussion of this case.

or improvement of luxuries, while some important necessities remain high or even rise in price. An important feature of post-war economic growth in the West has been the reduced cost and increased availability of kitchen appliances and other consumers' durables.[1] Although public opinion is gradually reclassifying many of these from luxuries to necessities, they cater to less urgent and less essential needs than do some personal services whose accessibility to the masses has increased little, if at all. When development takes this form, the public may well be dissatisfied with its course and demand that additional necessities be made available outside the market system on an egalitarian basis. The main example is the demand for free medical care. The growing demand for comprehensive national health service or insurance has been voiced in most advanced countries since the war; and you may well ask why. After all, real *per capita* income has been growing in all these countries at a very fast rate; more people than ever before can afford to *pay* for medical care as a result; why, at such a time, should the public be impatient with the progress already made and demand socialized medicine? There may be many reasons, but one of the most important is the one mentioned above. The public seems impatient that the post-war rise in incomes was accompanied by less social progress than it had hoped for or anticipated on the basis of past experience. As though society would resent the kind of economic progress that puts a second car in every garage sooner than it makes available medical care for all.

Another and similar example of this newly arising demand for the free and egalitarian distribution of necessities not generally available before is the move, in the United States, for establishing the Office of Public Defender. This would provide the funds to finance and the attorneys to conduct the legal defence of those accused of certain crimes, and thereby give the full protection of the law to many who hitherto have not been able to afford that expensive commodity.

Yet another attempt at increasing equity through public action is the campaign of Governor Brown of the State of California to abolish the death penalty. For life is a necessity

---

[1] The effect on farm prices of the even greater increases in agricultural productivity has been largely offset by public policies aimed at protecting the farmer by maintaining farm prices.

R

of life, and one which should be equitably distributed. Evidence, however, shows that all inhabitants of death row come from low income groups, and that the well-to-do can get away with murder—at least to the extent of escaping the death penalty.[1]

One more good that is coming to be considered a necessity that ought to be available to all is the assurance for one's old age of a standard of living commensurate to that achieved during one's active life. For a variety of reasons, this good is not likely to become generally available through the market mechanism and will probably have to be provided collectively. One reason is that its cost is likely to remain high or even rise, partly because life expectancy is on the increase and partly because the aged, often lonely and subject to chronic illness, require more than their proportionate share of personal services, whose price rises with the secular rise in labour productivity. The second reason is that the price of buying, during one's active life, a given standard of living for one's old age is greatly dependent on two unpredictable factors: one's time of death and the cost of living during one's old age. One can insure against the uncertainty of the first by buying a retirement or pension policy, against the uncertainty of the second by putting one's savings into a diversified portfolio of common stock; one can divide one's savings between the two; but one cannot insure against both risks simultaneously. This means that one cannot buy in the market a financially secure old age at a predetermined price; only the State can insure fully against the double hazard of rising prices and a long life.[2]

All the above examples illustrate the same point, which is this. The secular rise in the standard of living lengthens the list of goods society regards as necessities and wants to have distributed in an egalitarian way; and as this list becomes longer, it includes an increasing number of goods whose egalitarian distribution cannot be accomplished by the pricing system in the private sector and will therefore have to be effected outside of the market mechanism. Hence my prediction that

---

[1] Cf. Clinton T. Duffy, *88 Men and 2 Women*, Chap. 23; Edward B. Williams, *One Man's Freedom*, Chap. 14.
[2] The reason why insurance companies cannot insure against changes in the cost of living should be obvious. At the same time, they ought to be able to sell retirement policies tied, if not to the consumers' price index, at least to some stock index.

future social progress (increase in equity) will probably have to be implemented by the public sector to a greater extent than was the case with past social progress. The same point is implied by much of J. K. Galbraith's argument in *The Affluent Society*, and also by the deliberate bias in France's last (fourth) Modernization and Equipment Plan toward increasing investment in collective services rather than in the private sector.

Having discussed the motives for and the likelihood of the future transfer of some services from the private to the public sector of the economy, it may be fitting to end with a reminder of the possibility of shifts also in the opposite direction, prompted by the already mentioned inefficiency and cumbersomeness of distribution outside of the market mechanism. Goods and services paid out of taxes and made available free will be equitably distributed but are also likely to involve inefficient resource allocation. This is so because the demand for free goods is filled to saturation, which necessitates an undue diversion of scarce resources from goods that are not available free. The resulting loss of welfare may be a small price well worth paying for the equitable distribution of services whose social cost is low and the demand for which is quickly saturated. On the other hand, the free availability of services that do not meet these conditions may lead to resource misallocation too costly to be tolerated; and in such cases, ways must be found of restricting consumption without making distribution inequitable. Demand for free education is restricted (though perhaps not sufficiently) by making access to higher education conditional upon certain minimum achievement at lower levels. In the case of free medical care, British experience has shown that, after an initial period of transition, the physician's sensible attitude can restrain his patients from taking up his time and using his services for every trifle. Wartime rationing is another example of circumventing the market for the sake of equity and yet restricting consumption at the same time. This was accomplished partly by the administratively enforced equal distribution of specific commodities, partly by the issuance and equal distribution of a ration currency to circulate side by side with money.[1] The last-mentioned is in many ways the best way of achieving both

[1] Cf. my 'The Political Economy of Consumers' Rationing', *op. cit.*

equity and efficiency but is far too cumbersome to be tolerated except under the stress of war. For peacetime use, no solution has yet been developed (apart from the two examples mentioned), although the need is likely to become more pressing. One reason for this is the increasing density of population.

The increased density of population and its higher standard of living mean that more and more people crowd in upon each other, generating ever larger quantities of noise, exhaust fumes and debris on their way. As a result, many amenities that used to be either naturally free or provided free by government are in the process of being rendered scarce and expensive. Highways, metropolitan thoroughfares, unpolluted water, smogless air, places where man can commune undisturbed with nature are examples. To discuss just one of these, estimates of what city traffic will be twenty-five years from now in this country are totally incompatible not only with the nature but with the very concept of present-day cities. To solve the resulting problem, Professor Vickrey would restrict the use of city streets by charging a price for it—just as he would use prices for solving many similar problems in other areas as well.[1] To reject such proposals as utopian shows a lack of imagination and inability to realize that we are entering a new world in which many of the good things in life we now take for granted and regard as part of nature will become carefully husbanded commodities whose use or consumption must be rationed. The only question is whether rationing them by price would not create problems of equity and whether it would not be preferable therefore to develop other means of rationing free from this objection.

Society is bound to insist on the equitable distribution of goods that were once free; and the larger the number of such goods to be rationed by price, and the greater their scarcity, the smaller the likelihood that the market will distribute them equitably. Indeed, bringing hitherto free goods or amenities into the realm of the pricing system has the opposite effect on the degree of equity from that of a rise in real incomes. To prevent a retrogression in equity therefore, hitherto free goods may have to be rationed through means other and more equitable than the pricing system. I have no new general

[1] Cf. William S. Vickrey, 'Pricing in Urban and Suburban Transport', *American Economic Review* (PROCEEDINGS), vol. 53, pp. 452-65.

principle to suggest; and *ad hoc* methods with no overall principle may well be the best solution. An example, additional to those already mentioned, may be worth discussing.

Consider a country or region in which unspoilt nature is getting scarce. As more and more people seek the great outdoors, the time will come when nature cannot both be free and remain unspoilt. The present tendency is for the State to hasten the spoiling of nature by providing better and wider roads, more and faster transportation; for society still believes in man's natural right to the free enjoyment of nature and the State's duty to fill to saturation the public's demand for highway capacity. But should people come to believe that free access to nature is not the better alternative and wish to ration it rather than letting it be spoiled, they would have the choice of either charging an entrance fee to nature or limiting access through narrow, winding or rough roads. The first would be efficient but inequitable if the fee had to be high in order to be effective. The second would limit access to nature to those who value it highly enough to put up with the inconvenience of a long or difficult drive; and while this too can create inequities (e.g. it discriminates in favour of good drivers and people with much time on their hands), these are likely to be less resented than those created by the inequality of income and wealth distribution. More problematic is society's willingness to tolerate unsatisfactory roads as a rationing device. Yet, we may increasingly be forced to accept and learn to live with such *ad hoc* methods of restraint on our freedom to consume if increasing population and its increasing affluence reduce our elbow room much further.

Chapter 17

INTERNATIONAL PAYMENTS IN LAPUTA

1963

In case you should not remember your *Gulliver's Travels*, let me remind you that Laputa is a utopia—the third country Captain Gulliver visited and the one that was ruled by scientists and experts. What I propose to do therefore is to present to you a utopian system of international payments.

A utopia, as you know, is not unlike an economist's model. A model is a simplified picture of society or the economy, with some realistic, some unrealistic assumptions; and with the unrealistic assumptions so chosen that the model retains some of the essential features of the real world.

A utopia is also a model of society, with some realistic and some unrealistic assumptions; but here the purpose of the unrealistic assumptions is no longer that of simplifying, stripping away the inessentials in order to bring into sharper relief the essentials. Most utopias aim at showing up the consequences for society of human folly and human limitations, or of the folly and limitations of social institutions; and they do this either by assuming away the folly or the limitations, or by exaggerating them, carrying them to their logical extremes. In the first case, the utopia becomes an ideal society; in the second, it becomes a nightmare. Curiously enough, all utopia builders are pessimists. For those who build nightmares usually place them into the future; whereas those who build ideal societies place them in never-never land.

The utopia I want to present to you belongs to the family of ideal societies. I propose to make the realistic assumptions of rigid cost and price structures, of people concerned with full employment, growth and price stability, and of governments pursuing with varying success policies aimed primarily at maintaining full employment, growth and price stability. Such policies, as you know, often go counter and rule out fiscal and monetary policies aimed at external equilibrium; and besides, their existence and very success eliminate what automatic equilibrating forces may operate, in the absence of such policies, to assure or bring closer external equilibrium. In short, I am assuming the typical modern situation, where deliberate policy is needed to solve balance-of-payments difficulties; and where such policy may, as often as not, conflict with and take second place to domestic economic policies.

I shall also assume that central bankers, finance ministers, politicians, secretaries of the treasury, are intelligent, imaginative, forward-looking people, with some knowledge of economics; and while quite human and ordinary in their daily routine, when it comes to the framing of rules and the development of institutions, they are able and willing to appraise alternative plans on their merits and adopt them if good, even if they are unfamiliar or go counter to the prejudices of the past. The purpose of these admittedly unrealistic assumptions is to find out whether in the modern world, composed of modern economies, it is at all possible, at least conceptually, to have a satisfactory international payments mechanism.

Having stated our assumptions, we can proceed to imagine an ideal international payments mechanism to our hearts' content. This seems like an exercise no less useful and much less frustrating than the trade theorist's usual procedure, which is to lean over backwards in accepting the constraints of political feasibility and waste a lot of ingenuity on clothing in conservative garb some very modest and very partial reform, only to see it rejected on the ground that it is far too revolutionary and does not even solve *all* our economic ills. My main trouble with the utopian approach is that it may require more imagination than I possess. But it is a good game; and at least I should like to start you off with an example and show you how to play it. I shall have time to deal only with two subjects: balance-of-payments adjustment and the problem of external reserves.

As far as payments adjustment is concerned, Laputans believe that automatic forces of adjustment can be utilized and relied upon only inside an economy that is fully integrated. By this they mean an economy that has both an integrated capital market and an integrated economic policy, the latter comprising centrally directed and financed fiscal and monetary policies aimed at employment stability and investment for growth. They place a high value on the painlessness of balance-of-payments adjustment and regard this as a good reason for forming large economies. Between one economy and another, payments adjustment is brought about by deliberate policy, which they recognize as a necessary evil. The best one can do, they say, is to have the kind of adjustment that is the least painful. That is why they refuse to let payments adjustment affect overall levels of employment and rates of growth, and compromise by throwing the burden of adjustment on the industries involved in or directly affected by foreign trade. They accomplish this by an arrangement that amounts to flexible exchange rates within rigidly fixed limits of two kinds. International agreement binds each central bank to maintain the value of its currency in terms of international reserve units between limits as narrow as ours for some but as far apart as 5 or 6 per cent for most economies. The latter is comparable to what the situation would be in this country if the dollar value of gold were fixed between, say, $34 and $36, and the Federal Reserve, while maintaining day-by-day stability, adapted exchange rates within these limits in response to or in anticipation to balance-of-payments disequilibria. In addition to the flexibility of exchange rates within such limits, they have another type of flexibility as well: the limits themselves can drift up or down at an annual rate of 2 per cent. For example, if the dollar value of gold were kept between $34 and $36 this year, it could be kept betweent $34.68 and $36.72 next year should the Federal Reserve consider this desirable. They say that such flexibility is sufficient for exchange-rate adjustments to maintain payments equilibrium, although the limits are narrow enough to keep speculation within bounds and make possible long-term contracts for the main staples of foreign trade. They seem to feel that the effectiveness of their relatively small exchange-rate adjustments is explained partly by the promptness with which exchange rates are made or allowed to respond to payments imbalance, partly by the importance in their external accounts of foreign travel and luxury goods, items that respond quickly and massively even to small price changes.

I suspect, however, that they greatly exaggerate the importance of these factors. It is true that they get along with much smaller exchange-rate variations than the occasional massive devaluations we experience and seem to require; but I would seek the key to their success not in any such utopian foreign-trade elasticities but rather in their peculiar and ingenious system and management of international reserves.

As you know, we look upon international reserves as a means of providing deficit countries with breathing space in which automatic forces can exert their equilibrating pressure and the authorities can put equilibrating policies into action. The main characteristic of a breathing space is that the more you have of it the better off you are; on this argument therefore external reserves should be as large as possible. On the other hand, there is also something else, called balance-of-payments discipline. We should like to see some pressure brought to bear upon deficit countries sooner or later to remove the deficit. So between the conflicting desires to provide enough breathing space and yet to maintain balance-of-payments discipline we are forever undecided. None of our economists has succeeded as yet in providing a yardstick for measuring the adequacy of reserves; and we are forever quarrelling in a rather unscientific way over what yardstick to use and whether actual reserves are or are not adequate.

On this subject our colleagues from over there are more enlightened than we are. They maintain that in addition to providing a breathing space for deficit countries, reserves must also fulfil the additional function of putting pressure on surplus countries to remove surplus. The nature of reserves must be such as to assure the existence of such pressure; also, since the pressure on surplus countries increases while that on deficit countries diminishes with the quantity of reserves, they have a carefully conceived policy of keeping the total supply of international reserves at such a level that the pressure on surplus and deficit countries to restore payments equilibrium is equalized. Their reason for this is partly their wish to minimize the burden of adjustment on any individual economy by dividing, and dividing equally, the burden between deficit and surplus countries. Partly also they believe that the need for international payments adjustment should interfere as little as possible with the other economic-policy aims of each economy; and this reserve policy is their way of minimizing such interference.

These notions are so alien to us that I should begin perhaps with a discussion of our own attitude to all this. Needless to say, most of us consider a payments surplus a good thing. We call it a *favourable* balance and consider it, like other good things, too dull and uninteresting even to mention. That is why, if one were to judge the state of the world by the newspapers, one would come to the impossible and absurd conclusion that balance-of-payments deficits the world over greatly outweigh payments surpluses in both number and severity.

The only argument that a surplus may, after all, be undesirable I found in a 1957 report of the Scientific Council of Dr Erhard, the West German Minister of Economics; and I should like to read you a passage from this. According to the Council, 'A persistently active (positive) payments balance means that domestically produced goods and services are surrendered to foreigners and hence not available for domestic consumption and investment. . . . Such involuntary capital export may be acceptable when insufficient domestic demand creates excess productive capacity; but at a time of full employment, when price stabilization is the main concern of economic policy, a substantial involuntary capital export leads to great disturbances, since it creates domestic incomes whose real counterpart disappears abroad.'[1] The Council then proceeded to recommend raising the value of the mark; but the German Government, as you know, did not follow this advice until very much later, and then only under external pressure; instead it pursued a high-interest rate policy, which proved less than a complete success in stabilizing prices and increased rather than diminished Germany's payments imbalance. So, to summarize our attitude to an external payments surplus, one might say that few of us think of it as something bad and harmful to the economy; and even those few who do are not likely to do anything calculated to eliminate the surplus.

By their standards, this is topsy-turvy economics. They believe as firmly as we do in the need for long-run equilibrium

[1] Cf. *Der Wissenschaftliche Beirat beim Bundeswirtschaftsministerium, 5. Band Gutachten vom Januar 1957 bis Maerz 1961*, pp. 24-5. (Verlag Otto Schwartz & Co., Goettingen, 1961.)

in international payments; but as far as national points of view are concerned, their attitude is the very opposite of our attitude. They see few things wrong with a payment deficit, other than the fact that it gradually draws down external reserves and so can ultimately lead to the inconvenience and humiliation of bankruptcy. In times of underemployment, of course, a deficit compounds the problem by adding its deflationary influence; but at a time of full employment, a payments deficit exerts a price-stabilizing anti-inflationary pressure and adds to the growth potential of the economy.

By contrast, they see many things wrong with a payments surplus. In addition to the inflationary pressures feared also by the Germans, they point to the fact that the involuntary capital export implied by the surplus amounts to a wasting of scarce resources, which slows down the economy's own growth and does not even benefit the outside world as deliberate and voluntary capital exports would. They readily admit that these disadvantages of a payments surplus are long-run disadvantages, which become apparent in the long run only; and that is why they favour reserves big enough to enable the deficit countries to wait with their adjustment until the surplus countries have had time to wake up to their own need of making adjustment too.

This explains why their reserves are so much larger than ours; and in addition, their reserve arrangements are different too. These differences can all be explained by their desire to render the accumulation and the holding of reserves distasteful, or at least such that their presence is a constant reminder of the waste that their accumulation has entailed.

For one thing, they use as reserves only credit instruments and never credit. They say that since the acquisition of credit instruments involves a cost, objections will sooner or later be raised to the continued hoarding of credit instruments whose very presence is a reminder of past resource waste; whereas the presence of unused credit implies no such thing. For another thing, they insist that no credit instruments used as external reserves may earn interest. With the aid of this rule, they hope to drive home the lesson that involuntary capital exports waste resources. They regard as sheer folly our gold-exchange standard, where the holding of reserves is made more palatable to central banks by letting them hold their reserves in interest-bearing dollar and sterling securities. They would hardly believe me when I told them, with some embarrassment, that the United States and the United Kingdom, our two main deficit countries, pay more than $½ billion interest annually to the surplus countries merely to enable these, as they put it, to live longer and more happily with their surpluses and thus put off making the very adjustments which would relieve and benefit the deficit countries. I must admit that seeing the matter in this new light, I was quite embarrassed having to own up to such folly on behalf of my beloved country's government.

Let me now report to you on the ingenious way in which they adjust the supply of international reserves so as to equalize the pressure on surplus and deficit countries to adjust the exchange rates of their currencies. They have an international organization they call NIMF, which has nothing to do with our nymphs, those lovely female deities, and is spelt quite differently. NIMF is a kind of bank, a central banker's central bank, which issues their international reserve currency and puts this into circulation partly by giving aid to what they call their poor economies, partly by buying bonds in the open market, which represent loans given to poor countries by other banks. They insist that most of NIMF's reserves must represent some form of aid to poor countries, which according to them are the only deficit countries whose deficits should be subsidized. Indirectly, however, NIMF gives aid and comfort to *all* deficit countries, rich and poor; and this indirect aid has to do with the way in which and the rate at which NIMF issues additional reserves. For NIMF is bound by its charter so to regulate the supply of international reserves that their value remains stable in terms of national currencies. For example, if a couple of large economies, having payments deficits, keep lowering the values of their currencies or keep them persistently low (near the limit of the agreed-upon range), while no economy is trying to eliminate a payments surplus by raising the value of its currency or keeping it high, NIMF steps in to intervene. Its open market committee arranges to have bonds bought in the market and the supply of reserves increased, with a view to restoring to parity the weighted average of the value of national currencies in terms of the international reserve unit. Conversely, if some economies with payments surpluses are trying to contain inflation by raising the values of their currencies while none are sufficiently concerned over deficits to lower the values of theirs, NIMF must come to the aid of those fighting inflation by selling bonds in the market and *reducing* the supply of international reserves. Over the years, they say, NIMF has been increasing the supply of international reserves more or less in proportion with the increase in the supplies of national currencies; and this partly explains, according to them, the satisfactory working of their international payments mechanism.

Now my first reaction to this ingenious scheme was that it is inflationary; but they deny this. They point out, to begin with, that an increase in the supply of international reserves is not inflationary by itself—not even in the sense in which an increase in the supply of a national currency might be said by some to be inflationary. All that an increase in the supply of international reserves does is to cause the sum total of payments surpluses temporarily to exceed the sum total of payments deficits—and they concede that balance-of-payments surpluses can be and often are inflationary, just as balance-of-payments deficits can be and often are deflationary. They argue, however, that the authorities of the surplus countries themselves can and must be trusted to combat these inflationary pressures—especially since their system provides exceptional facilities and extra inducement to do so. The raising of a currency's exchange value is an exceptionally quick and effective means of containing inflationary pressures exerted through a payments surplus, since it reduces effective demand, stops or slows the increase in the supply of money, and directly lowers a part of the price structure, all in one stroke. As to the extra inducement, they claim that the accumulation of large non-interest-bearing reserves forcibly drives home the fact, to central bankers and the general public alike, that a payments surplus involves a squandering and improductive hoarding of national resources, quite apart from and independently of whatever inflationary pressures may also be involved.

Let me return now to the subject of inflationary pressures. They argue that since a payments surplus exerts inflationary pressures only under full-employment conditions, just as a payments deficit exerts deflationary pressures only when there is unemployment, a mechanical policy of equating the sum total of payments surpluses to the sum total of payments deficits makes little sense; for it can be either inflationary or deflationary depending on circumstances, and only accidentally will it be neutral. They do insist that international reserve policy should be neutral; and they mean by this a policy that gives the authorities of each economy the maximum freedom of action to deal as best they see fit with their own problems of employment, growth and price stability. They argue that when NIMF aims at keeping the average value of national currencies stable, it is pursuing just such a policy of neutrality, because it is exactly balancing, on a world-wide scale, the inflationary pressures of the payments surpluses against the deflationary pressures of the payments deficits.

I had to admit that such a policy does, indeed, distinguish between actual and potential inflationary and deflationary pressures, and offsets against each other only the actual pressures; but I argued that such a policy is not truly neutral either, because it offsets these pressures one against the other only to the extent that they influence, or that national policies make them or allow them to influence exchange rates. They readily conceded this, but pointed out two things. First, they said, when exchange rates are flexible, as theirs are within limits, then they usually respond right away to inflationary or deflationary pressures and bear the brunt of adjustment to such pressures. Secondly, they pointed out that the open-market operations of NIMF allow plenty of flexibility to take care of such problems and to enable NIMF to pursue a truly neutral international reserve policy. This is so, thanks to this agency's power to buy or sell in any national market it pleases. For example, if a world-wide bias toward currency depreciation induces NIMF to engage in the open-market buying of development bonds, it can buy them in deficit countries and so relieve the pressure they are under to depreciate; but it can also buy them in surplus countries and add to the pressure on them to appreciate. The special circumstances of each particular occasion determine which is the best market for NIMF to operate in; in case of indifference, NIMF buys in deficit countries, since this promotes exchange-rate stability between economies.

In further discussions of this whole programme, they also

told me that when they stabilize the value of international reserves in terms of national currencies, they omit from their calculations the currencies of those economies that are frankly inflationary, in the sense that their national authorities place a low value on price stability and use inflation as a source of government finance. In this way, they feel, the reserve policy of NIMF is a truly neutral policy, which allows the greatest possible scope for national economic policies compatible with international balance and the maintenance of a high volume of international trade, with all the benefits that this entails. There is a constraint of course: the value of different currencies cannot, in the long run, drift apart at more than 4 per cent per annum (twice the 2 per cent drift of the limits within which the value of each currency must remain); and this likewise restrains the degree to which domestic price levels can drift apart in different economies. They believe, however, that this leaves ample scope for differences in national policies and for the different solutions of different national problems.

Indeed, this arrangement of theirs seems so natural to them, so much the only rational arrangement possible that, irked by my incessant questioning, they began to ask how our system worked. I told them that our international payments mechanism, while superficially resembling theirs, was really very different, because we hardly ever faced the problems uppermost in their minds. We had no control over the supply of international reserves, which depended largely on whether the reserve-currency countries ran surpluses or deficits; but I had no doubt that, by their standards, our reserves were woefully inadequate. Our surplus countries hardly ever had a chance of becoming aware of inflationary pressures and the unproductive use of resources; for the pressure on the deficit countries to remove their deficits was so great that they had usually eliminated their deficits—and with them the surplus countries' surpluses—before these latter had time to engage in corrective policies of their own or even to consider whether or not to engage in such policies.

My colleagues from over there thought that this was bound to create a deflationary bias in our economies; and I was forced to admit that it did—to an even greater extent than they realized. For not only was there usually an excess of economies in which the external payments imbalance exerted deflationary pressures; but our fear of devaluation as a symbol of weakness often forced the countries already under deflationary pressure to compound the evil by using deflationary policies (instead of devaluation) to eliminate their payments deficits. They inquired whether our deficit countries did not find too great the burden of adjustment imposed on them, whether they did not protest against an arrangement so inequitable and to their mind so irrational; but I tried to explain that since we regard a payments deficit as something slightly shameful and a sign of economic weakness or faulty economic policies, the deficit countries are always at a slight disadvantage when it comes to a discussion of these matters and in no position to throw their weight around in international financial circles. This was clearly incomprehensible to my Laputan colleagues; and rather than to enlarge upon so delicate and difficult a topic, I hastened to change the subject.

INDEX

SCITOVSKY. Papers on welfare
and growth.